Catalogue of Choral Music Arranged in Biblical Order

Supplement

James H. Laster

The Scarecrow Press, Inc.
Lanham, Maryland, and London
2002

SCARECROW PRESS, INC.

Published in the United States of America
by Scarecrow Press, Inc.
4720 Boston Way, Lanham, Maryland 20706
www.scarecrowpress.com

4 Pleydell Gardens, Folkestone
Kent CT20 2DN, England

British Library Cataloguing-in-Publication Information Available

Library of Congress Cataloging-in-Publication Data

Laster, James, 1934–
    Catalogue of choral music arranged in Biblical order. Supplement / James H. Laster.
        p. cm.
    Includes indexes.
    ISBN 0-8108-4138-X (alk. paper)
    1. Church music—Bibliography. 2. Choral music—Bibliography. I. Title.

    ML 128.C54 L4 1996 Suppl.
    016782'2—dc21   2001049502

Contents

PREFACE
to the
Supplement

When the second edition of the *Catalogue of Choral Music Arranged in Biblical Order* appeared in 1995, the size of the volume surprised us all! Granted, it did contain the entire first edition, but the amount of new material was sizable. Plans for a third edition began immediately, but this volume would only be a supplement to the second edition and would emphasize music published since 1995, or titles that were overlooked in the previous editions.

The *Supplement* continues the tradition of the *Catalogue* in that it is designed as an aid for the church musician and/or pastor seeking to plan unified worship services.

Grateful appreciation is expressed to the publishers who sent music for examination, including Augsburg, Beckenhorst, Concordia, Lorenz, MorningStar, Presser, and Walton.

The entries in the *Catalogue* are either single octavos or titles found in anthem collections. If an entry is found in a collection, the title of the collection is given at the end of the citation. Publisher, date, and compiler for each anthem collection can be located in the Collection Information, page 105.

The format for citations in the *Supplement* remains the same as in the previous editions. All titles are listed as they appear on the octavo. No attempt is made to incorporate Uniform Titles. This will account for the variation in titles and in the various spellings of composers' names. Texts from the Psalms are entered according to the King James numbering. Canticles from English Services are included only if published as a single title, e.g., a setting of the *Magnificat* or the *Nunc Dimittis,* but are not included if listed as a Service.

There are two types of entries found in the *Catalogue*: a Main Entry and a SEE reference. An annotated Main Entry is as follows:

(1) Proverbs 3:5, 6; ((2) Psalm 121:7, 8)
(3) Wetzler, Robert. (4) *He shall direct your paths.* (5) SATB, kbd. (6) Concordia (1999) 98-3531

(1) Biblical reference—Book, chapter, and verse.
(2) Additional Scripture used in the anthem; or the name of the author of a paraphrased text, or a translator of the text.
(3) Composer's name, including arranger or editor.
(4) Title. All texts are assumed to be in English unless otherwise indicated.
(5) Voicing, solos, accompaniment.
   (A) When an anthem has the voice parts reduced for keyboard playing, but the work is intended for unaccompanied singing, it is listed as 'kro' (keyboard rehearsal only).
   (B) When an anthem is printed in open score with no keyboard reduction and is intended for unaccompanied singing, it is listed as 'no acc.' (no accompaniment).
   (C) When an anthem has an accompaniment, it is listed as 'kbd.' (keyboard), organ, or piano. Additional instruments are indicated here.
(6) The name of the publisher, the most recent date of publication, and the octavo number appear at the end of each citation. Information concerning instrumental parts, other versions

of the same title, and the name of collections where the work might appear are included. Items where no date is given are listed as (n.d.) or left blank. Items for which there is no octavo number are listed as (n.#.) or left blank.

An annotated SEE reference is as follows:

(1) Psalm 121:7, 8 (2) SEE: Proverbs 3:5, 6 (3) Wetzler, Robert. (4) *He shall direct your paths*

(1) Biblical reference—Book, Chapter and verse.
(2) The SEE reference which refers to the Main Scripture Heading where the complete citation is located.
(3) and (4) Composer and title for the Main Heading are repeated in the SEE reference.

As before, the Biblical reference which appears on the printed music has been used as the entry point for cataloging. When there were errors, corrections were attempted. If an anthem listed the text as "from the Psalms" or "from Scripture," every effort was made to try to determine the specific passage. When the text could be located it was listed; when it could not be found, the selection was excluded.

A work such as this is always out of date the minute it is frozen into print. Due to the vast amount of choral music, there are numerous titles that have been overlooked. Do share what you have found so that it can be included in the next supplement.

List of Abbreviations

S	Soprano
A	Alto
T	Tenor
B	Bass
Bar.	Baritone
divsi	voice parts are divided
SATB/SATB	Double choir
SA(T)B	Voice part in parentheses is optional
kbd.	Keyboard
kro	Keyboard rehearsal only
n.d.	No date
n.#.	No number
U	Unison

The Old Testament

GENESIS

7:00 (based on)
> Harlan, Benjamin. *Noah.* 2-part, kbd. Fred Bock (1994) BG 2189

12:1-4 (based on) (Psalm 33:12; John 1:36-39)
> Haas, David. *I am the voice of God.* SATB, kbd. GIA (1991) G-3701

15:1, 2, 11, 13, 17
> Wright, Paul Leddington. *I will sing to the Lord.* SATB, organ. Hinshaw (1995) HMC 1397

28:10-22 (based on)
> Haan, Raymond H. *As Jacob with travel* (based on English folk song *Jacob's Ladder*). SATB, piano, optional second pianist or handbells. MorningStar (1997) MSM-50-9087

28:10-22 Rogers, Sharon Elery, arr. *A song of faith.* SATB, kbd. Coronet (Presser) (1995) 392-41974

28:10-22 Smith, Lani. *Jacob's vision.* SATB, kbd. Sacred Music Press (1993) 10/1027

28:10-22 (based on)
> Spiritual (arr. Marc Robinson). *Jacob's ladder/Hold on.* SATB, B/solo, piano. Kjos (2000) 8934

28:10-22 (based on)
> Spiritual (arr. Roger C. Wilson). *Jacob's ladder.* SAB, kbd. Lorenz, found in *Anthems for limited choirs*

28:16, 17 Lau, Robert. *Surely the Lord is in this place* (found in *Choral responses for worship*). SATB, kbd. Coronet (Presser) (1995) 392-41857

28:16b, 17b
> Lovelace, Austin. *Surely God is in this place* (#1 of *Introit and blessing*). SATB, organ. Hinshaw (1998) HMC 1631

28:17 SEE: Psalm 122:1-2. Pethel, Stan. *The gate of heaven*

28:17 SEE: Matthew 16:18. Locklair, Dan. *St. Peter's rock*

31:40 (II Corinthians 13:14)
> Grotenhuis, Dale. *May the Lord watch over you and me* (#1 of *Two choral benedictions*). SATB, kro. Sacred Music Press (Lorenz) (1994) 10/1117

32:23-30 (Wesley)
> Mennicke, David L. *Come, O Thou traveler unknown* (uses tune *Candler*). SATB, or 2-part, or unison, 2 instruments in C, kbd. MorningStar (2000) MSM-50-8109

EXODUS

15:00 (adapted)
> Soper, Scott. *Song of Moses.* Unison, 2 instruments in C, kbd. GIA (1997) G-4623

15:1-2 (Psalm 118:21-22, and other)
> Powell, Robert J. *He hath triumphed gloriously.* SATB, kbd. Coronet (Alexander Broude) (1983) CP 246

15:2, 11 (paraphrased)
> Schwoebel, David. *The Lord is my strength and my song.* SATB, kbd. Hinshaw (1997) HMC 1547

LEVITICUS

19:9 (Isaiah 9:3)
> Zabel, Albert. *Come, joy!* SATB, optional handbells, kbd. Shawnee Press (1995) A-6949

25:8-17 SEE: Isaiah 61:2. Courtney, Craig. *Blow ye the trumpet!*

NUMBERS

6:22-27 Walker, Christopher. *May God bless and keep you.* SATB, kbd. OCP (1989) 9225

6:24-26 (based on)
Brown, Grayson Warren. *May the Lord bless you.* SATB, guitar, kbd. OCP (1992) 10298

6:24-26 Lau, Robert. *The Lord bless you and keep you* (found in *Choral responses for worship*). SATB, kbd. Coronet (Presser) (1995) 392-41857

6:24-26 Lovelace, Austin. *May God bless and keep you.* SAB or SATB, solo instrument, kbd. OCP (1989) 9459

6:24-26 Spevacek, Linda Steen. *The blessing of Aaron.* SAB, kro. Heritage (1994) 15/1088

24:17 Mendelssohn, Felix (ed. Ken Fleet). *There shall a star* (from *Christus*). SATB, kbd. Kjos (1995) 8773

24:17-18 McCray, James. *Orietur stella.* SATB, organ. Mark Foster (1996) MF 583

DEUTERONOMY

4:29 SEE: Joel 2:12, 13. Mendelssohn, Felix. *If with all your hearts*

4:29 Murphy, Michael Patrick (arr. Dick Averre). *If with all your hearts.* SATB, kbd. Coronet (Presser) (1995) 392-42000

6:4 Löwenthal, Tom. *These words.* Unison, kbd. OCP (1992) 10342

8:2 (Revelation 21:3; Habakkuk 3:17-19)
Powell, Robert J. *Remember your Lord God (Prayer of Habakkuk).* Unison, kbd. Augsburg Fortress (1997) 11-10776

11:18 (based on)
Schurr, Walter W. *Fix these words.* SATB, kbd. Kjos (1996) 8836

32:1-4 Day, James R. *Listen, O heavens.* SATB, kbd. Roger Dean (1998) 10/1894R

33:27 Showalter, Anthony (arr. David M. Hines). *Leaning* (uses hymn tune *Showalter*). SATB, kbd. Coronet (Presser) (1996) 392-42978

JOSHUA

1:5-6 (Jeremiah 31:3; Isaiah 43:1; Isaiah 49:16; Psalm 37:3-4, 7)
Grotenhuis, Dale. *Song of commitment.* SATB, flute, kbd. Birnamwood (MorningStar) (2001) MSM-50-8826

5:9-12 (Psalm 34:00; II Corinthians 5:17-21; Luke 15:1-32)
Thompson, J. Michael. *Taste and see the Lord is good.* SATB, oboe, organ. Augsburg (1997) 11-10842

6:00 (based on)
African-American spiritual (arr. Marylou India Jackson). *Joshua fit de battle of Jericho.* SSAA, kro. Treble Clef Press (1996) TC-107.

24:15 (based on)
McDonald, Mary. *We will serve the Lord.* SATB, kbd. Purifoy Publishing (Lorenz) (1994) 10/1152

JUDGES

5:1-5, 10-12 (paraphrased)
DeLong, Richard. *Sing to the God of Israel (Canticle of Deborah).* 2-part, organ, percussion, optional instrument in C. Choristers Guild (1994) CGA 670

5:2-3, 12 Lindh, Jody W. *Israel, awake!* Unison, organ and percussion. Choristers Guild (1996) CGA714

I SAMUEL

2:10 (Luke 1:46-55)
Jennings, Carolyn. *A new magnificat.*
SATB, organ. Augsburg (1998)
11-10817, found in *The Augsburg
choirbook, Sacred choral music of the
twentieth century,* ed. Kenneth
Jennings

I CHRONICLES

16:00 (taken from)
Pelz, Walter L. *O give thanks to the
Lord.* SATB, trumpet in C, organ.
Concordia (1998) 98-3449

16:25-34 (adapted)
Curry, Craig. *Everlasting praise.*
SATB, kbd., with optional brass.
Monarch Music (Lorenz) (1996)
10/1462M

II CHRONICLES

5:13 Young, Gordon. *The trumpeters and
the singers were as one.* SATB, kbd,
optional 3 trumpets. Coronet (Presser)
(1995) 392-41954

5:13-14 SEE: Job 38:7. Scott, K. Lee. *When
the morning stars together*

7:16 Wold, Wayne L. *Alleluia, I have
chosen.* SATB, organ. MorningStar
(1993) MSM-80-870

NEHEMIAH

9:5, 6 Starr, David. *Stand up and bless the
Lord.* SATB, kbd. Coronet (Presser)
(1998) 392-42204

9:5b, 6 (based on)
Berry, Cindy. *Stand up and bless the
Lord.* SATB, kbd. GlorySound
(Shawnee) (1999) A-7324

JOB

19:25 (and S. Medley)
Kosche, Kenneth T. *I know that my
redeemer lives.* SATB, kbd. Coronet
(Presser) (1998) 392-42206

19:25 (and S. Medley)
Williams, David H. *I know that my
redeemer lives.* SATB, organ.
Coronet (Presser) (1998) 392-42215

19:25-27 (Samuely Medley)
Behnke, John, arr. *I know that my
redeemer lives* (uses *Duke Street*).
SAB, organ, optional trumpet, optional
2-3 octave handbells. Concordia
(1995) 98-3197

19:25-27 (Samuely Medley)
Bunjes, Paul G. (setting by). *I know
that my redeemer lives* (uses *Duke
Street*). SATB, trumpet, organ.
Concordia (1990) 98-2933

19:25-27 (Samuely Medley)
Cox, Michael, arr. *I know that my
redeemer lives* (uses 19th-century
American folk hymn). SATB, kbd.
Hinshaw (1991) HMC 1221

19:25-27 Hughes, Howard. *I know that my
redeemer lives.* Unison, kbd. GIA
(n.d.) 2281

19:25-27 SEE: John 20:18. Hurd, Bob. *I have
seen the Lord*

19:25-27 MacAller, Dominic. *I know that my
redeemer lives.* SATB, kbd. OCP
(1990) 9436

22:21, 26, 28b
Haan, Raymond H. *Acquaint now
thyself with him.* SATB, piano
Birnamwood (MorningStar) (2001)
MSM-50-6025

23:3 SEE: Joel 2:12, 13. Mendelssohn,
Felix. *If with all your hearts*

28:20-21, 23-24, 28
Rollins, Joan E. *When then comes
wisdom.* SATB, organ. Randall Egan
(1993) EC 274

38:7 (II Chronicles 5:13-14)
Scott, K. Lee. *When the morning stars together* (uses tune *Sorrell*). SATB, organ, optional children's choir, handbells, and trumpet. Choristers Guild (Lorenz) (1995) CGA707

PSALMS

1:00 Cooney, Rory. *Psalm 1: Roots in the earth.* Unison, kbd. GIA (1993) G 3969

1:00 (adapted)
Killman, Daniel. *You shall be as the tree.* SATB, kbd. MorningStar (2000) MSM-50-7041

1:00 (Psalm 91:00)
McCabe, Michael. *A Psalm of the redeemed.* SATB, organ. Randall M. Egan (1994) EC 309

2:7-8 Schramm, Charles W., Jr. *You are my son.* SA(T)B, organ. Concordia (2000) 98-3571

4:00 Ure, James. *Psalm 4.* SATB, kro. Plymouth (1995) CC-109

4:1 (Psalm 5:2)
Schütz, Heinrich (arr. David W. Music). *Lord, hear my prayer (Erhöre mich)* (English/German). 2-part, kbd. Concordia (2000) 98-3563

4:8 SEE: Psalm 17:8. West, John E. (arr. Bonnie Barrett). *Hide me under the shadow of thy wings*

4:8 SEE: Psalm 5:8. Wesley, Samuel B. *Lead me, Lord*

5:00 (adapted)
Wagner, Douglas E. *O be joyful.* SATB, kbd. Lorenz (1986) found in *Exaltation*

5:2 SEE: Psalm 4:1. Schütz, Heinrich (arr. David W. Music). *Lord, hear my prayer*

5:8 (Psalm 23:4)
Molique, Wilhelm B. (arr. Lani Smith). *Lead me, O Lord.* SAB, kbd. Lorenz (1971) found in *Anthems for limited choirs,* II

5:8 (Psalm 4:8)
Wesley, Samuel S. *Lead me, Lord.* SATB, kbd. Lorenz (1949) found in *Easy standard anthems,* I

6:9 SEE: Psalm 96:1-4. White, David Ashley. *Cantate Domino*

8:00 (Haas)
Haas, David. *Your wonderful name.* 2-part mixed, instrument in C, kbd. GIA (1995) 4340

8:00 Hassell, Michael. *How exalted is your name.* SATB, piano. Augsburg (1997) 11-10854

8:00 Hoekstra, Thomas. *Psalm 8.* SSA, TTB, or mixed, kro. Concordia (1996) 98-3293

8:00 (taken from)
Hopson, Hal H. *Lord, O Lord, your name is wonderful.* Unison, 6 handbells, kbd. Choristers Guild (1997) CGA762

8:00 Johengen, Carl. *How wonderful is your name.* SATB, piano. GIA (1992) G-3652

8:00 (based on)
Lung, Richard Ho (arr. Jon and Wynton Williams). *When I look at the heavens.* SATB, piano. OCP (1997) 10746

8:00 Marcello, Benedetto (ed. and arr. Dale Grotenhuis). *O God, creator.* 2-part, kbd. MorningStar (1998) MSM-50-9420

8:00 Wold, Wayne L. *O sovereign God.* SATB, S/solo, organ. Kjos (2000) 8930

8:1 Handel, G. F. (ed. Robert S. Hines). *How excellent thy name.* SATB, organ or piano. Hoffman (Alexandria House) (1973, 1982) H-2016

8:1, 3-9   Levine, Elliot Z. *Psalm 8 (O Lord our God).* SSA (TBB), no acc. E. Henry Davids (Presser) (1995) 392-02520

8:1, 4-7, 10
Hancock, Gerre. *O Lord our governor.* SATB, organ. Oxford (1998) 94/267

8:1-6, 9   Powell, Robert J. *O Lord, our Lord.* SATB, French horn, organ. Concordia (1997) 98-3312

8:5 6   SEE: Matthew 28:6 7. Kosche, Kenneth T. *Alleluia! Christ has risen*

9:1-2 (paraphrased)
SEE: Ephesians 5.19. Clemens, James E. *Sing and make music to the Lord*

9:1, 2, 10   Nelson, Ronald A. *With my whole heart.* SAB, kbd. Concordia (1999) 98-3511

9:1-10   Larson, Lloyd. *I will praise you, O Lord, with all my heart.* SATB, kbd. Beckenhorst (1997) BP 1510

9:11-12   Schütz, Heinrich (arr. David W. Music). *Praise God in heaven (Lobet den Herren)* (English/German). 2-part, kbd. Concordia (2000) 98-3587

11:1b (based on)
Spanish folk tune (arr. Leland B. Sateren). *Flee as a bird.* SATB, no acc. Kjos (1996) 8824

13:00   Bell, John L. *How long, O Lord.* Unison, cello, kbd. GIA (1987) G-4531

13:00   Grotenhuis, Dale. *How long, O Lord?* SATB, kro. Hinshaw (1997) HMC 1567

13:00 (Psalm 22:00)
Schutte, Dan. *How long, O Lord.* 2-part choir, oboe, kbd. OCP (1929) 9918

13:1, 3, 5   Pflueger, Carl (arr. Ellen Jane Lorenz). *Consider and hear me.* SATB, B/solo, kbd. Lorenz (1949) found in *Easy standard anthems,* I

13:5   SEE: Psalm 46:10, 11. Nelson, Ronald A. *Be still and know*

14:00   Ives, Charles (ed. John Kirkpatrick and Gregg Smith). *Psalm 14.* SATB, kro. Merion (Presser) (1995) 342-40161

15:00   Bell, John L. *Lord, who may enter your house?* SATB, cantor, kbd. GIA (1998) G-4669

16:00 (adapted)
Haas, David. *Show me the path.* SATB, kbd. GIA (1993) G-3927

16:00 (Psalm 118:00)
Pollock, Gail Leven. *I will sing to the Lord.* SATD, kbd. Flammer (Shawnee) (1999) A 7348

17:1, 5-6, 8, 15
Cooney, Rory. *Psalm 17: When your glory appears.* SATB, kbd. OCP (1981) 10463

17:6, 8   Owens, Sam Batt. *Hide me under the shadow of your wings.* 2-part mixed, organ. MorningStar (1997) MSM-50-9207

17:8 (Psalm 91:11; Psalm 4:8)
West, John E. (arr. Bonnie Barrett). *Hide me under the shadow of thy wings.* SATB, kbd. Lorenz (1994) 10/1409U

18:00 (based on)
Brown, Grayson Warren (arr. Val Parker and Grayson Warren Brown). *I love you, O Lord.* Unison, kbd. Found in *If God is for us,* OCP (1995) 10114

18:47-48   SEE: Psalm 143:9-10. Haydn, Johann Michael (ed. David Stein). *Eripe me, Domine*

19:00   Beethoven, Ludwig van (arr. Arthur Frackenpohl). *The heavens are praising.* SATB, kbd. Mark Foster (1990) MF 2062

19:00   Handel, G. F. (arr. Hal H. Hopson). *The heav'ns declare God's mighty power* (from *Samson*). SAB, kbd. Mark Foster (1990) MF 2059

19:00 (paraphrased)
McKinney, Richard. *The heavens are telling.* SAB, kbd. Concordia (1999) 98-3517

19:1-6 (II Corinthians 5:17)
Courtney, Craig. *Creation hymn.* SATB, kbd. Beckenhorst (1995) BP 1468

19:1-6
Lassus, Rudolf de (ed. Richard Proulx). *Stars in the sky proclaim.* SAB, kro. Augsburg (1995) 12-400004

19:1-6, 14
Bach, J. S. (arr. Michael Burkhardt). *The heavens declare Thy glory* (from Cantata 68, *My heart ever faithful*). Unison, 2 treble instruments, kbd., optional bass. MorningStar (1997) MSM-50-7503

19:8-11
SEE: John 6:68. Joncas, Michael. *Lord, you have the words*

19:14
Baumbach, Adolph. *Let the words of my mouth.* SAB, kbd. Lorenz (1969) found in *Anthems for limited choirs,* II

19:14
Wetzler, Robert. *Always, only, for my king.* SATB, organ. AMSI (1994) 675

20:00
Brown, Grayson Warren (arr. Val Parker and Grayson Warren Brown). *Psalm 20.* Unison, kbd. Found in *If God is for us,* OCP (1995) 10114

20:00
SEE: Psalm 43:3, 4. Gounod, Charles. *Send out Thy light*

22:00
SEE: Psalm 13:00. Schutte, Dan. *How long, O Lord*

22:27
Schalk, Carl. *All the ends of the earth.* SATB, organ. Concordia (1999) 98-3546

23:00 (Watts)
American folk melody (setting by Howard Helvey). *My shepherd will supply my need* (uses tune *Resignation*). Unison, optional 2-part or SATB, piano, optional cello or trombone. Providence (Hope) 1998 PP 154

23:00 (Watts)
American folk tune (arr. Austin Lovelace). *My shepherd will supply my need.* SATB, kbd. AMSI (1992) 634

23:00
Behnke, John A. *The Lord's my shepherd.* SATB, piano, optional 3-octave handbells, cantor and congregation. Concordia (1997) 98-3400

23:00
Bell, John L. *The Lord is my shepherd.* SATB, cantor, kbd. GIA (1998) G-4669

23:00
Burkhardt, Michael. *Psalm 23.* SATB, instrument in C, organ. MorningStar (1997) MSM-50-9051

23:00 (based on)
Choplin, Pepper. *My shepherd is the Lord.* SATB, optional flute, kbd. Shawnee Press (1995) A-6956

23:00
Dvořák, Antonin (arr. Dale Grotenhuis). *God is my shepherd* (from *Ten Biblical songs*, Op. 99) (#2 in *Two Dvořák Biblical songs for male chorus*). TTBB, piano. MorningStar (1998) MSM-50-9700

23:00
Grier, Gene and Lowell Everson. *The Lord is my shepherd.* SATB, kbd. Lorenz (1990) found in *Exaltation*

23:00 (Herbert, adapted)
Hayes, Mark. *The God of love my shepherd is.* SATB, organ (optional oboe and orchestra). Beckenhorst (1998) BP 1525, orchestra parts available from publisher

23:00 (Baker)
Kimberling, Clark. *The king of love my shepherd is.* 2-part, optional instrument in C, kbd. GIA (1997) G-4480

23:00 (*Scottish Psalter 1650*)
Kosche, Kenneth T. *The Lord's my shepherd* (based on tune *Crimond*). SATB, organ with optional congregation and strings. MorningStar (1999) MSM-60-9081A; full score MSM-60-9018; instrumental parts MSM-60-9018B

23:00 (*The Key Note,* 1863)
Lau, Robert C. *To Thy pastures.* SATB, kbd. Lorenz (1996) 10/1378L

23:00 Lawson, Gordon. *Psalm 23.* S, organ. Randall Egan (1992) 90-102

23:00 Leavitt, John. *The Lord is my shepherd* (from *Requiem*). SATB, piano. Concordia (2000) 98-3583

23:00 Liddle, Samuel (arr. William Livingston). *The Lord is my shepherd.* SATB, piano or organ. Coronet (Presser) (1960, 1995) 392-41986

23:00 (adapted)
McCabe, Michael. *The shepherd's song.* 2-part, flute and kbd. Lorenz (1980), found in *Songs of joy*

23:00 Mengel, Dana. *My shepherd will supply my need.* SATB, kbd. Coronet (Presser) (1995) 392-41928

23:00 Mozart, W. A. (ed. Ellen Jane Lorenz). *The Lord is my shepherd.* SATB, kbd. Lorenz (1951) found in *Simplified standard anthems,* I

23:00 Mulholland, James Quitman. *Psalm 23* (from *Canticle of Psalms*). SATB, piano (optional instrumental ensemble). Plymouth (1994) JM-110; all three Psalms published as *Canticle of Psalms,* JM-109

23:00 (adapted)
Murphy, Michael Patrick (arr. Dick Averre). *In the arms of my shepherd.* Bar. solo/SATB, optional flute, kbd. Coronet (Presser) (1998) 392-42149

23:00 (Baker)
Near, Gerald. *The king of love my shepherd is.* SATB, organ. Aureoloe (MorningStar) (2001) AE 123

23:00 (based on)
Pooler, Marie. *Truly blest.* 2-part, kbd. AMSI (1998) 798

23:00 Roth, John. *David's Song.* SA, instrument in C, kbd. Concordia (1995) 98-3184

23:00 (Herbert)
Schalk, Carl. *The God of love my shepherd is.* SATB, 2 violins, organ. MorningStar (1998) MSM-50-8812; violin MSM-50-8812A

23:00 Schubert, Franz (arr. Walter Ehret). *The Lord is my shepherd.* SATB, no acc. AMSI (1995) 702

23:00 (Baker)
Shelley, Harry Rowe (arr. Ellen Jane Lorenz). *The King of love my shepherd is.* A/solo, SATB, kbd. Lorenz (1951) found in *Simplified standard anthems,* I

23:00 (Baker)
Young, Gordon. *The king of love.* SATB, kbd. Flammer (1996) A 7073

23:00 Sensmeier, Randall. *The Lord is my shepherd.* SATB, instrument in C, kbd. GIA (1995) G4132

23:00 Smith, Timothy R. *The Lord is my shepherd.* SATB, kbd. OCP (1994) 10581

23:00 Stearns, Peter Pindar. *The Lord is my shepherd,* Op. 152. SATB, organ. Paraclete (1998) PPM 09822

23:00 Zimmermann, Heinz Werner. *Psalm 23 (The Lord is my shepherd).* SATB, kbd., string bass. Augsburg (1998) 11-10817, found in *The Augsburg choirbook, Sacred choral music of the twentieth century,* ed. Kenneth Jennings

23:1 Haan, Raymond H. *The shepherd song.* Unison or 2-part, piano. AMSI (1989) 567

23:4 SEE: Psalm 5:8. Molique, Wilhelm B. *Lead me, O Lord*

24:00 (based on)
Hampton, Keith. *My God is an awesome God.* SATB, piano. Augsburg Fortress (2000) 0-8006 5917-1

24:00 McCray, James. *Lift up your heads.* SATB, kro. Mark Foster (1996) MF 2121

24:7-10 (and Weissel) Handel, George F. (setting by Hal H. Hopson). *He is the king of glory* (based on tune *Truro*). SATB, piano or organ. Hope (1999) C 5022

24:7-10 (adapted) Holden-Holloway, Deborah. *Lift up your heads.* SATB, organ, percussion. Selah (1999) 410-647

24:7-10 Larson, Lloyd. *Lift up your heads.* SATB, kbd. Hope (1996) PP145

24:7-10 Owens, Sam Batt. *Lift up your heads, O gates.* 2-part mixed, organ. Morning Star (1996) MSM-50-0302

24:7-10 (Weissel) Williams, Thomas J. (arr. Stan Pethel). *Lift up your heads.* SATB, kbd. Coronet (Presser) (1998) 392-42190

25:00 (adapted Hopson) Beethoven, Ludwig van (arr. Hal H. Hopson). *My soul longs for you, O God.* SAB, kbd. Belwin-Mills (1981) GCMR 3442

25:00 Burkhardt, Michael. *Thy holy wings (I lift my soul)* (based on Swedish folk tune *Bred dina vida vingar*). Unison/2-part, piano, with optional oboe, clarinet, and cello. MorningStar (1999) 50-5552; parts 50-5552-A

25:00 Haugen, Marty. *To you, O Lord.* SATB, 2 treble instruments, kbd. GIA (1985) G 2653

25:00 Hobby, Robert A. *Thy holy wings (I lift my soul)* (based on Swedish folk tune *Bred dina vida vingar*). Unison, flute, piano. MorningStar (1996) MSM-50-9453; part MSM-50-9453A

25:00 Roberts, Leon C. *To you, O Lord, I lift my soul.* SATB, kbd. GIA (1997) G-4601

25:1-2 Kalinnikoff, P. *To thee, O Lord, do I lift up my soul.* SATTBB, kro. J. Fischer. Found in *Twenty-five anthems from the Russian liturgy*

25:1, 2 Rachmaninoff, Sergi. *To thee, O Lord do I lift up my soul.* SATB, kro. J. Fischer. Found in *Twenty-five anthems from the Russian liturgy*

25:1-21 Schalk, Carl. *Show me your ways, O Lord.* SATB, kro. Concordia (1995) 98-3207

25:3 (Isaiah 40:3; James 5:8; Zephaniah 3:14-18; Luke 1:45, based on) Hurd, Bob (arr. Craig Kingsbury). *Await the Lord with hope.* SATB, kbd., oboe. OCP (1996) 10579

25:4, 5 Pelz, Walter. *Show me thy ways.* SATB, oboe, guitar. Augsburg (1998) 11-10817, found in *The Augsburg choirbook, Sacred choral music of the twentieth century,* ed. Kenneth Jennings

25:4-8 Scott, K. Lee. *All the day long.* SATB, kbd. Concordia (1996) 98-3275

25:17-18 Haydn, Johann Michael (ed. David Stein). *Tribulations cordis mei (Many are the sorrows).* SATB, kbd. Presser (1999) 312-41743

27:00 (adapted) Burson, John Wyatt. *The Lord is my light.* SATB, kbd. Lorenz (1995) 10/1407U

27:00 (based on) Drennan, Patti. *The Lord is my light.* SATB, kbd. Beckenhorst (1996) BP 1473

27:00 Honoré, Jeffrey. *Psalm 27: The Lord is my light* (found in *Psalter for bells and voices, Set I*). SATB, congregation, handbells (3-5 octaves), kbd. Concordia (1999) 98-3508, handbells 97-6781

27:00 Johengen, Carl. *In the land of the living.* SB, flute, piano. GIA (1993) G-3816

27:00 (from)
> Leavitt, John. *The Lord is my light and my salvation* (from *Requiem*). SATB, piano. Concordia (2000) 98-3583

27:00   Mulholland, James Quitman. *Psalm 27* (from *Canticle of Psalms*). SATB, piano (optional instrumental accompaniment). Plymouth (1994) JM-113; all three Psalms published as *Canticle of Psalms* JM-109

27:00   Murphy, Michael Patrick. *The Lord is my light and my salvation.* SATB, kbd. Coronet (Presser) (1996) 392-42076

27:00   O'Hearn, Arletta. *Psalm 27 – Trust in God.* SATB, piano. Kjos (2000) 8909

27:00 (based on)
> Soper, Scott. *The goodness of the Lord.* SAB, solo instrument, kbd. OCP (1993) 9587

27:00   Walker, Christopher. *The Lord is my light.* SATB, kbd. OCP (1996) 10448

27:1, 3   Cox, Michael. *The Lord is my light.* 2-part, kbd. Coronet (Presser) (1998) 392-42158

27:1, 3   Cox, Michael. *The Lord is my light.* SAB, kbd. Coronet (Presser) (1998, 2000) 392-42315

27:1-4 (based on)
> South African freedom song (arr. Hal H. Hopson). *We are singing for the Lord is our light* (based on traditional Zulu song). Unison or SAB, kbd. Hope (1999) C5060

27:1-4 (based on)
> Zulu traditional song (arr. Hal H. Hopson). *We are singing for the Lord is our light.* Unison, or SATB, kbd. Agape (Hope) (1994) HH3949

27:1, 4, 6 Rudolph, Glenn L. *One thing I ask of the Lord.* SATB, organ. GIA (1995) G-4103

27:1, 7, 11
> Kosche, Kenneth T. *The Lord is my light and my salvation.* SATB, organ. Coronet (Presser) (1996) 392-42013

27:4   Schütz, Heinrich (ed. David W. Music). *I ask one thing of the Lord (Eins bitte ich vom Herren)* (German/English). 2-part, kbd. Concordia (1999) 98-3540

27:5 (Psalm 84:3-4, 12)
> Proulx, Richard. *One thing I seek.* 2-part mixed, organ. AMSI (1998) 797

27:10   Farrant, Richard (arr. Kenneth T. Kosche). *Hide not Thou thy face from us, O Lord.* SAB, optional kbd. Coronet (Presser) (1997) 392-42086

27:10-13 Neswick, Bruce. *Hearken to my voice, O Lord, when I call.* 2-part treble, kbd. Augsburg (1998) 11-10817, found in *The Augsburg choirbook, Sacred choral music of the twentieth century,* ed. Kenneth Jennings.

28:10-11 SEE: I Corinthians 10:17. Proulx, Richard. *Though we are many, in Christ we are one*

29:1-2 (and Carl P. Daw, Jr.)
> Scott, K. Lee. *O God of font and altar.* SATB, organ, optional brass quartet. MorningStar (2000) MSM-50-7043

30:00 (adapted)
> Young, Philip M. *I will extol you, O Lord.* SATB, brass quintet or organ. MorningStar (1995) MSM-50-7016

30:1-5, 12-13
> Schramm, Charles W., Jr. *I will exalt you, O Lord.* SATB, organ. Concordia (1999) 98-3532

30:4, 5, 12
> Baker, Richard C. *Sing unto the Lord.* SATB, kro. Randall Egan (1974, 1991) n.#.

31:00 (paraphrase)
> Haas, David. *I put my life in your hands (Pongo mi vida en tus manos)* (English/Spanish). SATB, instrument in C, kbd. GIA (1993) G-3949

31:00   Soper, Scott. *My life is in your hands.* 2-part mixed, kbd. GIA (1997) G-4620

31:1-2 Proulx, Richard. *In te speravi, Domine (In you have I hoped, O Lord).* Treble voices, organ. Paraclete (1995) PPMO 9521

31:1, 3 SEE: Psalm 141:1, 2, 3, 8. Tschaikovsky, P. *Lord, I cry unto thee*

31:1-4 Ippolitoff-Ivanoff, M. *Incline thine ear.* SATB, kro. J. Fischer. Found in *Twenty-five anthems from the Russian liturgy*

31:2, 6, 12-13, 15-17, 25
Talbot, John Michael. *Father, I put my life in your hands.* SATB, kbd. OCP (1997) 10666

31:5 Fritschel, James. *Into your hands.* SATB, kro. AMSI (1997) 774

31:14-15 Proulx, Richard. *Trust.* 2-part, organ. AMSI (1998) 786

32:00 Callahan, Charles. *Psalm 32.* SATB, cantor, organ. Randall Egan (1994) EC 335

33:00 (based on)
Cortez, Jaime (arr. Craig Kingsbury). *Rain down.* SATB, kbd. OCP (1991) 9771

33:1, 5a, 6, 9 (based on)
Proulx, Richard. *Of the kindness of the Lord.* Unison or SA, organ. GIA (1968) G 3274

33:12 (based on)
SEE: Genesis 12:1-4. Haas, David. *I am the voice of God*

33:12, 18-22 (Wesley)
Darwall, John (setting by Craig Courtney). *Rejoice, the Lord is king (uses tune Darwall's 148th).* SATB, optional brass quartet, kbd. Beckenhorst (1995) BP 1476

33:20-22 Schalk, Carl. *Our soul waits for the Lord.* SATB, kro. Concordia (1996) 98-3252

34:00 (adapted)
Barnard, Mark (arr. John Purifoy). *Taste and see.* SATB, kbd. Lorenz (1994) 15/1150

34:00 Chepponis, James. *Psalm 34.* SATB, organ, congregation, optional strings, woodwinds, timpani, cymbal, hand-bells. MorningStar (1999) MSM-80-848A; full score MSM-80-848; choir score MSM-80-848A; instrumental parts MSM-80-848B

34:00 Cooney, Rory. *Every morning in your eyes.* 2-part, optional flute and string quartet, guitar, kbd. GIA (1995) G-4112

34:00 Larkin, Michael. *O taste and see.* SATB, kbd. Coronet (Presser) (1995) 392-41993

34:00 (Psalm 50:00, based on)
Lias, Stephen. *Come glorify the Lord!* SATB, kbd. Sacred Music Press (1995) 10/1203

34:00 (based on)
Schulz-Widmar, Russell. *Through all the changing scenes of life.* SATB, kbd. Concordia (1997) 98-3355

34:00 Schutte, Dan. *Ever on my lips.* SATB, guitar, kbd. OCP (1992) 10321

34:00 SEE: Joshua 5:9-12. Thompson, J. Michael. *Taste and see the Lord is good*

34:1 (adapted)
Carter, John. *I will always give thanks (includes setting of tune St. George's Windsor).* SATB, kbd. Hope (1994) PP 138

34:1 Soper, Scott. *I will always thank the Lord.* Unison, solo instrument, kbd. OCP (1988) 9556

34:1 Telemann, Georg Philipp (arr. Susan Palo Cherwien). *I want to praise the Lord all of my life.* 2/3-part choir, optional solo instrument, kbd. Concordia (1997) 98-3350

34:1-7, 9   Smith, Timothy R. *Taste and see.*
SATB, kbd. OCP (1996) 10699

34:1-8   Kosche, Kenneth T. *O taste and see.*
SATB, organ. OCP (1993) 10352

34:1-9   Busarow, Donald. *Proclaim with me.*
SATB, optional trumpet, organ.
Concordia (1994) 98-3127

34:2-11   Proulx, Richard. *Taste and see.*
SATB, organ. GIA (1997) G-4471

34:3   Lewis, Eric. *Glorify the Lord with me.*
SATB, kbd. Triune Music (Lorenz)
(1996) 10/11431T

34.8   Neswick, Bruce. *O taste and see.*
SATB, S/solo, kro. Augsburg (1995)
11-10592

34:8   Nikolsky, A. *O taste and see how
gracious is the Lord.* SSATB, kro.
J. Fischer. Found in *Twenty-five
anthems from the Russian liturgy*

34:8-9   SEE: I Corinthians 5:7b-8. Schalk,
Carl. *Be known to us, Lord Jesus*

34:8-10   Gehring, Philip. *Taste and see that the
Lord is good* (from *Choral offertories*).
SATB, kro. Concordia (2000) 98-
3585

34:8-10   Goss, Sir John (arr. Robert J. Hughes).
O taste and see. SATB, organ. Lorenz
(1969) found in *Easy standard
anthems, II*

37:00 (based on)
Grown, Grayson Warren. *Don't be
worried.* SATB, kbd. OCP (1992)
10307

37:1-10   Bell, John L. *Do not be vexed.*
SATB, kbd. GIA (1998) 4668

37:3-4, 7   SEE: Joshua 1:5-6. Grotenhuis, Dale.
Song of commitment

37:7   Mendelssohn, Felix (arr. Jonathan
Willcocks). *O rest in the Lord*
(*Elijah*). SATB, kbd. Triune Music
(Lorenz) (1995) 10/1359T

40:00 (based on)
Christianson, Donald G. and Carrie L.
Kraft. *Lord have mercy.* SATB,
piano. Kjos (2000) 8832

40:00   Lord, Suzanne. *I will praise my God.*
2-part mixed, or SA, or TB, kbd.
Coronet (Presser) (1995) 392-41916

40:00   Pote, Allen. *I waited patiently for the
Lord.* SATB, flute, kbd. Coronet
(Presser) (1995) 392-41972

40:1   Bales, Gerald. *I waited patiently for
the Lord.* SATB, organ. Randall Egan
(1981) n.#.

40:1   Mendelssohn, Felix (ed & arr Walter
Ehret). *I waited for the Lord* (from
Hymn of Praise). SAB, kbd. Presser
(1999) 312-41754

40:1, 4   Mendelssohn, Felix (arr. James
Denton). *I waited for the Lord.*
SATB, kbd. Lorenz (1969) found
in *Easy standard anthems,* II

40:4-8   Powell, Robert J. *Thy law is within
my heart.* SATB, instrument in C,
organ. Concordia (1997) 98-3331

41:1-2   Sr. Maria of the Cross. *Like the deer.*
SSA, no acc. Dominican Nuns (1970)
n.#.

42:00   Brown, Grayson Warren. *Psalm 42:
My soul is thirsting.* SATB, kbd.
OCP (1992) 10009

42:00 (Tate and Brady)
Mengel, Dana. *As pants the hart for
cooling streams.* SATB, kbd. Coronet
(Presser) (1996) 392-42015

42:00 (based on)
Pethel, Stan. *I shall yet praise him.*
SATB, kbd. Shawnee Press (1995)
A 7002

42:00 (Psalm 150:00)
Schutte, Dan. *Let us go to the altar.*
SATB, kbd. OCP (1996) 10509

42:00 (Psalm 43:00, adapted)
Shepperd, Mark. *I will yet praise him.* SATB, piano. Augsburg (1997) 11-10853

42:00 (Tate and Brady)
Wetzler, Robert. *As the hart.* 2-part or unison, optional flute or other instrument, kbd. AMSI (1997) 762

42:1-5 Young, Philip M. *As a hart longs for flowing streams.* SATB, organ. MorningStar (1999) 50-6013

42:2 (Psalm 43:3-5)
Joncas, Michael. *As the deer.* SATB, optional instruments, kbd. GIA (1998) G-4883

42:4-8 (based on)
Drennan, Patti. *With a voice of joy.* SATB, kbd. optional brass sextet. Beckenhorst (1995) BP 1444

42:7-10 Brahms, Johannes (arr. Hal H. Hopson). *Let all the gates be opened wide.* Unison or 2-part treble or mixed, kbd. Choristers Guild (1996) CGA 736

43:00 SEE: Psalm 42:00. Shepperd, Mark. *I will yet praise him*

43:3, 4 (Psalm 20:00)
Gounod, Charles (arr. Walter Price). *Send out Thy light.* SAB, kbd. found in *Anthems for limited choirs*

43:3, 4 (Psalm 20:00)
Gounod, Charles (arr. Walter Price). *Send out thy light.* SATB, kbd. Lorenz (1944) found in *Easy standard anthems,* I

43:3-5 SEE: Psalm 42:2. Joncas, Michael. *As the deer*

45:00 (taken from)
Grotenhuis, Dale. *I will exalt you, my God and king.* SATB, kbd. Sacred Music Press (Lorenz) (1994) 10/113

45:2 Blersch, Jeffrey. *The transfiguration of our Lord.* (*Alleluia verses,* set 2). SATB, organ. Concordia (1996) 98-3285

46:00 Burkhardt, Michael. *Psalm 46 (Three Psalm settings).* Unison or mixed, optional kbd., tambourine, handbells. MorningStar (1998) 80-705

46:00 Kosche, Kenneth T. and John A. Behnke. *Psalm 46.* (#1 of *3 festival Psalms*) SATB, 3 octave handbells. Concordia (1997) 98-3365

46:00 Luther, Martin (setting by John Ness Beck). *Psalm XLVI* (uses tune *Ein feste Burg*). SATB, brass sextet and organ. Beckenhorst (1983) BP 1153

46:00 Schultz, Timothy P. *God is our refuge and strength.* SATB, piano. Concordia (1994) 98-3156

46:4, 5 (Revelation 22:2, 3)
Traditional Irish melody (arr. Richard Dickinson). *There is a river.* 2-part, kbd. Coronet (Presser) (2000) 392-42280

46:10, 11 (Isaiah 43:1, 2; Psalm 13:5; Psalm 131:2, 3)
Nelson, Ronald A. *Be still and know.* SATB, organ. Birnamwood (MorningStar) (2001) MSM-50-9117

47:00 Butler, Eugene. *God has gone up with a merry shout.* SATB, kbd. Sacred Music Press (1996) 10/1242

47:00 Handl, Jacob (ed. Lawrence Doebler). *Psalm 47 (Omnes gentes plaudite manibus).* SATB/SATB, kro. Roger Dean (1994) 15/1083

47:00 Hopson, Hal H. *Antiphonal praise.* 2-part, organ. Lorenz (1981) found in *NINE BY TWO*

47:00 Lau, Robert C. *O clap your hands.* SATB, organ, optional brass and timpani. H. W. Gray (1996) GCMR 9705; parts GCMR 9705A

47:00 (adapted)
Leavitt, John. *Oh, clap your hands* (from *Requiem*). SATB, piano. Concordia (2000) 98-3583

47:00   Palmer, Nicholas. *Psalm 47: God mounts his throne.* Unison, trumpet, organ. GIA (1995) G 4063

47:00   Staplin, Carl. *O clap your hands, all ye people!* SATB, kro. Augsburg (1994) 11-10370

47:00   Staplin, Carl. *O clap your hands, all ye people!* SSAATTBB, kro. Augsburg (1994) 11-10567

47:00 (Revelation 4:11, based on).
Wilkinson, Sandy. *Come, celebrate our God and king.* SATB, kbd. Purifoy Publishing (Lorenz) (1995) 10/1287P

47:1-2, 5-8
Innwood, Paul. *God mounts his throne.* SATB, kbd. OCP (1986) 10287

47:1, 2, 6
McChesney, Kevin. *O clap your hands.* SATB, kbd. Lorenz (1996) 10/13761

47:2-3, 6-7, 8-9
SEE: Psalm 118:1-2. Chipponis, James J. *Eastertime Psalm*

47:5   McCabe, Michael. *God is gone up!* SATB, organ. Randall Egan (1992) 92-105

47:5-6 (Psalm 68:18)
Lawson, Gordon. *God is gone up.* SATB, organ. Oecumuse (1992) n.#.

48:14   Blersch, Jeffrey. *Festival of the Reformation* (based on *Ein feste Burg*) (*Alleluia verses*, set 2). SATB, organ. Concordia (1996) 98-3285

50:00   SEE: Psalm 34:00. Lias, Stephen. *Come glorify the Lord!*

50:14-15 Christiansen, F. Melius. *Psalm 50, Offer unto God.* SATB, kro. Augsburg (1998) 11-10817, found in *The Augsburg choirbook, Sacred choral music of the twentieth century,* ed. Kenneth Jennings

51:00   Castillo, Eugene. *Have mercy on us, Lord* (English/Spanish). Unison, kbd., guitar. OCP (1993) 9988

51:00   Cooney, Rory. *Psalm 51: Create me again.* SATB, instrument in C, optional strings, kbd. GIA (1993) 3975

51:00   Ferris, William. *Be merciful, O God.* SAB, organ. Paraclete (1998) PPM09814

51:00   Jenkins, Steve. *Create in me.* Unison or 2-part, kbd. MorningStar (1998) 80-302

51:00 (paraphrased)
Mendelssohn, Felix (arr. Hal H. Hopson). *Hear, O Lord* (from *Christus*). 2-part, organ. Lorenz (1981) found in *NINE BY TWO*

51:00 (based on)
Mozart, W. A. (arr. Theron Kirk). *Mercy, God have mercy.* 2-part mixed, kbd. (Music is adapted from the *Miserere nobis* from a Litany that Mozart composed in 1776.) Coronet (Presser) (1997) 392-42082

51:00 (paraphrase)
Purcell, Henry (arr. Hal H. Hopson). *O God, have mercy* (from *Pafunsanias the betrayer*). 2-part mixed, kbd. Lorenz (1981) found in *NINE BY TWO*

51:1   White, David Ashley. *Miserere mei.* SATB, kro. Paraclete (1996) PPMO 9632

51:1a, 2, 7, 9, 13
Schalk, Carl. *Have mercy on me, O God.* SATB, kro. Augsburg (1998) 11-10937

51:1-4, 7-9
Hopson, Hal H. *A Psalm of confession.* SATB, optional solo, kro. Augsburg Fortress (2001) 0-8006-5952-X

51:1-8, 10-12
> White, David Ashley. *Psalm 51, have mercy on me, O God* (under title *Two Lenten anthems*). SATB, organ. Randall Egan (1993) EC 254

51:3-4, 9 Gregorian Chant (setting by Richard Keys Biggs). *The Asperges.* SATB, optional organ. OCP (1987) 9055

51:3-4, 12, 14, 17, 19
> Hurd, Bob (arr. Craig Kingsbury). *Psalm 51: Create in me.* SATB, alto saxophone, kbd. OCP (1996) 10251

51:9-13 Locke, Matthew (ed. George Guest). *Turn thy face from my sins* (#3 of *Three penitential anthems from the Gostling manuscript c. 1706*). SSATB, organ. Paraclete (1996) PPMO 9629

51:9-13 (based on)
> Wilkinson, Sandy. *Take my heart* (uses hymn tune *Ellers*). SATB, kbd. GlorySound (Shawnee) (1999) A 7376

51:10-12 Roth, John. *Create in me.* Unison, 1 or 2 instruments in C, kbd. Concordia (1997) 98-3389

51:10-12 Willan, Healey (arr. Henry V. Gerike). *Create in me a clean heart, O God.* TTBB, kro. Concordia (2000) 98-3605

51:10-13 James, Layton. *Create in me.* SATB, S/solo, piano or harp. MorningStar (1999) 50-3043

51:11-13 (10-12)
> Schultz, Ralph C. *Create in me.* SATB, organ. MorningStar (1997) MSM-50-3034

51:17, 19 Handel, G. F. (arr. Richard Langdon). *The sacrifice of God* (from *Rinaldo*). SATB, kbd. Coronet (Presser) (1999) 392-42276

51:20-15 Wagner, Douglas E. *Create in me a clean heart.* SAB, organ. Sacred Music Press (Lorenz) (1993) 10/1088

51:20-15 Wagner, Douglas E. *Create in me a clean heart.* SATB, organ. Sacred Music Press (Lorenz) (1993) 10/1089

55:1-7 Mendelssohn, Felix (ed. & arr. Robert S. Hines). *Hymne - Hear my prayer.* S/solo, SATB, organ. Concordia (2000) 98-3513

55:22 (Kirkland)
> Kirkland, Terry. *Cast your burden upon the Lord.* SATB, kbd. Triune Music (Lorenz) (1994) 10/1227T

55:22 Mendelssohn, Felix (ed. Nancy Telfer). *Cast your burden upon the Lord* (*Elijah*). SATB, kro. Kjos (1992) 8738

57:5, 7-8 Handel, George F. (arr. Mark Mataranglo). *O exult yourself above the heavens* (duet from *Judas Maccabaeus*). 2-part mixed, organ. Augsburg (1994) 11-10549

57:7-11 Powell, Robert J. *My heart is steadfast, O God.* SATB, organ. Concordia (1997) 98-3352

57:7-11 Young, Philip M. *My heart is steadfast, O God.* SATB, organ, optional brass (2 trumpets, horn, trombone, tuba). Concordia (1996) 98-3290

59:16-17 Nesheim, Paul. *I will sing of Thy might.* SATB divsi, no acc. Roger Dean (1998) 10/1821R

60:00 Gastoldi, Giovanni G. (ed. Harry Johansen). *Deus in adjutorium* (#1 of *Vesper Psalms*). SSATTB, organ continuo. Roger Dean (1995) 10/1296R-3

63:00 (and other)
> Joncas, Michael. *As morning breaks.* SATB, kbd. OCP (1994) 10755

63:00 Kosche, Kenneth T. and John A. Behnke. *Psalm 63* (#3 of *3 festival Psalms*). SATB, 3 octave handbells. Concordia (1997) 98-3365

63:00 (based on)
    Medema, Ken and Ron Harris (arr. Ron Harris). *In the shadow of your wings.* SATB, kbd. Ron Harris Music (1999) RH 0709

63:00 (based on)
    Pethel, Stan. *We come rejoicing.* SATB, kbd. Choristers Guild (1998) CGA 816

63:1-8   Hurd, Bob (arr. Craig S. Kingsbury) *My soul is thirsting.* OCP (1991) 9450

63:2-6   Callahan, Charles. *My soul is thirsting for you, O Lord, my God.* SATB, organ, optional flute.

63:2-9   Haugen, Marty. *In the morning I will sing.* 2-part, woodwind in C, kbd. GIA (1993) G-4276

65:00 (Psalm 66)
    Bober, Melody (arr. Gregg Sewell). *Praise awaits you.* Any 2 voices, kbd. Laurel (Lorenz) (1999) 10/2148L

65:00 (paraphrased)
    Haydn, Franz Joseph (arr. Walter Ehret). *Fields are dancing with ripened corn* (from *The Seasons*). SATB, kbd. Concordia (1999) 98-3523

65:00   SEE: I Thessalonians 2:19. McDonald, Mary. *Call forth with songs of joy*

65:10-11, 14
    Bell, John L. *With grace and carefulness.* SATB, kbd. GIA (1998) 4670

66:00   SEE: Psalm 65:00. Bober, Melody. *Praise awaits you*

66:1-2   SEE: Isaiah 48:20b. Jennings, Kenneth. *With a voice of singing.*

66:1-2   SEE: Psalm 100:00. Mozart, W. A. (ed. Robert Kendall). *Jubilate Deo (O be joyful)*

66:1, 2   Schultz, Ralph C. *Sing for joy.* SATB, kro. Concordia (2000) 98-3597

67:00   Bales, Gerald. *Deus misereatur (Psalm 67).* SATB, organ. Randall Egan (1987)

67:00   Bouman, Paul. *God be merciful.* 2-part, kbd. MorningStar (2000) MSM-50-7039

67:00   Carter, Andrew. *God be merciful unto us and bless us.* SATB, organ. Oxford (1994) A 420

67:00   Christopherson, Dorothy. *Let all the peoples praise God.* SSA, kbd. Concordia (1998) 98-3453

67:00   Johengen, Carl. *Let all the peoples praise you!* SAB, kbd. GIA (1994) G-3997

67:00   Kauffmann, Ronald. *Let the people praise Thee, O God.* SATB, organ. Concordia (1998) 98-3428

67:00 (with George Herbert)
    Pasatieri, Thomas. *Canticle of praise.* SATB, organ. Presser (1997) 312-41707

67:1-2   Lantz, David, III. *May God be gracious* (#2 of *Introit and Benediction*). SATB, kbd. Shawnee (1995) A 6991

67:3 (based on)
    Sleeth, Natalie. *Let all the people praise thee* (quotes tune *St. Anne*). 2-part mixed or SATB, kbd., optional trumpet. Found in *10 anthems for about 10 singers.* Lorenz (1990) 45/1094L

67:3-5   Scott, K. Lee. *Let all the world.* SATB, organ. Hinshaw (1994) HMC 1365

68:00 (paraphrased)
    SEE: Isaiah 35:4c-61. Westra, Evret. *The Lord, our God, will come*

68:18   SEE: Psalm 47:5-6. Lawson, Gordon. *God is gone up*

69:00 Gastoldi, Giovanni (Harry Johansen, ed). *Deus in adjutorium* (Psalm 69, #1 of *Vesper Psalms*). SSATTB, continuo. Latin only. Roger Dean (1995) 10/1296R

69:1, 3, 7, 10, 13, 14
Blow, John (ed. George Guest). *Save me, O God* (#2 of *Three penitential anthems from the Gostling Manuscript c. 1706*). SATB, organ. Paraclete (1996) PPMO 9628

69:30 (based on)
McDonald, Mary. *Praise the Lord in a song.* SATB, kbd. Purifoy (Lorenz) (1993) 10/1051

70:1 (Psalm 71:2, Psalm 109:26)
Himmel, F. H. (arr. and abridged by Ellen Jane Lorenz). *Incline thine ear.* A/ or B/solo, SATB, kbd. Lorenz (1951) found in *Simplified standard anthems,* I

71:2 SEE: Psalm 70:1. Himmel, F. H. *Incline thine ear*

72:00 Cornell, Garry A. *Hail to the Lord's annointed.* SATB, organ. AMSI (1995) 704

72:00 (Psalm 84:00)
Mozart, W. A. (arr. Jay Daniels). *Holy be Thy glorious name.* SAB, kbd. Coronet (Presser) (1999) 392-42259; also available SATB, 392-41475

72:00 (Psalm 84:00)
Mozart, W. A. (arr. Jay Daniels). *Holy be Thy glorious name.* SATB, kbd. Coronet (Presser) (1999) 392-41475

72:00 Owens, Sam Batt. *He shall come down like rain.* SATB, no acc. Paraclete (1995) PPMO 9533

72:00 Schröter, Leonhart (setting by Mark Bender). *Hail to the Lord's annointed.* SATB, trumpet, optional timpani, organ. Concordia (1990) 98-2888

72:6, 8, 11a
Owens, Sam Batt. *He shall come down.* SAB, organ. MorningStar (1997) MSM-50-0302

72:18-19 McDonald, Mary. *Blessed be our Lord.* SSATB, kbd. Purifoy Publishing (Lorenz) (1994) 10/1146

74:1-3 Blow, John (ed. George Guest). *O God, wherefore art thou absent* (#1 of *Three penitential anthems from the Gostling Manuscript c. 1706*). SSATB, organ. Paraclete (1996) PPMO 96630

77:00 Bell, John L. *I cry to God.* SATB, solo voice, flute or oboe, organ. GIA (1996) G-4530

80:00 (Watts)
Croft, William (arr. Hal H. Hopson). *Festival 'St. Anne.'* SATB, brass, handbells, organ. AMSI (1985) 498, brass parts available separately

80:00 Powell, Robert J. *Give ear, O shepherd of Israel.* SATB, organ. Paraclete (1995) PPMO 9529

80:2-3, 15-16, 18-19
Roberts, Leon C. *Lord, make us turn to you.* SATB, piano. OCP (1996) 10783

81:00 (taken from)
Butler, Eugene. *God our strength.* SATB, kbd. Hal Leonard (1997) 08741032

81:1 (Psalm 145:1-4, 10, 11a, 12, 21)
Bisbee, B. Wayne. *Sing for joy to God our strength.* SATB, 2 trumpets, organ. GIA (1994) G 3825

81:1-3 Scott, K. Lee. *Sing aloud to God our strength.* SATB, brass quartet or organ. Augsburg Fortress (2001) 0-8006-5971-6

81:3 SEE: I Corinthians 15:20, 55, 57. Wagner, Douglas E. *Easter fanfare.*

82:8 Handel, G. F. (arr. Walter Ehret). *Arise, O God, and judge the nations* (from *Joshua*). SATB, kbd. Elkan-Vogel (Presser) (1999) 392-03413

84:00 Albrecht, Ronald. *Even the sparrow.* SAB, kbd. Mark Foster (1994) MF 2107

84:00   Alstott, Owen. *How lovely is your dwelling place.* Unison, kbd. OCP (1983) 8431

84:00 (Psalm 141, Watts)
             Croft, William (arr. John Ferguson). *A song of hope* (based on tune *St. Anne*). SATB, 2 trumpets, 2 trombones, handbells. GIA (1993) G-3891

84:00   Goebel-Komala, Felix. *How lovely is your dwelling place.* SATB, kbd. GIA (1996) G-4406

84:00   Horman, John D. *Oh, how beautiful!* SATB, optional flute, and handbells, kbd. Choristers Guild (1997) CGA 773

84:00   Mackie, Ruth E. *Psalm 84.* SATB, optional descanting instrument, organ. Concordia (1966) 98-3305

84:00   Marshall, Jane. *How lovely is your dwelling place.* SATB, organ. Augsburg (1998) 11-10817, found in *The Augsburg choirbook, Sacred choral music of the twentieth century,* ed. Kenneth Jennings

84:00   SEE: Psalm 72:00. Mozart, W. A. (arr. Jay Daniels). *Holy be Thy glorious name*

84:00   Mulholland, James Quitman. *Psalm 84.* SATB, piano (optional instrumental ensemble). Plymouth (1994) JM-112

84:00   Rutter, John. *O how amiable are Thy dwellings.* SATB, kbd. Hinshaw (1994) HMC 1393 (parts for 2 flutes, harp, strings available from publisher)

84:1, 2, 4 SEE: Psalm 122:1. Pote, Allen. *In this house of worship*

84:1, 2, 4, 12
             Bales, Gerald. *Quam Dilecta (How lovely are thy dwellings)* (English). SATB, organ. Randall M. Egan (1995) EC-342

84:3-4, 12
             SEE: Psalm 27:5. Proulx, Richard. *One thing I seek*

84:4, 5, 12 SEE: Romans 8:35-39. Young, Jeremy. *Nothing can come between us*

85:00   Hurd, Bob (arr. Craig Kingsbury). *Psalm 85: Show us your kindness.* SATB, kbd. OCP (1993) 9874

85:00   Martinson, Joel. *Psalm 85.* Soloist or cantor, congregation, flute, organ. Concordia (1996) 97-6587

85:6, 7   Dietterich, Philip R. *Wilt not thou turn again, O God?* SAB, organ. Lorenz (1985) found in *Sacred anthem book*

85:8-9, 13
             Behnke, John A. *Listen to what the Lord is saying* (from *Three Psalms for unison choir*). Unison, kbd. Concordia (2000) 98-3578

85:9, 12-13
             Kohrs, Jonathan. *Surely his salvation is at hand* (Offertory: Advent I). SAB, organ. Concordia (1996) 98-3279

86:00 (paraphrased)
             Handel, G. F. (arr. Geoffrey Allen). *Bow down and hear me* (adapted from *Rinaldo*). SATB, kbd. Coronet (Presser) (1997) 392-42135

86:00 (based on)
             Rogner, James A. *Give ear, O Lord, and visit me.* SATB, organ. MorningStar (2000) MSM-50-6501

86:00   Sedio, Mark. *Teach me your way, O Lord.* 2-part, kbd. AMSI (1995) 711

86:1, 3, 5 Arensky, Anton. *Bow down thine ear, O Lord.* SATB, kro. J. Fischer. Found in *Twenty-five anthems from the Russian liturgy*

86:9   SEE: Revelation 15:3-4. Callahan, Charles. *Revelation canticle*

86:11-12, 15-16a
             Bisbee, B. Wayne. *Teach me your way, O Lord.* 2-part mixed, kbd. Augsburg (1995) 11-10603

89:00   Butler, Eugene. *Let the heavens praise your wonders.* SATB, optional trumpet, kbd. Coronet (Presser) (1998) 392-42179

89:1   SEE: Jeremiah 33:10-11, 14-16. Weber, Paul. *I will sing the story of your love*

89:1, 2   Levi, Michael. *Canticle.* SSA, no acc. Henry David Music (Presser) (2000) 392-02526

89:2, 21-22, 25 27, 29, 34   Inwood, Paul. *I will sing for ever of your love, O Lord.* Unison, kbd. OCP (1977) 10144

89:26-28, 51 (Psalm 132:14, 16-17)   Neswick, Bruce. *I will set his dominion in the sea.* SATB, organ. Paraclete (1995) PPM 90519

90:00   Bell, John L. *Lord, you have been our refuge.* SATB, no acc. GIA (1995) G-4297

90:00   Breedlove, Jennifer. *Throughout every age.* SATB, flute, kbd. OCP (1989) 9575

90:00   Keil, Kevin. *Guide us, Lord.* SATB, kbd. OCP (1993) 10045

90:1 (Lamentations 3:22; Psalm 100:5)   Ferguson, John. *A song of thanksgiving.* SATB organ. Augsburg (1998) 11-10817, found in *The Augsburg choirbook, Sacred choral music of the twentieth century,* ed. Kenneth Jennings.

90:1, 2 (and other)   Martin, Gilbert M. *True builder of the house.* SATB, organ. Sacred Music (1995) 10/1205

90:1-6, 12, 17   Landes, Rob. *Lord, Thou hast been our dwelling place.* T/solo, SATB, organ. MorningStar (1998) MSM-50-9097

91:00   Hurd, Bob (arr. Craig Kingsbury). *Psalm 91: Be with me.* SATB, kbd. OCP (1991) 1-250

91:00   Joncas, Michael (arr. Edwin Earle Ferguson). *On eagles' wings.* SATB, kbd. North American Liturgy Resources (1983) n.#.

91:00 (based on)   Lisicky, Paul. *Shelter.* SAB, optional flute, kbd. GIA (1997) G-4426

91:00   SEE: Psalm 1. McCabe, Michael. *A Psalm of the redeemed*

91:1, 4   SEE: Psalm 121:5, 7. Page, Anna Laura. *The Lord is my keeper*

91:1-6, 10-11   Janco, Steven R. *God has put the angels in charge of you.* Unison, 2 instruments in C, kbd. GIA (1997) G-4215

91:1-7, 9-12   Courtney, Craig. *Psalm 91.* SATB, flute, harp, or piano and optional string quartet. Beckenhorst (1998) BP150, parts available from publisher

91:4, 11-12   Busarow, Donald. *He shall give his angels charge over thee.* SA, optional C/B-flat instrument, kbd. Concordia (1994) 98-3168

91:9-12, 15-16   Hillert, Richard. *He shall give his angels charge over you.* Unison, organ, oboe, optional string quartet. GIA (1993) G-3983

91:11   SEE: Psalm 17:8. West, John E. (arr. Bonnie Barrett). *Hide me under the shadow of thy wings*

91:11, 12 (Luke 2:9-14; Luke 24:1-5; Psalm 103:20)   Nelson, Ronald A. *Angels.* 2-part, kbd. AMSI (1996) 726

92:00 (Scottish Psalter, 1650)   Butler, Eugene. *To render thanks.* SATB, kbd. Coronet (Presser) (1997) 392-41208

92:00   Schutte, Dan (arr. Randall DeBruyn). *Like cedars.* SATB, optional instruments, kbd. OCP (1992) 10322

92:00 (adapted from)
Starr, David. *It is a good thing to sing.* SAB, kbd. Presser (1998) 392-42189

92:1-3
Kosche, Kenneth T. *It is a good thing.* SATB divsi, no acc. Augsburg Fortress (2001) 0-8006-5963-5

92:1-5
Bouman, Paul. *It is a good thing to give thanks.* SATB, kbd. MorningStar (2000) MSM-50-6503

92:1-5, 12
Busarow, Donald. *It is a good thing to give thanks (Psalm 92).* SATB, handbells (4 octaves), organ. Concordia (1994) 98-3126

93:00 (adapted from)
Barrett, Michael. *Truly God is good (#2 of Two S.A.B. praise anthems).* SAB, kbd, optional electric bass. Shawnee Press (1995) D-5450

93:00
Willcock, Christopher. *The Lord now rules.* SATB, organ. OCP (1994) 10893

95:00 (adapted)
Aks, Catherine. *Venite, exultemus Domino (Let us come and praise the Lord* (Latin/English). SSA, kro. E. Henry David (Presser) 392-02522

95:00
Bertalot, John. *Alleluia, come, let us sing.* Two equal voices, kbd. Choristers Guild (1994) CGA679

95:00 (based on)
Choplin, Papper. *Psalm of joy.* SATB, kbd. Monarch Music (Lorenz) (1996) 10/1455M

95:00
SEE: Psalm 118:24. Fischer, David. *Sing praise and celebrate*

95:00 (based on)
Haugen, Marty. *Come, O come, let us sing (Venite).* 2-part mixed, woodwind in C, kbd. GIA (1995) G-4275

95:00
Hurd, Bob and Joe Bellamy (arr. Craig Kingsbury). *Psalm 95: If today.* SATB, flute, kbd. OCP (1995) 10249

95:00 (Psalm 96:00; Psalm 100 adapted)
Jordan, Alice. *Sing with joy.* SATB, organ. Birnamwood (MorningStar) (2001) MSM-80-709

95:00 (Psalm 96:00)
Lantz, David, III. *O come, let us sing unto the Lord* (#1 of *Introit and Benediction*). SATB, kbd. Shawnee Press (1995) A 6991

95:00 (adapted)
Larson, Lloyd. *O God we do exalt your name.* 2-part any combination, kbd. Found in *Instant anthems of praise,* Lorenz (2000) 45/1091L

95:00
Sedio, Mark. *Raise a joyful sound (Sing alleluia! Jesus lives!)* SATB, brass quartet, organ. Selah (1997) 410-895; instruments 410-896

95:1 (Isaiah 61:1, and other)
Clay, Crystal Davis. *A jubilant song.* SSATB, kbd. Purifoy Publishing (Lorenz) (1994) 10/1233P

95:1 (Psalm 96:9, 13)
Martin, Gilbert M. *Canticle of praise (Venite exultemus).* SATB, organ. Sacred Music Press (1992) S-523

95:1-7
Romer, Charles B. *Come, let us sing to the Lord!* SATB, optional flute, kbd. Singspiration (Zondervan) (1982) ZJP 7424

96:00
Bell, John L. *Sing a new song* SATB, kbd. GIA (1998) G4672

96:00 (Scottish Psalter)
Butler, Eugene. *Sing all the earth to God.* SATB, kbd. Coronet (Presser) (1995) 392-41847

96:00
Cortez, Jaime. *Vayan al mundo/Go out to the world* (English/Spanish). SATB, kbd. OCP (1994) 10494

96:00 (Psalm 98:00; Psalm 100:00)
Courtney, Craig. *Sing to the Lord a new song* (III of *Three sacred canticles*). SATB, organ, brass quintet, timpani, cymbals. Beckenhorst (1999) BP1549

96:00　SEE: Psalm 118:24. Fischer, David. *Sing praise and celebrate*

96:00 (paraphrased)
　　Haydn, Franz Joseph (arr. Hal H. Hopson). *Sing to the Lord a new song.* SATB, kbd. (optional orchestra). Birnamwood (MorningStar) (1999) MSM-50-2503A; full score MSM-50-2503; choir score MSM-50-2503A; instrumental parts MSM-50-2503B

96:00 (based on)
　　Martin, Joseph M. *Come, sing unto the Lord.* 2-part mixed, kbd. Found in *Instant anthems of praise,* Lorenz (2000) 45/1091L

96:00 (paraphrased)
　　Scott, K. Lee. *Declare God's glory.* SATB, organ, handbells, brass, percussion. Concordia (2000) 98-3555

96:00　SEE: Psalm 95:00. Jordan, Alice. *Sing with joy*

96:00　SEE: Psalm 95:00. Lantz, David, III. *O come, let us sing unto the Lord*

96:00 (adapted)
　　Larson, Lloyd. *Declare the glory among the nations!* SATB, kbd., optional brass. Hinshaw (1995) HMC 1416

96:00 (taken from)
　　Pelz, Walter L. *A Psalm of cele-bration.* SATB, brass quartet, organ. Augsburg (1994) 11-10356; instruments 11-10357

96:00 (based on)
　　Martin, Joseph M. *Come, sing unto the Lord.* 2-part mixed, kbd. Timespan Music (Lorenz) (1994) 10/1236T

96:00　Matthews, Thomas. *Sing, sing to the Lord.* SATB, organ. FitzSimons (1967, 1993) F2221

96:00 (Isaiah 43:1b-3a, based on)
　　Pote, Allen. *A new song.* SATB, optional flutes and tambourine, kbd. Hope (1994) A685

96:00 (paraphrased)
　　Scott, K. Lee. *Sing to the Lord a new song.* SATB, children's choir, handbells (3 or 4 octaves), organ. Concordia (1994) 98-3124

96:1　Handel, G. F. (arr. Robert N. Roth). *O sing unto the Lord.* SAB, kbd. Coronet (Presser) (1995) 392-41818

96:1　Handel, G. F. (arr. Robert N. Roth). *O sing unto the Lord.* SATB, kbd. Coronet (Presser) (1995) 392-41829

96:1　Sweelinck, Jan P. (ed. and arr. Robert S. Hines). *Sing to the Lord.* SATB, kro. Concordia (1995) 98-3211

96:1-3　Hassler, Hans Leo (ed. John Hooper) *Cantate Domino* (English/Latin). SATB, kro. Concordia (1994) 98-3147

96:1, 3　Mozart, W. A. (arr. Henry Kihlken). *Sing to the Lord a new song* (from *Vespers,* K. 321). SATB, kbd. Coronet (Presser) (1995) 392-41874

96:1-3, 7-8, 10 (adapted)
　　Connolly, Michael. *Tell all the nations.* SATB, 2 flutes, kbd. GIA (1995) G-4029

96:1-4　Martinson, Joel. *O sing to the Lord a new song* (from *Salvation unto us has come*). SSAA, organ. Paraclete (1997) 9710

96:1-4 (paraphrase, Hopson)
　　Swedish folk tune (setting by Hal H. Hopson). *Oh, sing to God a new song.* (Also has text for *Prepare the royal highway.*) Unison or 2-part, kbd. MorningStar (1995) MSM-50-0301

96:1-4 (Psalm 6:9)
　　White, David Ashley. *Cantate Domino.* SATB, brass quintet, organ. Paraclete (1996) PPMO 9605S, full score; PPMO 9605, choral part; PPMO 9605, brass parts

96:1-4a, 7a, 8, 11-12
　　Behnke, John A. *Sing to the Lord a new song.* 2-part choir, kbd, optional handbells (3 octaves). Concordia (1999) 98-3503; handbells 97-6800

96:1-10   Sharpe, Carlyle. *Sing unto the Lord a new song.* SATB, brass quartet, percussion, organ. Hinshaw (1996) HMC 1483

96:7-9   SEE: Psalm 107:1, 9-10, 20, 22. Beethoven, Ludwig van (ed. Richard Proulx). *Give thanks to God*

96:9, 13 SEE: Psalm 95:1. Martin, Gilbert M. *Canticle of praise (Venite exultemus)*

97:00   Manalo, Ricky. *Be glad in the Lord.* Unison, optional instrument in C, kbd. GIA (1997) G-4363

97:00   Zaimont, Judith Lang. *Psalm 97* (from *Sacred service*). SAATB/solos, SATB, piano (orchestra material on rental). Galaxy (1981) I.2878

98:00   See Psalm 96:00. Courtney, Craig. *Sing to the Lord a new song*

98:00 (Wesley)
          Glaser, Carl G. (arr. Theron Kirk). *O for a thousand tongues.* SATB, organ. Oxford (1992) 94.243

98:00   Glaser, Carl (arr. David W. Music). *O for a thousand tongues to sing* (based on *Azmon*). SATB, brass (2 trumpets, 2 trombones, timpani, optional tuba), organ. GIA (1994) G 3788

98:00   Glaser, Charles (arr. Walter Pelz). *O for a thousand tongues to sing* (based on *Azmon*). SATB, cello, organ. Augsburg (1990) 11-2556

98:00   SEE: Isaiah 9:6. Kosche, Kenneth T. *Unto us a child is born*

98:00   Martinson, Joel. *Psalm 98.* SATB, trumpet, organ. Concordia (1995) 98-3225

98:00 (based on)
          McClellan, Michael. *A new song of praise.* SAB, cantor, optional congregation, kbd. Lorenz (1997) 10/1554U

98:00   Monteverdi, Claudio (ed. Karl-Heinz Schnee). *Cantate Domino (Sing ye unto the Lord)* (Latin/English). SSATBB, kbd, optional instruments. Walton (1980) W2315

98:00   Schweizer, Mark. *Let all the rivers clap their hands.* SATB, kbd. Concordia (1998) 98-3427

98:00 (Wesley) (Isaiah 43:1, 3)
          Wetzler, Robert. *Oh, for a thousand tongues.* SATB, organ. Concordia (1996) 98-3295

98:00   Young, Gordon. *O for a thousand tongues to sing* (based on tune *Richmond*). SATB, kbd. Flammer (1988) A 6382

98:1, 2, 5-8
          SEE: Psalm 118:24. Wright, Paul Leddington. *This is the day*

98:1-3, 8 Pachelbel, Johann (ed. Donald Rotermund). *Sing to the Lord a new song.* SATB/SATB, no acc. Concordia (1997) 98-3329

98:1-3, 9 Pachelbel, Johann (arr. William Braun). *Sing to the Lord a new song.* 2-part mixed, kbd. Concordia (1994) 98-3151

98:4-6 (based on)
          Wyrtzen, Don. *Fanfare of praise.* SATB, kbd. Singspiration (Zondervan) (1986) ZJP7014

99:1-3   Behnke, John A. *The Lord is king* (from *Three Psalms for unison choir*). Unison, kbd. Concordia (2000) 98-3578

99:1-3, 9 White, David Ashley. *The Lord is king.* SATB, organ. Randall M. Egan (1990) EC 184

100:00 (based on)
          Akins, John R. *Enter his gates with thanksgiving.* SATB, kbd. Sound III (1987) ES3007B

100:00 (Ken)
> Anonymous (ed. William P. Rowan). *Praise God from whom all blessings flow* (19th-century American tune). SATB, no acc. GIA (1997) G-4398

100:00 Bales, Gerald. *Jubilate Deo.* SATB, 3 trumpets, 3 trombones, percussion (timpani, suspended cymbal, snare drum), organ. Waterloo Music (Randall M. Egan) (1966, 1990) EC92-108

100:00 SEE: Acts 13:47, 52. Canedo, Ken. *We are a light*

100:00 Carr, Benjamin. *O be joyful.* SAB, kbd. Boston Music (1992) found in *Early American sacred choral library,* vol. 1

100:00 SEE: Psalm 96:00. Courtney, Craig. *Sing to the Lord a new song*

100:00 (Lee)
> Dean, Stephen. *Peoples of earth.* SATB, kbd. OCP (1993) 10667

100:00 Diemer, Emma Lou. *Psalm 100.* SATB, organ, drum and optional brass quartet. Sacred Music Press (1996) 10/1252; brass parts 30/1158

100:00 Halmos, László. *Jubilate deo.* SATB, no acc. Santa Barbara Music (1990) SBMP 24

100:00 Handel, G. F. (arr. Hal H. Hopson). *Lift up your voice and sing* (adapted from *Joshua*). 2-part mixed, kbd. Coronet (Presser) (1995) 392-41856

100:00 (adapted)
> Harlan, Benjamin. *Make a joyful noise.* SATB, kbd. Shawnee (1986) A-6258

100:00 Heck, Lyle. *Make a joyful noise unto the Lord.* 2-part (SA, TB, or SB), flute, kbd. Augsburg (1995) 11-10601

100:00 Hodges, Edward. *O praise the Lord.* SATB, kbd. Boston Music (1992) found in *Early American sacred choral library,* vol. 2

100:00 Hopson, Hal H. *Jubilate Deo (Be joyful you people).* SATB, organ, optional handbells. MorningStar (2000) MSM-50-2508

100:00 James, Donald. *O be joyful in the Lord.* SATB, organ. Paraclete (1996) 9640

100:00 James, Layton. *Make a joyful noise unto the Lord.* SATB, organ. MorningStar (1997) MSM-50-7022

100:00 SEE: Psalm 95:00. Jordan, Alice. *Sing with joy*

100:00 Kalbach, Don. *Make a joyful noise.* SATB, piano. Presser (1998) 312-41715

100:00 Kerrick, Mary Ellen. *Shout for joy.* 2-part, optional handbells (3 octaves), kbd. Choristers Guild (1997) CGA 771

100:00 McHugh, Charles R. *Psalm 100.* SATB, kro. Randall Egan (1992) n.#.

100:00 (and other)
> McDonald, Mary. *Unto God be glory.* SSATB with orchestra. Monarch Music (Lorenz) (1996) 10/1457

100:00 (paraphrased)
> Mozart, W. A. (arr. Hal H. Hopson). *To God be joyful* (from *Regina coeli,* K. 108). SAB, kbd. Shawnee Press (1984) D-5371

100:00 (paraphrased)
> Mozart, W. A. (arr. Hal H. Hopson). *To God be joyful* (from *Regina coeli,* K. 108). SATB, kbd. Shawnee Press (1984) A-6142

100:00 (Psalm 66:1, 2)
> Mozart, W. A. (ed. Robert Kendall). *Jubilate Deo (O be joyful)* (Latin/ English), K. 117. SATB, kbd. Concordia (1995) 98-3191; instrumental parts 97-6513

100:00 Patterson, Joy F. *Be joyful in the Lord.* SATB, kbd. MorningStar (1997) MSM-50-7026

100:00 (paraphrased)
> Pergolesi, Gian Battista (arr. Hal H. Hopson). *O bless the Lord, O my soul.* 2-part voices, kbd. GIA (1997) G-4387

100:00 Powell, Robert J. *Be joyful in the Lord.* Unison, optional flute, kbd. Choristers Guild (1997) CGA765

100:00 Praetorius, Hieronymus. *Gaudete omnes.* SSATTB, continuo. J&W Chester (1970) ABC 5

100:00 Scott, K. Lee. *Festival jubilate.* SATB, organ (or horn, 3 trumpets, 2 trombones, timpani). Concordia (1995) 98-3195

100:00 Selby, William. *O be joyful in the Lord.* SATB, kbd. Boston Music, found in *Early American sacred choral library,* vol. 2

100:00 Schubert, Franz (arr. Walter Rodby). *O be joyful, joyful in the Lord (Jubilate Deo).* SATB, kbd. Coronet (Presser) (1996) 392-41998

100:00 Schütz, Heinrich (ed. Leonard Van Camp). *O be joyful, all ye nations (Jubilate Deo omnia terra)* (English/ Latin). Unison (or solo), 2 treble instruments, kbd. Unicorn (1981) 1.0023.2

100:00 Star, David. *Shout for joy.* SATB, kbd. Coronet (Presser) (1999) 392-42218

100:00 (and other)
> Sweelinck, Jan P. (ed. Leonard Van Camp). *Gaudete omnes (Rejoice, ye people)* (Latin/English). SSATB, kro. Concordia (1995) 98-3212

100:1, 2 (based on)
> Mozart, W. A. (arr. Hal H. Hopson). *Come be joyful* (from *Thamaos, König in Ägypten*). 2-part mixed, kbd. MorningStar (1997) MSM-50-7302

100:1-2a Schiavone, John. *Cry out with joy.* SATB, kro. GIA (1992) 9806

100:1, 2, 4
> SEE: Psalm 122:1. Hallquist, Gary. *I was glad*

100:2 (and other)
> Handel, George F. (arr. Theron Kirk). *Sing his praise!* SATB, kbd. Coronet (Presser) (1995) 392-41945

100:4 (Matthew 6:13)
> Bish, Diane. *Introit and prayer.* Hinshaw (1988) SATB, organ. Hinshaw (1988) C22

100:4-5 Nickson, John. *A festive alleluia.* SATB, organ. Kjos (1981) 5999

100:5 SEE: Psalm 90:1. Ferguson, John. *A song of thanksgiving*

103:00 (based on)
> Dengler, Lee. *Bless the Lord, O my soul.* SATB, optional youth choir, optional percussion, kbd. GlorySound (Shawnee) (1999) A 7361

103:00 Ellis, John. *Praise, my soul, the king of heaven.* SATB, kbd. Presser (1998) 392-42203

103:00 Honoré, Jeffrey. *Psalm 103: The Lord is compassionate* (found in *Psalter for bells and voices,* Set I). SATB, congregation, handbells (3-5 octaves), kbd. Concordia (1999) 98-3508; handbells 97-6781

103:00 Jennings, Carol, arr. *Praise, my soul, the God of heaven* (based on tune *Lauda anima*). SATB, organ. Augsburg Fortress (1977) 11-10811

103:00 Jennings, Carolyn. *Bless the Lord, O my soul.* SATB, kbd. Kjos (2000) 8925

103:00 Kosche, Kenneth T. and John A. Behnke. *Psalm 103 (#2 of 3 festival Psalms).* SATB, 3 octave handbells. Concordia (1997) 98-3365

103:00 Lovelace, Austin C. *Bless thou the Lord, O my soul.* SATB, kro. Randall Egan (1960, 1993) EC 215

103:00   Moore, Bob. *Psalm 103: Our God is rich in love.* SATB, kbd. GIA (1993) G3858

103:00   Mulholland, James Quitman. *Psalm 103* (from *Canticle of Psalms*). SATB, piano (optional instrumental ensemble). Plymouth (1994) JM-111; all three Psalms published as *Canticle of Psalms,* JM-109

103:00 (Vajda, based on)
Schütz, Heinrich (arr. John Leavitt). *Give glory all creation.* SATB, solo instrument, percussion. Concordia (2000) 98-3558

103:00 (based on)
Soper, Scott. *Loving and forgiving.* SATB, kbd. OCP (1992) 9893

103:1   Lau, Robert. *Bless the Lord, O my soul* (found in *Choral responses for worship*). SATB, kbd. Coronet (Presser) (1995) 392-41857

103, 1, 2, 8, 11
Ippolitov-Ivanov, Michael (arr. Ellen Jane Lorenz). *Bless the Lord, O my soul.* SAB, kbd. Lorenz (1949, 1969) found in *Anthems for limited choirs,* II

103, 1, 2, 8, 11
Ippolitov-Ivanov, Michael (arr. Ellen Jane Lorenz). *Bless the Lord, O my soul.* SATB, kro. Lorenz (1949) found in *Easy standard anthems,* I

103:1-4   Larson, Sonia. *Psalm 103.* 2-part, optional flute or recorder, kbd. AMSI (1992) 636

103:1-4, 15, 16
James, Gary. *Bless the Lord, O my soul.* SATB, no acc. Randall Egan (1992) n.#.

103:1-5   SEE: Psalm 104:33-34. Hayes, Mark. *Rejoice and sing out his praises*

103:1-5 (Isaiah 40:29-31)
McDonald, Mary. *Like eagles, you will fly!* SATB, kbd. Purifoy (1994) 10/1176

103:1-5, 20-22
Bell, John L. *Bless, O my soul* SATB, kbd. GIA (1998) 4673

103:1-5, 22
Malone, Matthew. *Bless the Lord, O my soul.* SATB, kbd. Triune Music (Lorenz) (1996) 10/1440T

103:1-6 (based on)
Hughes, Robert J. *Praise to the Lord, the almighty.* SAB, kbd. Lorenz (1965) found in *Anthems for limited choirs*

103:1-6 (based on)
Steffy, Thurlow T., arr. *Praise to the Lord, the almighty.* SATB, kbd. Coronet (Presser) (1995) 392-41926

103:1, 8, 11
Cobb, Nancy Hill. *Bless the Lord, O my soul.* 2-part, kbd. Lorenz (1995) 10/1339K

103:13   Haan, Raymond H. *Like as a father.* SATB, organ. MorningStar (1997) MSM-50-9091

103:20   SEE: Psalm 91:11, 12. Nelson, Ronald A. *Angels*

104:00 (based on)
Boyce, William (alt. and arr. Jane McFadden and Janet Linker). *Psalm of joy.* 2-part, kbd, optional handbells (2 octaves). Choristers Guild (1997) CGA 760

104:00   Cooney, Rory. *Psalm 104: Send out your spirit.* SATB, flute, kbd. OCP (1991) 5896

104:00   Cotter, Jeanne. *Lord, send out your spirit.* Unison, kbd. GIA (1995) G-4630

104:00 (based on)
Foley, John S. J. *Your works, O God.* SATB, kbd. OCP (1997) 10761

104:1, 24, 29-30, 31, 34
SEE: Psalm 118:1-2. Chipponis, James J. *Eastertime Psalm*

104:1-12 (The Grail)
Callahan, Charles. *The spirit of the Lord.* SATB, cantor, flute, organ. Concordia (1996) 98-3256

104:6-10 (The Grail)
Callahan, Charles. *Send us your strength, O God.* SATB, cantor, organ. Concordia (1996) 98-3257

104:11-15a (The Grail)
Callahan, Charles. *How many are your works, O Lord.* SAB, flute, organ. Concordia (1996) 98-3258

104:24   Young, Gordon. *Glorious and everlasting God.* SATB, kbd. Harold Flammer (1981) A-5957

104:25, 31, 32, 34
Schalk, Carl. *I will sing to the Lord as long as I live* (found in *Alleluia, I will sing*). Unison, kbd. Augsburg (1986) 11-5115

104:33-34 (Psalm 108:1b; Psalm 103:1-5)
Hayes, Mark. *Rejoice and sing out his praises.* TTBB, kbd. Hinshaw (1985) HMC 1350

105:00 (based on)
Brown, Jody and Jeff McGaha. *O give thanks to the Lord.* SATB, kbd. Purifoy (1995) 10/1370P

107:00   Haas, David. *God shepherds the poor.* 2-part, instrument in C, kbd. GIA (1996) G-4564

107:8 (and Carlton C. Buck)
Butler, Eugene. *Praise him, Alleluia!* 2-part, kbd. Sacred Music Press (1990) found in *Sing to the Lord a new song*

107:8 (and other)
Butler, Eugene. *Praise him, Alleluia!* 2-part any combination, kbd. Found in *10 anthems for about 10 singers.* Lorenz (1990) 45/1094L

107:9-10, 20, 22 (Psalm 96:7-9)
Beethoven, Ludwig van (ed. Richard Proulx). *Give thanks to God,* Op. 48, No. 1. SAB, kbd. Augsburg (1995) 11-10648

108:00 (and other)
Barnard, Mark. *My heart is ready.* SATB, optional flute, handbells, congregation. Lorenz (1995) 10/1398U

108:00   Butler, Eugene. *My heart is ready.* SATB, kbd. Coronet (Presser) (1998) 392-42177

108:00 (Psalm 119:00)
Lindley, Simon. *O God, my heart is ready.* 2-part equal voices, organ. Banks (1986) ECS 162

108:1b   SEE: Psalm 104:33-34. Hayes, Mark. *Rejoice and sing out his praises*

108:1-5   Leaf, Robert. *My heart is ready to sing.* Unison or 2-part, organ. Choristers Guild (1994) CGA676

108:1-5   Martin, Joseph M. *I will awaken the dawn.* SATB, piano. Belwin-Mills (1995) BSC 9514

108:1-6   Nelson, Ronald A. *Higher than the heavens.* Unison, organ. Choristers Guild (1994) CGA671

109:00   Gastoldi, Giovanni (ed. Harry Johansen). *Dixit Dominus* (Psalm 109) (#2 of *Vesper Psalms*). SSATTB, continuo. Latin only. Roger Dean (1995) 10/1296R

109:26   SEE: Psalm 70:1. Himmel, F. H. *Incline thine ear*

110:00   Kosche, Kenneth T. (handbell parts by John A. Behnke). *Psalm 110* (#2 of *3 festival Psalms,* Set 2). SATB, 3 octave handbells. Concordia (1998) 98-3468

111:00   Proulx, Richard. *My heart is full today.* 2-part choir, triangle, tambourine, handbells (or glockenspiel), kbd. Concordia (1997) 98-3361

111:1-3   Kosche, Kenneth T. *Canticle of praise* (based on *Allein Gott in der Höh sei Ehr*). SATB, 3 octave handbells. AMSI (1996) 745

112:00   Vivaldi, Antonio (ed. Joan Whittemore). *Beatus Vir.* SSAA, SS/soli, kbd. JEHMS (1997)

113:00 (Psalm 118:00)
    Ellingboe, Bradley. *The house of the Lord.* SATB, organ, piano, handbells. Kjos (2000) 8926

113:00   Hailstork, Adolpheus. *How long?* (a movement from cantata, *I will lift up mine eyes*). T/solo, SATB, orchestra. Presser (1997, 1998) 312-41723

113:00   Wienhorst, Richard. *Give praise, you servants of the Lord.* SAB, handbells (3 octaves), optional kbd. Concordia (1987) 98-2782

114:00   Bell, John L. *When Israel came out of Egypt's land.* SATB, kbd. GIA (1998) G-4674

115:00 (based on)
    Mendelssohn, Felix (arr. Ellen Jane Lorenz). *The Lord is mindful of his own.* SATB, kbd. Lorenz (1949) found in *Easy standard anthems,* I

115:1 (Zephaniah 3:17, 20)
    Busarow, Donald. *Not unto us, O Lord.* TTBB, no acc. MorningStar (1998) MSM-50-9755

115:1 (Zephaniah 3:17, 20)
    Busarow, Donald. *Not unto us, O Lord.* SATB, organ, optional congregation. Augsburg Fortress (2001) 0-8006-5965-1

115:1, 2   Mozart, W. A. (arr. Willian Livingston). *Not unto us, O Lord* (from *Offertorium in festo St. Benedicti,* K. 34). SATB, kbd. Coronet (Presser) (2000) 302-42281

115:12   Mendelssohn, Felix (arr. Jean Martin). *But the Lord is mindful of His own* (from *St. Paul*). 2-part, kbd. Coronet (Presser) (1931, 1955) 392-41988

115:14   Bach, J. S. (arr. David W. Music). *May God bless you now* (from Cantata 196, *Der Herr denket an uns*). 2-part, kbd. Selah (1997) 410-815

116:00 (taken from)
    Mengel, Dana. *How can I repay the Lord* (#2 in *Triptych for holy week*). SATB, kbd. Logia (Concordia) (1998) 98-3483

116:00   Soper, Scott. *What shall I give.* SATB, kbd. OCP (1992) 9794

116:1-8, 12-13
    Haugen, Marty. *I will walk in the presence of God.* SATB, two woodwinds in C, guitar. GIA (1995) G-4282

116:10-13
    Ducis, Benedictus (ed. Henry V. Gerike). *My faith is sure* (found in set of 3 anthems for men's voices called *Proclaim the mercy of Christ*). TTBB, kro. Concordia (1996) 98-3274

116:12-13, 17-18
    SEE: I Corinthians 10:16. Joncas, Michael. *Our blessing cup*

116:12-14, 17-19
    Tiefenbach, Peter. *What shall I render to the Lord?* SATB, kro. Augsburg (1998) 11-10817, found in *The Augsburg choirbook, Sacred choral music of the twentieth century,* ed. Kenneth Jennings

117:00   Busarow, Donald. *Psalm 117. Praise the Lord, all you nations.* SATB, no acc. MorningStar (1998) MSM-50-7029

117:00   Chant (ed. J. Ritter Werner). *Laudate Dominum* (found in *Gregorian chant, music from antiquity for modern liturgy*). Unison, kbd. Lorenz (1995) 10/1273U

117:00 (based on)
    Larson, Lloyd. *Take up the tambourine.* Unison/2-part, kbd. Choristers Guild (1998) CGA 819

117:00   Mozart, W. A. (ed. Nancy Telfer). *Laudate Dominum* (Latin/English). S/solo, SATB, kbd. Kjos (1992) 8731

117:00   Mulet, Henri (ed. Kenneth Saslaw). *Laudate Dominum* (Latin). STB, organ. Randall M. Egan (1983) n.#.

117:00   Pitoni, Giuseppi O. (ed. Patrick M. Liebergen). *Laudate Dominum (Sing praise to God above)* (Latin/English). SATB, kro. GIA (1997) G-4455

117:00   Roth, John. *From all who dwell below the skies* (uses tune *O Waly, Waly*). SATB, kbd. Concordia (1997) 98-3369

118:00   Barnard, Mark (arr. Bryan Verhoye). *Give thanks to the Lord.* 2-part any combination, kbd. Lorenz (1995) 10/1276U

118:00   SEE: Psalm 113:00. Ellingboe, Bradley. *The house of the Lord*

118:00   SEE: Psalm 16:00. Pollock, Gail Leven. *I will sing to the Lord*

118:00   Renick, Charles R. *This is the day the Lord has made.* SATB, organ, brass quartet, timpani. OCP (1999) G-4804

118:00 (adapted)
          Roberts, Leon C. *This is the day.* SATB, piano. GIA (1997) G-4600

118:00   Shute, Linda Cable. *This is the day* (uses tune *Land of rest*). SATB, kbd, optional handbells, congregation and instrument in C. Augsburg Fortress (2001) 0-8006-5974-0

118:00 (paraphrased)
          Roth, John. *O give thanks unto the Lord.* SATB, optional instruments (synthesizer, bass, percussion), kbd. Concordia (1996) 98-3277; instrumental score 97-6600

118:1-2, 15-24
          Kosche, Kenneth T. (handbell parts by John A. Behnke). *Psalm 118* (#1 of *3 festival Psalms,* Set 2). SATB, 3 octave handbells. Concordia (1998) 98-3468

118:1-2, 16-17, 22-23 (Psalm 47:2-3, 6-7, 8-9; Psalm 104:1, 24, 29-30, 31, 34)
          Chepponis, James J. *Eastertime Psalm (Psalms for Easter, Ascension, and Pentecost).* SATB, kbd, optional trumpets and handbells. GIA (1994) G 3907

118:1-2, 16-17, 22-23, 24
          Joncas, Michael. *This is the day.* SATB, piano or organ, Glockenspiel, handbells. OCP (1982) 10090

118:1, 4, 24
          Brown, Grayson Warren (arr. Val Parker and Grayson Warren Brown). *This is the day.* Unison, kbd. Found in *If God is for us.* OCP (1995) 10114

118:1, 17, 24
          Fedak, Alfred V. *This is the day.* SATB, organ. MorningStar (1997) MSM-50-4030

118:14-17, 22-24
          Farlee, Robert Buckley. *God is my strength and song* (#1 in *Three Biblical songs*). Unison, kbd. Augsburg (1995) 11-10604

118:17   Luther, Martin (ed. William Braun). *I shall not die (Non moriar).* SATB, kro. Concordia (1995) 98-3196

118:19-22, 24 (paraphrased)
          Scott, K. Lee. *Open to me the gates of righteousness.* SATB, organ, optional brass. Concordia (1999) 98-3501

118:21-22
          SEE: Exodus 15:1-2. Powell, Robert J. *He hath triumphed gloriously*

118:22 (Psalm 145:2; Isaiah 22:21, based on)
          Barnard, Mark. *Sing Alleluia to our king.* 2-part, kbd. Lorenz (1995) 10/1399U

118:24   Caceres, Abraham. *This is the day.* U or SAB, kbd. Augsburg Fortress (1997) 11-10682

118:24   Callahan, Charles. *This is the day!* SATB, organ. Randall Egan (1994) EC 320

118:24 (I Corinthians 15:20-22, 57)
Cooke, S. Charles (simplified by Ellen Jane Lorenz). *This is the day.* SATB, kbd. Lorenz (1949) found in *Easy standard anthems,* vol. I

118:24 (Psalm 95:00; Psalm 96:00 adapted)
Fischer, Dave. *Sing praise and celebrate.* SATB, kbd. Shawnee Press (1995) A-6951

118:24 (adapted)
Hayes, Mark. *This is the day the Lord has made.* SATB, optional winds and percussion, kbd. Beckenhorst (1995) BP 1442; instruments BP 1442A

118:24 (and other)
Kirkland, Terry. *This is the day!* 2-part, optional drum, cymbals and 2 octave handbells, kbd. Unity (Lorenz) (1995) 15/1156

118:24 (Isaac Watts)
Owens, Sam Batt. *This is the day.* 2-part mixed, organ. MorningStar (1997) MSM-50-4502

118:24 SEE: I Corinthians 5:7b-8. Schalk, Carl. *Be known to us, Lord Jesus*

118:24 (Luke 24:34)
Shields, Valerie. *Easter acclamation.* SATB, organ, 1 or 2 trumpets. Kjos (1996) 8829

118:24 Schultz, Larry E. *Let us rejoice and sing.* Unison or 2-part, kbd. Choristers Guild (1998) CGA 802

118:24 (Psalm 98:1, 2, 5-8)
Wright, Paul Leddington. *This is the day.* SATB, organ. Hinshaw (1997) HMC 1563

118:24 Young, Gordon. *This is the day the Lord hath made* (#1 of *A collection of responses and service music*). SATB, no acc. Flammer (1999) GA 5046

118:24, 27-29
Shoemaker-Lohmeyer, Lisa. *This is the day the Lord has made.* SATB, optional children's choir, trumpet, organ. MorningStar (1998) MSM-50-7030

118:26 (John 12:13)
Nystedt, Knut. *Hosanna! Blessed is he.* SATB, organ. Augsburg (1998) 11-10817, found in *The Augsburg choirbook, Sacred choral music of the twentieth century,* ed. Kenneth Jennings

119:00 (based on)
SEE: Luke 24:32. Englert, Eugene. *Make our hearts burn with love*

119:00 SEE: Psalm 108:00. Lindley, Simon. *O God, my heart is ready*

119:00 Marcello, Benedetto (ed. and arr. Dale Grotenhuis). *Teach me now, O Lord.* 2-part mixed, kbd. MorningStar (1998) MSM-50-9418

119:00 Mitchell, Tom. *Teach me, O Lord, the way of your statutes.* SATB, kbd. Coronet (Presser) (1995) 392-41903

119:105 (and Bruce Vantine)
Vantine, Bruce. *Your word is a candle* (based on spiritual *All night long*). SATB, kro. MorningStar (1999) MSM-50-7037

119:175 SEE: Isaiah 26:3. Neswick, Bruce. *Thou wilt keep Him in perfect peace*

121:00 Barta, Daniel. *Psalm 121.* 2-part, piano. Logia (Concordia) (1994) 98-3158

121:00 Berger, Jean. *I to the hills lift up mine eyes.* SATB, kro. Augsburg (1998) 11-10817, found in *The Augsburg choirbook, Sacred choral music of the twentieth century,* ed. Kenneth Jennings

121:00 Brown, Charles F. *I will lift up mine eyes.* SATB, kbd. Hinshaw (1997) HMC 1544

121:00 Caesar, Anthony. *Psalm 121.* SATB, organ. Paraclete (1997) PPM 09722

121:00 (paraphrased)
Dengler, Lee. *I lift my eyes.* SATB, Organ. Concordia (1995) 98-3215

121:00 Hailstork, Adolpheus. *I will lift up mine eyes.* Cantata for T/solo, SATB, orchestra. Presser (1997, 1998) 312-41723

121:00   Harris, Ed. *I will lift my eyes.* Solo, SATB, kbd. Coronet (Presser) (2000) 392-42294

121:00   Hildebrand, Kevin. *Psalm 121.* 2-part treble, instrument in C or B-flat, organ. Concordia (1998) 98-3437

121:00 (and other)
Mengel, Dana. *I to the hills will lift my eyes.* SATB, kbd. Concordia (1999) 98-3498

121:00   Nelson, Daniel. *I will lift my eyes unto the hills.* SSA, piano. Concordia (1998) 98-3475

121:00   Roberts, Leon C. *Let us go rejoicing* (from *Mass of Saint Augustine*). SATB, solo, kbd. GIA (1997) G-4606

121:1-3, 5, 7
Young, Philip. *I will lift up my eyes.* SATB, organ. MorningStar (1996) MSM-60-9080

121:4 (Psalm 138:7)
Mendelssohn, Felix (arr. Gene Grier and Lowell Everson). *He watching over Israel.* SAB, kbd. Coronet (Presser) (1999) 392-42270

121:5, 7 (Psalm 91:1, 4)
Page, Anna Laura. *The Lord is my keeper.* SATB, piano, optional handbells, flute. MorningStar (2000) MSM-50-2506A

121:7, 8   SEE: Proverbs 3:5-6. Wetzler, Robert. *He shall direct your paths*

122:00   Chassidic melody (arr. Richard Proulx). *I rejoice when I heard them say.* 2-part chorus, optional flute and string bass. GIA (1993) G-3780

122:00   Cotter, Jeanne. *Let us go rejoicing.* SAB, kbd. GIA (1995) G-4631

122:00   Haas, David. *I was glad.* Unison, kbd. GIA (1994) G-4133

122:1 (Psalm 100:1, 2, 4)
Hallquist, Gary. *I was glad.* SATB, kbd (or orchestra). GlorySound (1999) A7317

122:1   SEE: Matthew 16:18. Locklair, Dan. *St. Peter's rock*

122:1 (Psalm 84:1, 2, 4, adapted)
Pote, Allen. *In this house of worship.* SATB, 2 trumpets, kbd. Hinshaw (1996) HMC 1459

122:1-2 (Habakkuk 2:20; Genesis 28:17)
Pethel, Stan. *The gate of heaven.* SATB, kbd. Coronet (Presser) (1989) 392-41517

122:1-9   Hurd, Bob (arr. Craig Kingsbury). *Let us go rejoicing* (based on tune *Point Hill*). SATB, kbd. OCP (1996) 10622

123:00   Bullard, Janice M. *Psalm 123.* SATB, piano. Presser (1999) 312-41729.

125:00   Foley, John. *Our God has done great things for us.* SATB, optional instruments, kbd. GIA (1993) G 3941

125:00   Gastoldi, Giovanni (ed. Harry Johansen). *In convertendo* (Psalm 125) (#3 of *Vesper Psalms*). SSATTB, continuo. Latin only. Roger Dean (1995) 10/1341R

126:00   Farrell, Bernadette. *Those who sow in tears.* Unison, flute and violin, organ or piano. OCP (1994) 10339

126:00   Honoré, Jeffrey. *Psalm 126: The Lord has done great things for us* (found in *Psalter for bells and voices, Set I*). SATB, congregation, handbells (3-5 octaves), kbd. Concordia (1999) 98-3508; handbells 97-6781

126:00 (based on)
Voorhaar, Richard E. *Sing out to God.* SAB, kbd. Lorenz (1985) found in *The two-part mixed choir*

127:00 (based on)
Lentz, Roger. *A Lord-built house.* SATB, kbd. Beckenhorst (1987) BP 1278

127:1 (based on)
Causey, C. Harry. *To build your kingdom.* SATB, piano or guitar. Valley Press (1982) VP 8201

127:1-2   Kosche, Kenneth T. *Unless the Lord builds the house.* SATB, instrument in C, kbd. Augsburg (1994) 11-10429

128:00 (based on)
Cooney, Rory. *Psalm 128: All the days of our lives.* SAB, 2 flutes, kbd. OCP (1997) 10473

128:00   Guimont, Michel. *Blessed are you.* SATB, kbd. GIA (1993) G-3690

130:00   Ferguson, John. *Psalm 130, Out of the depths* (from *Psalm set*). SATB, organ, found in *The Augsburg choirbook, Sacred choral music of the twentieth century,* ed. Kenneth Jennings

130:00 (paraphrased)
Hopson, Hal H. arr. *O Lord from the depths I cry.* 2-part mixed, SA/TB, organ. Augsburg Fortress (2001) 0-8006-5968-6

130:00   Johnson, Stephen P. *Psalm 130: Out of the depths.* SATB, kro. Concordia (1998) 98-3487

130:00   Schalk, Carl. *Out of the depths.* SAB, organ. MorningStar (1998) 50-3410

130:1, 4   Owens, Sam Batt. *Out of the depths.* 2-part mixed, organ. MorningStar (1997) MSM-50-3501

131:2, 3   SEE: Psalm 46:10, 11. Nelson, Ronald A. *Be still and know*

132:14, 16-17
SEE: Psalm 89:26-28, 51. Neswick, Bruce. *I will set his dominion in the sea*

133:00 (Ephesians 4:4-6; I Peter 1:22)
Scott, K. Lee. *How very good and pleasant.* SATB, organ. MorningStar (1995) MSM-50-9072

133:1 (I Corinthians 1:10; Ephesians 4:1-3, 5-6; Philippians 2:2-4)
Chepponis, James. *In unity and peace.* SATB, optional instrument in C, kbd. GIA (1997) G-4452

134:00 (and other)
Pote, Allen. *Lord, for the years.* SATB, organ and 2 optional trumpets. Sacred Music Press (1994) 10/1131

134:1 (plus additional text)
Lau, Robert. *Come bless the Lord.* SAB, optional flute, kbd. Triune Music (Lorenz) (1996) 10/1434T

134:1 (with additional)
Lau, Robert. *Come bless the Lord.* SAB, optional flute, kbd. Found in *10 Anthems for about 10 singers.* Lorenz (1990) 45/1094L

134:1-3   Victoria, Tomás Luis de (arr. Robert J. Powell). *Ecce nunc benedicite Dominum (Hearken, bless ye the Lord).* SATB/SATB, kro. Concordia (1998) 98-3424

135:00   Handel, G. F. (arr. Walter Rodby). *O Praise the Lord with one accord* (from *Chandos anthem #9*). SATB, kbd. Coronet (Presser) (1996) 392-41976

135:1, 3, 21
Tschaikovsky, P. I. *Praise ye the name of the Lord* (from *Vesper service,* Op. 52). SATB, kro. J. Fischer. Found in *Twenty-five anthems from the Russian liturgy.*

135:1, 21 (Psalm 136:1)
Ivanov, P. (arr. Ellen Jane Lorenz). *Psalm of praise.* 2-part mixed, kbd. Lorenz (1986) found in *The two-part mixed choir*

135:1, 21 (Psalm 136:1)
Ivanov, P. (arr. Ellen Jane Lorenz). *Psalm of praise.* SATB, kbd. Lorenz (1949) found in *Easy standard anthems,* I

135:2, 3 (Revelation 15:3)
Spinney, Walter (arr. Roger C. Wilson). *Ye that stand in the house of the Lord.* SATB, organ (extended section for TTBB). Lorenz (1951) found in *Simplified standard anthems,* I

136:00 (paraphrased)
Latvian melody (arr. Mark Sedio). *By the Babylonian rivers.* SATB, violin, viola or C instrument. Selah (1994) 410-850

136:00 Purcell, Henry (arr. Rosemary Hadler). *O give thanks!* 2-part mixed, kbd. Lorenz (1986) found in *The two-part mixed choir*

136:1 SEE: Psalm 135:1, 21. Ivanov, P. *Psalm of praise*

136:1, 7, 25
Hopson, Hal H. *Let us with a gladsome mind (Christ the Lord is risen today)* (based on tune *Llanfair*). SATB, organ, optional electric bass or synthesizer. MorningStar (1998) MSM-50-7031

136:1-9, 23-24
Scandinavian Folk Melody (arr. Dale Grotenhuis). *Give thanks to God.* SATB, kbd. Coronet (Presser) (1999) 39-42266

137:00 Anonymous. *By the rivers of Babylon.* 3-part round (taken from *The Psaltery*, 1846). Boston Music (1992) found in *Early American sacred choral library*, vol. 2

137:00 (Ewald Bash)
Latvian folk tune, arr. Richard Erickson. *By the Babylonian rivers* (based on Latvian folk tune *Kas Dziedaja*). SATB, organ. Augsburg (1997) 11-10814

137:00 Loeffler, Charles M. *By the rivers of Babylon.* SSAA, organ, or piano, or organ, harp, 2 flutes, cello. Paraclete (1995) 9514

137:1-5, 7-9
Vedel, Artemiy (ed. Anthony Antolini). *By the banks of Babylon's streams (Na rekakh Vavilonskikh)* (English/ Russian, Latin & Cyrillic alphabets). SSAATTBB, kro. Paraclete (1995) 9503

138:00 Hoekstra, Thomas. *Psalm 138.* SATB, optional organ. Concordia (1997) 98-3292

138:1-3, 7-8
Bender, Mark. *I will praise you, O Lord, with all my heart.* 2-part mixed, organ. Concordia (2000) 98-3559

138:1, 8 Behnke, John A. *I thank you, Lord* (from *Three Psalms for unison choir*). Unison, kbd. Concordia (2000) 98-3578

138:7 SEE: Psalm 121:4. Mendelssohn, Felix (arr. Gene Grier and Lowell Everson). *He watching over Israel*

139:00 (adapted)
Canedo, Ken (arr. Mark Barnard). *Fly like a bird.* SATB, optional congregation, kbd. Unity (Lorenz) (1995) 10/1271U

139:00 (based on)
Farrell, Bernadette. *O God, you search me.* SATB, optional oboe and French horn, kbd. OCP (1992) 10057

139:00 (taken from)
Ford, Sandra T. *O Lord, you know my heart.* SAB, kbd. Hinshaw (1996) HMC 1491

139:00 (based on)
Hobby, Robert A. *Lord, you have searched me.* SATB, S/solo, flute, kbd. MorningStar (2000) MSM-50-6026

139:00 Lisicky, Paul. *Filling me with joy.* 2-part, optional viola, guitar, kbd. GIA (1993) G-3678

139:00 (based on)
Spencer, Linda. *Wings of the dawn.* SATB, piano. Shawnee Press (1995) A 6183

139:8-9 Dams, Julian. *If I take the wings of the morning.* SATB, organ. GIA (1994) G-4311

139:11, 12
SEE: Isaiah 26:3. Neswick, Bruce. *Thou wilt keep Him in perfect peace*

139:23-24
Day, J. R. *Search me, O God.* SATB, kro. Roger Dean (1998) 10/1864R

141:00 (Watts)
SEE: Psalm 84:00. Croft, William (arr. John Ferguson). *A song of hope*

141:00 Inwood, Paul. *Let my prayer rise before you (Evening Psalm).* Unison choir, kbd. OCP (1985) 7138

141:1, 2, 3, 8 (Psalm 31:1, 3)
Tschaikovsky, P. *Lord I cry unto Thee.* S/S/A/solos, SATB, kro. J. Fischer. Found in *Twenty-five anthems from the Russian liturgy.*

141:2 Walker, Christopher. *Let my prayer rise.* SATB, solo instrument, kbd. OCP (1988) 10231

142:00 Clemens, James E. *With my voice I cry out to the Lord.* SATB, no acc. Concordia (1997) 98-3306

143:00 (taken from)
Holyoke, Samuel. *Hear our prayer.* SATB, kbd. Boston Music, found in *Early American sacred choral library,* vol. 1

143:00 (paraphrased)
Hopson, Hal H. *O Lord, hear me* (based on ground bass from *Seventh suite* of G. F. Handel). SAB, kbd. Laurel Press (Lorenz) (2000) 10/2152LA

143:00 Kosche, Kenneth T. (handbell parts by John A. Behnke). *Psalm 143* (#3 of *3 festival Psalms, Set 2*). SATB, 3 octave handbells. Concordia (1998) 98-3468

143:9-10 (Psalm 18:47-48)
Haydn, Johann Michael (ed. David Stein). *Eripe me, Domine* (Latin/English). SATB, kbd. Presser (1998) 312-41743

144:00 (Psalm 145:00)
Dvorák, Antonin (arr. Dale Grotenhuis). *I will sing new songs of gladness* from *Ten Biblical songs,* Op. 99 (#1

in *Two Dvorák Biblical songs for male chorus*). TTBB, piano. MorningStar (1998) MSM-50-9700

144:15 SEE: I Corinthians 10:17. Proulx, Richard. *Though we are many, in Christ we are one*

145:00 Cotter, Jeanne. *I will praise your name.* Unison, piano and guitar. GIA (1996) G-4634

145:00 SEE: Psalm 144:00. Dvorak, Antonin (arr. Dale Grotenhuis). *I will sing new songs of gladness*

145:00 (based on)
Pote, Allen. *Praise the goodness of God.* SATB, kbd. Choristers Guild (1995) GCA 733

145:00 (based on)
Wright, Vicki Hancock. *I will praise God.* Unison, kbd. (Optional handchimes, resonator bells, or 2 octave set of handbells). Choristers Guild (1998) CGA822

145:1-2 (Monsell)
Buck, Pery C. (setting Robert Below). *Sing to the Lord a joyful song* (uses tune *Gonfalon Royal*). SATB, organ. Augsburg (1987) 11-2380

145:1-2 (Monsell)
Powell, Robert J. *Sing to the Lord a joyful song.* Unison, kbd. Choristers Guild (1988) CGA 443

145:1-2 (Monsell)
Story, Donald J. *Sing to the Lord a joyful song.* SATB, organ. Mark Foster (1994) MF 2105

145:1-2, 8-10, 21-22
Powell, Robert J. *I will magnify Thee.* SATB, brass quartet, timpani, organ. MorningStar (1996) MSM-50-7019; parts MSM-50-7019A

145:1-3, 8-13
Parry, C. Hubert (arr. Donald Busarow). *O Lord, you are my God and king* (based on tune *Jerusalem*). SAB, trumpet, handbells (4 octaves), organ. Augsburg (1998) 11-10892

145:1-4, 10, 11a, 12, 21 SEE: Psalm 81:1.
Bisbee, B. Wayne. *Sing for joy to God our strength*

145:2   SEE: Psalm 118:22. Barnard, Mark. *Sing alleluia to our king*

145:8-10 SEE: Psalm 147:12-13. Mauder, J. H. *Praise the Lord, O Jerusalem*

145:14-17
Proulx, Richard. *The eyes of all.* Unison, organ. Augsburg Fortress (1997) 12-109

145:15, 16
Berger, Jean. *The eyes of all wait upon thee.* SATB, kro. Augsburg (1998) 11-10817, found in *The Augsburg choirbook, Sacred choral music of the twentieth century,* ed. Kenneth Jennings

145:15-16
Larkin, Michael. *The eyes of all.* SATB, kbd. MorningStar (1999) 50-9110

146:00   Pelz, Walter L. *Praise the almighty, my soul adore him.* SATB, organ, brass quartet, timpani. Concordia (1996) 98-3282; full score, brass parts 97-6642

146:2, 6-10
Chepponis, James J. *Psalm 146.* SATB, instrument in C, handbells, kbd. GIA (1997) G-4227

147:00 (paraphrase)
Proulx, Richard. *How good it is to sing praise.* SAB, organ. Sacred Music Press (1996) 10/1390

147:00   Routley, Erik (arr. Austin C. Lovelace). *The music of earth* (based on tune *Lac du Flambeau*). SATB, organ. Randall Egan (1989) n.#.

147:1-11 Courtney, Craig. *Psalm 147.* SATB, kbd. optional handbells. Sacred Music Press (1996) 10/1256; handbells 30/1157

147:3 (Matthew 11:28-30; Isaiah 53:45, based on)
Scott, K. Lee. *God shall the broken heart repair.* SATB, kbd. Augsburg (1994) 11-10530

147:12-13 (Psalm 145:8-10)
Maunder, J. H. (rev. Roger C. Wilson). *Praise the Lord, O Jerusalem.* SATB, kbd. Lorenz (1951) found in *Simplified standard anthems,* vol. I

148:00 (Psalm 150:00)
Callahan, Charles. *O praise ye the Lord.* SATB, optional brass quartet and timpani, organ. Concordia (1997) 98-3402

148:00 (based on)
Clemens, James E. *Praise the Lord in the highest.* SATB, kbd. Shawnee Press (1995) A6993

148:00   Diemer, Emma Lou. *Psalm 148.* SATB, organ, optional handbells (3 octaves). Sacred Music Press (1995) 10/1206

148:00   Hopson, Hal. *Praise the Lord! O heavens, adore him* (uses hymn tune *Holy Manna*). 2-part, organ. Lorenz (1981) found in *NINE BY TWO* and *Sing to the Lord a new song*

148:00   Leaf, Robert. *All praise.* SA, kbd. AMSI (1994) 686

148:00 (taken from)
Lovelace, Austin C. *The universal praises* (uses tune *Duke Street*). 2-part mixed, kbd. Sacred Music Press (1995) 10/1193

148:00   Mengel, Dana. *Let creation raise the strain.* SATB, organ. Coronet (Presser) (1996) 392-41963

148:00 (Psalm 150:00, based on)
Parry, C. Hubert (arr. S. Drummond Wolff). *O praise ye the Lord* (based on tune *Laudate Dominum*). SATB, trumpet, organ. Concordia (1994) 98-3137

148:00 Vivaldi, Antonio (arr. Hal H. Hopson). *Sing to the Lord* (from *Deus in Adjutorium*). SATB, kbd. Hope (1995) AA 1694

149:00 (taken from) Billings, William (ed. Leonard Van Camp). *Universal praise - O praise God.* SATB, kro. Concordia (1973) 98-3321

149:00 (Psalm 150:00) Emig, Louis Myers. *Let us sing to the Lord.* SAB, kbd. Lorenz (1970) found in *Anthems for limited choirs*

149:00 (paraphrase) Mengel, Dana. *Sing to the Lord a new song.* SATB, kbd. Concordia (2000) 98-3569

149:1-3 Raminsh, Imant. *Cantata Domino.* SSAA, strings, percussion, trumpet. Hinshaw (1995) HMC 1401

149:1, 3-4 Beck, Theodore. *Sing to the Lord a new song.* SATB, kro. Concordia (1997) 98-3386

150:00 Aguiar, Ernani. *Salmo 150 (Psalm 150).* SATB, no acc. earthsongs (1993) n.#.

150:00 Busarow, Donald. *A festival Psalm* (incorporates tune *St. Anne*). SATB, 2 trumpets, 2 trombones, tuba, organ. Concordia (1990) 98-2849

150:00 SEE: Psalm 148:00. Callahan, Charles. *O praise ye the Lord*

150:00 Cann, Jesse. *Psalm 150 - Hallelujah!* SATB, organ. Kjos (1996) 8766

150:00 (Wesley) Courtney, Craig. *Praise the Lord who reigns above.* SATB, kbd. Beckenhorst (1996) BP 1489

150:00 SEE: Psalm 149:00. Emig, Louis Myers. *Let us sing to the Lord*

150:00 (Wesley) Foundry Collection (arr. Alice Parker). *Praise the Lord who reigns above* (uses tune *Amsterdam*). SATB, brass, timpani, organ. Concordia (1991) 11-10094; instruments 11-10096

150:00 (based on) Friedman, Mark. *Make a joyful noise.* 2-part, guitar, kbd. OCP (1997) 10488

150:00 (based on) Hayes, Mark. *Psalm 150.* SATB, kbd., optional instruments. Hinshaw (1997) HMC 1545

150:00 (paraphrased) Hilton, John (arr. Hal H. Hopson). *Sing a round of praise.* SAB, kbd. Coronet (Presser) (1998) 392-42201

150:00 Hopson, Hal H. *Hallelujah! Sing praise to the Lord.* SATB, organ. MorningStar (1998) MSM-50-7034

150:00 Hovland, Egil. *Laudate Dominum (O let us praise the Lord)* (English/Latin). 3-part treble. Egan (1976) n.#.

150:00 Liebergen, Patrick M. *Laudate!* SSA, optional trumpet, kbd. Shawnee (1997) B 0571

150:00 Mason, Lowell. *O praise God in his holiness.* SATB, kbd. Boston Music (1992) found in *Early American sacred choral library,* vol. 1

150:00 Neaveill, Ryan. *Let everything that has breath praise the Lord.* SATB, kbd. Concordia (1998) 98-3459

150:00 Niedmann, Peter. *Praise the Lord, his glories show.* Unison/2-part, kbd. GIA (1998) G-4743

150:00 Parry, C. Hubert (arr. Mark White). *O praise ye the Lord.* SATB, kbd. Coronet (Presser) (1999) 392-2238

150:00 (based on) SEE: Psalm 148:00. Parry, C. Hubert (arr. S. Drummond Wolff). *O praise ye the Lord*

150:00   Rowan, William P. *Psalm 150.* SATB, kbd. Concordia (2000) 98-3603

150:00 (taken from)
Schubert, Franz (arr. Dale Grotenhuis). *Strike the cymbal.* 2-part, kbd. MorningStar (2000) MMS-50-9421

150:00   Schütz, Heinrich (arr. B. Wayne Bisbee). *Psalm 150.* SATB, organ and percussion. MorningStar (2000) MSM-50-7040

150:00   SEE: Psalm 42:00. Schutte, Dan. *Let us go to the altar*

150:00   Young, Jeremy. *Praise God with the trumpet.* SAB, kbd. (optional brass quintet). Augsburg (1998) 11-10893; instruments 11-10907

150:2, 3 Tschaikovsky, P. I. (arr. Homer Whitford). *Praise ye the Lord.* SATB, kbd. Found in *Praise ye the Lord.*

PROVERBS

3:5   Martin, Joseph M. *Trust in the Lord.* SATB, kbd. Lorenz (1993) 10/1033

3:5-6 (based on)
McDonald, Mary. *Trust in the Lord.* SATB, kbd. Purifoy (1995) 10/1368P

3:5-6 (Psalm 121:7, 8)
Wetzler, Robert. *He shall direct your paths.* SATB, kbd. Concordia (1999) 98-3531

6:20-22 (based on)
Martin, Joseph M. *My friend, do not forget.* SATB, kbd. Triune (1994) 10/1121

22:6 (inspired by)
Choplin, Pepper. *Train up a child.* SAB, kbd. GlorySound (Shawnee) (1995) D 554

ECCLESIASTES

1:00 (12:00 adapted)
Hayes, Mark. *To love our God.* SATB, kbd. Hinshaw (1997) HMC 1576

3:00   Caracciolo, Stephen. *To everything there is a season.* SATB divsi, harp and flute. Roger Dean (1995) 10/1420R

3:1 (adapted)
Wagner, Douglas E. *A time for all things* (based on Scottish folk tune). 2-part mixed, kbd. Found in *10 Anthems for about 10 singers.* Lorenz (1990) 45/1094L

3:1-8   Courtney, Craig. *There is a time.* SATB, kbd. Beckenhorst (1995) BP 1463

3:1-8 (Romans 8:28, adapted from)
Ore, Charles W. *A time and a purpose.* SATB, optional congregation, kbd. MorningStar (1998) MSM-80-845

3:1-9 (Matthew 13:4-8)
Ridge, M. E. (arr. Patrick Loomis). *Parable.* 3-part choir, solo instrument, kbd. OCP (1991) 8876

11:1, 2, 7, 8
McLarry, Beverly. *Send your bread forth.* SATB, kbd. Presser (1996) 312-41665

12:00   SEE: Ecclesiastes 1:00. Hayes, Mark. *To love our God*

SONG OF SONGS

2:8-13   Callahan, James. *Hark my beloved.* SATB, no acc. Paraclete (1996) PPMO 9613

2:10,11, 12
Entsminger, Deen E. *Rise up my love, my fair one.* SSAA, kro. Plymouth (1996) SC-220

2:10-12 Grotenhuis, Dale. *The time for singing.* SATB, piano. Kjos (1996) 8841

2:10-12 Laubengayer, Paul. *Rise up, my love.* SATB, kro. Concordia (2000) 98-3586

2:10-12 McConnell, David A. *Rise up, my love, my fair one.* SATB, T/solo, no acc. Augsburg (1994) 11-10537

2:10-12 McCray, James. *Rise up, my love, my fair one.* TTB, flute, piano. National Music (1993) WHC 173

2:10-12 Near, Gerald. *Arise, my love, my fair one.* SSATB, kro. Augsburg (1998) 11-10817, found in *The Augsburg choirbook, Sacred choral music of the twentieth century,* ed. Kenneth Jennings.

2:10-13 (Song of Songs 8:6, 7)
Hoddinott, Alun. *Set me as a seal upon thine heart.* SATB, organ. Paraclete (1994) 9404

2:11-12 (and Kathleen Black)
Snyder, Audrey. *The time of singing.* SSA, piano. Hal Leonard (1997) n.#.

8:6-7 Conte, David. *Set me as a seal.* SATB, organ. E. C. Schirmer (1994) 4272

8:6, 7 Grotenhuis, Dale. *Set me as a seal.* SATB, kro. Concordia (1999) 98-3515

8:6, 7 SEE: Song of Songs 2:10-13. Hoddinott, Alun. *Set me as a seal upon thine heart*

8:6-7 Micheltree, John. *Set me as a seal upon your heart.* Unison, kbd. Augsburg (1982) 11-2089

ISAIAH

2:00 (Isaiah 25:00; Isaiah 41:00)
Ridge, M. E. *In the day of the Lord.* SAB, flute, trumpet, kbd. OCP (1992) 9889

5:1-7 Pinkham, Daniel. *Vinea mea electa* (#4 of *Passion music*) (English/Latin). SATB, organ or string quartet. Thorpe (Presser) (1995) 392-03040

6:00 (based on, as well as additional text)
Hallquist, Gary and Benjamin Harlan. *Holy Lord of hosts.* SATB, kbd. (brass, clarinet, oboe, flute, percussion). Shawnee Press (1995) A6900

6:3 Blersch, Jeffrey. *Verse for the Holy Trinity* (based on tune *St. Patrick's Breastplate*) (found in *Alleluia Verses*). SATB, organ. Concordia (1996) 98-3230

6:3 Evans, John E. *Sanctus.* SATB, optional kbd. Kjos (1996) 8778

6:3 Fauré, Gabriel (ed. Nancy Telfer). *Sanctus* (from *Messe basse*). SA, kbd. Kjos (1993) 6228

6:3 Fauré, Gabriel (ed. and arr. Robert Roth). *Sanctus* (from *Requiem,* Op. 48) (Latin/English). SATB, organ. Coronet (Presser) (1995) 392-41853

6:3 Franck, César (arr. Donald Moore). *Holy, holy, holy (Sanctus)* (English/ Latin) (from *Prelude in b minor,* Op. 18). Belwin-Mills (1995) BSC 9612

6:3 Haydn, Franz J. (ed. Rod Walker). *Sanctus* (from *Missa cellenis*). SATB, kbd. National Music (1993) NMP 206

6:3 Mason, Lowell. *Holy is the Lord.* SATB, kbd. Boston Music, found in *Early American sacred choral library,* vol. 2

6:3 Mozart, W. A. (arr. Anthony Howells). *Sanctus* (English). SAB, kbd. Coronet (Presser) (1995) 392-41851

6:3 Mozart, W. A. (arr. Henry Kihlken). *Sanctus* (*Missa brevis,* K. 220) (Latin/ English). SATB, kbd. Coronet (Presser) (1999) 392-42246

6:3 North, Jack. *Holy, holy, holy.* SATB, optional keyboard. Alfred (1980) 7006

7:14   SEE: Isaiah 40:1, 3-5. Larson, Lloyd. *A voice cries out, 'Prepare the Way of the Lord'*

9:2   Malmin, Olaf G. *Advent proclamation.* SATB, kbd. AMSI (1996) 737

9:2, 6   Causey, C. Harry. *Prince of peace.* SAB, kbd. Fred Bock (1982) B-G0411

9:3   SEE: Leviticus 19:9. Zabel, Albert. *Come, joy!*

9:5, 6, 9   Proulx, Richard. *A radiant light.* Treble voices, flute, oboe, cello, organ, optional harp. GIA (1996) G-4351

9:6   Handel, G. F. (transcribed by Lynn S. Lund). *For unto us a child is born (Messiah).* SATB, optional C instrument, kbd. Presser (1996) 392-00884

9:6   Handel, G. F. (arr. and abridged by Sharon Elery Rogers). *For unto us a child is born (Messiah).* SATB, kbd. Coronet (Presser) (1995) 293-41944

9:6   Handel, G. F. (arr. Roger C. Wilson). *For unto us a child is born (Messiah).* SATB, kbd. Lorenz, 1951 (found in *Simplified standard anthems for mixed voices,* I)

9:6 (Psalm 98:00)   Kosche, Kenneth T. *Unto us a child is born* (incorporates tune *Lobt Gott, ihr Christen*). 2-part, optional instrument in C, kbd. Choristers Guild (1995) CGA 695

9:6, 40 (Isaiah 40:4, 11)   Roberts, Leon C. *He shall be called wonderful.* SATB, piano. OCP (1996) 10591

11:00 (Isaiah 35:00)   McRae, Shirley. *Carol of prophecy.* Unison voices, handbells. Choristers Guild (1996) GCA 720

11:6   SEE: Isaiah 40:1. Nelson, Ronald A. *Comfort, O comfort*

11:9   Peter, Johann Friedrich (ed. Nola Reed Knouse). *Das Land ist voll Erkenntnis des Herrn (The earth is full of the knowledge of God).* SSAB, kbd. Hinshaw (1998) HMC 1519, full score and string parts available from publisher.

12:2, 4   Lindh, Jody W. *Behold, God is my salvation.* Unison, optional 2nd voice, organ. Concordia (1993) 98-3193

12:2-6 (paraphrased)   Roberts, Leon C. *Cry out with joy and gladness.* SATB, kbd. GIA (1997) G-4602

12:5   Fortunato, Frank. *Praise the Lord in song.* 2-part mixed, piano. Fred Bock (1982) B-G0367

22:21   SEE: Psalm 118:22. Barnard, Mark. *Sing alleluia to our king*

25:00 (based on)   Martin, Joseph. *Canticle of hope.* SATB, kbd. Shawnee Press (1995) A6983

25:00   SEE: Isaiah 2:00. Ridge, M. E. *In the day of the Lord*

25:3, 4, 8   Stearns, Peter Pindar. *Thou wilt keep him in perfect peace.* SATB, organ. Paraclete (1998) PPM 09811

26:3 (Psalm 139:11, 12; I John 1:5; Psalm 119: 175)   Neswick, Bruce. *Thou wilt keep Him in perfect peace.* SATB, organ. Paraclete (1996) PPMO 9627

26:3-4   Kosche, Kenneth T. *You will keep in perfect peace.* 2 equal voices, kbd. Concordia (1999) 98-3506

30:15, 18 (adapted)   Dare, Carol R. *In quietness and confidence.* 2-part mixed, piano. Lorenz (1986) found in *The two-part mixed choir*

33:5, 9, 10   West, John E. (arr. and abridged by Ellen Jane Lorenz). *The Lord is exalted.* SATB, kbd. Lorenz (1951) found in *Simplified standard anthems,* I

35:00   SEE: Isaiah 11:00. McRae, Shirley.
         Carol of prophecy

35:00 (Romans 13:00; James 5:00)
         Schoenbachler, Tim (arr. Patrick
         Loomis). *Maranatha.* 3-part, organ,
         guitar, and solo instrument. OCP
         (1979, 1985) 10003

35:4   Fellows, Donald Kramer. *Behold, our
         God.* 2-part mixed, organ. Augsburg
         Fortress (1997) 11-10775

35:4c-6a (Psalm 68:00, paraphrased)
         Westra, Evert. *The Lord, your God,
         will come.* SATB, kro. Chantry
         (1965)

40:00 (adapted)
         Sartor, David P. *Thy light is come.*
         SATB, organ. E. C. Schirmer (1989)
         4270

40:1   Martinson, Joel. *Locus iste.* SATB
         divsi, kro. Paraclete (1992)
         PPM09206

40:1 (Isaiah 66:31a; Isaiah 51:3-4; Isaiah 11:6)
         Nelson, Ronald A. *Comfort, O
         comfort.* 2-part mixed, kbd.
         Concordia (2000) 98-3554

40:1-2, 11-31
         Purifoy, John. *They that wait upon the
         Lord.* SATB, medium voice solo, kbd.
         Triune (Lorenz) (1995) 10/1307T

40:1, 3, 4, 9
         Dufford, Bob (acc. by Rich Modlin).
         Every valley. 2-part choir, 2 flutes,
         kbd. OCP (1994) 10476

40:1, 3-5 (Isaiah 7:14)
         Larson, Lloyd. *A voice cries out,
         'Prepare the way of the Lord.'* SATB,
         kbd. Providence (1993) PP 136

40:1-4   Larkin, Michael. *Comfort, comfort
         now my people.* SATB, kbd.
         Birnamwood (MorningStar) (1999)
         MSM-50-0025

40:1-11 Joncas, Michael. *A voice cries out.*
         SATB, guitar, flute, oboe, kbd. OCP
         (1995) 10000

40:3 (based on)
         SEE: Psalm 25:3. Hurd, Bob. *Await
         the Lord with hope*

40:3 (and other Advent themes in Isaiah)
         Keesecker, Thomas. *Return, Lord.*
         SATB, organ, optional handbells.
         Concordia (1996) 98-3324

40:3 (Matthew 3:3; Mark 1:30; Luke 3:40)
         Robinson, Marc A. *Prepare ye.* SATB,
         percussion, kro. Kjos (1996) 8830

40:3-4 (Mark 1:3)
         Bach, J. S. (setting Hal H. Hopson).
         The Lord will soon appear (from Can-
         tata 24). SATB, kbd., optional solo
         violin. Augsburg (1998) 11-10888

40:3-5   Taulè, Alberto (arr. Jerry Gunderson).
         Toda la Tierra (All earth is waiting).
         SSA, piano. Logia (Concordia) (1995)
         98-3233

40:4, 11 SEE: Isaiah 9:6, 40. Roberts, Leon C.
         He shall be called wonderful

40:5   Handel, George F. (condensed and
         simplified by James Denton). *And the
         glory of the Lord (Messiah).* SATB,
         kbd. Lorenz (1965) found in *Easy
         standard anthems,* II

40:28-31 Hobby, Robert A. *Have you not
         known?* SATB, organ. MorningStar
         (1999) MSM-50-0024

40:29-31 SEE: Psalm 103:1-5. McDonald,
         Mary. *Like eagles, you will fly!*

40:31 (and other)
         Sanders, John. *The creator.* SATB,
         organ. Theodore Presser (1995) 312-
         41677

40:31   Wilson, Russell. *They that wait upon
         the Lord.* SATB, piano. Jackman
         (Presser) (1997, 1986) 00301

41:00   SEE: Isaiah 2:00. Ridge, M. E. *In the
         day of the Lord*

42:1, 6 Bengston, Bruce. *Behold my servant.*
         SATB, organ. Augsburg Fortress
         (2000) 0-8006-5912-0

43:1   SEE: Joshua 1:5-6. Grotenhuis, Dale. *Song of commitment*

43:1, 2   Donaghy, Emily (arr. Stewart Landon). *Fear thou not* (quoting tune *Portuguese Hymn*). SATB, kbd. Lorenz (1957) found in *Easy hymn tune anthems,* I

43:1, 2   SEE: Psalm 46:10, 11. Nelson, Ronald A. *Be still and know*

43:1, 2, 10   Hirten, John Karl. *Blest be God.* Unison, oboe, keyboard or handbells. GIA (1995) G-4128

43:1, 3   Wetzler, Robert. *Oh, for a thousand tongues to sing.* SATB, organ Concordia (1996) 98-3295

43:1b-3a (based on)   SEE: Psalm 96:00. Pote, Allen. *A new song.*

43:1, 3   SEE: Psalm 98:00. Wetzler, Robert. *Oh, for a thousand tongues.*

43:1-4   Courtney, Craig. *Be not afraid.* SATB, kbd. Beckenhorst (1992) BP 1388

43:1-4 (Luke 6:20)   Dufford, Bob (arr. Douglas Wagner). *Be not afraid.* SAB, kbd. Hope (1994) A 683

45:8   Proulx, Richard. *Rorate caeli* (based on plainsong, Mode I). SATB, kro. Paraclete Press (1992) PPM 09215

45:33 (Philippians 2:00, and other)   McDonald, Mary. *Holy, true and faithful God.* Medium voice solo, SATB, piano. Monarch Music (Lorenz) (1996) 10/1456M

48:20   Busch, Richard. *Vocem jucunditatis.* SATB, kro. Paraclete (1993) PPM 09313

48:20b (Psalm 66:1-2)   Jennings, Kenneth. *With a voice of singing.* SATB, kro. Augsburg (1998) 11-10817, found in *The Augsburg choirbook, Sacred choral music of the twentieth century,* ed. Kenneth Jennings

49:6   Schalk, Carl. *Arise, shine; for your light has come* (from *Songs from Isaiah*). SATB, no acc. Concordia (2000) 98-3600

49:16   SEE: Joshua 1:5-6. Grotenhuis, Dale. *Song of commitment*

51:3-4   SEE: Isaiah 40:1. Nelson, Ronald A. *Comfort, O comfort*

51:11   Schalk, Carl. *And the ransomed of the Lord shall return* (from *Songs from Isaiah*). SATB, no acc. Concordia (2000) 98-3600

52:7   Stainer, John (ed. John Carlton). *How beautiful upon the mountains* (from the anthem *Awake, awake; put on thy strength, O Zion*). SATB, kbd. Presser (1989) 312-41544

52:7   Stanford, C. Villiers. *How beauteous are their feet.* SATB, organ. Mayhew (1992) n.#.

52:7-8 (Romans 10:15)   Hassell, Michael. *How beautiful.* SATB, organ or piano. MorningStar (1997) MSM-50-6007

53:3   Graun, Karl (ed. and arr. Dale Grotenhuis). *He was despised.* SATB, kro. Coronet (Presser) (1999) 392-42261

53:3, 5   Dengler, Lee. *Lord, have mercy* (plus Latin, *Kyrie eleison*). SATB, kbd. Concordia (1996) 98-3248

53:3-5 (Matthew 11:28-29)   Dubois, Theodore (arr. Hal H. Hopson). *He was despised* (from *The seven last words of Christ*). S/solo, T/solo, SATB, kbd. MorningStar (1997) MSM-50-3038

53:3-5   SEE: Philippians 2:8. Malmin, Olaf C. *Meditations on the cross*

53:4   Victoria, Tomás Luis de (ed. John V. Mochnick). *Vere languores nostros (Truly our Lord has suffered).* SATB, kro. Roger Dean (1993) HRD 360

53:4, 5   SEE: I Peter 2:21-24. Dean, Stephen. *Ours were the griefs he bore*

53:4-5 (and other)
Larkin, Michael. *Crucifixus*. SATB, kbd. MorningStar (2000) MSM-50-3503

53:4-5   Lund, Lynn S. *Surely, He hath borne our griefs*. SATB, piano. Jackman Music (Presser) (1997) 392-00985

53:4-5 (with other text)
Mengel, Dana. *Kyrie eleison*. SATB, no acc. Concordia (1998) 98-3476

53:4-5   SEE: Luke 24:4-7. Nelson, Ronald A. *Risen! Go and tell*

53:4-5   Powell, Robert J. *Surely he hath borne our griefs*. SATB, kbd. Coronet (Alexander Broude) (1983) CP 245

53:4-5   Schiavone, John. *Surely he has borne our griefs*. SATB, kro. OCP (1993) 9851

53:4-6 (based on)
Larson, Lloyd. *Surely he has borne our griefs*. SATB, kbd. Beckenhorst (1998) BP1519

53:6   SEE: John 21:15-17. Hatton, Ray D. *Feed my lambs*

53:6   Martin, Joseph M. *All we like sheep*. 2-part mixed, optional flute, kbd. Timespan Music (Lorenz) (1994) 10/1225T

55:1 (John 4:14)
Malmin, Olaf G. *Come, drink of the water*. Unison, kbd. AMSI (1997) 757

55:1, 2 (based on)
Lotti, Antonio (ed. and arr. Hal H. Hopson). *Sing a song of joy* (from motet *Cum sancto spiritu*). SAB, kbd. MorningStar (1997) MSM-50-7203

55:3, 5   Dengler, Lee. *Lord, have mercy*. SATB, kbd. Logia (Concordia) (1996) 98-3248

55:6, 7   Roberts, J. V. (abridged by Roger C. Wilson). *Seek ye the Lord*. T/ or S/solo, SATB, kbd. Lorenz (1951) found in *Simplified standard anthems*, I

55:6-11   Callahan, Charles. *The second song of Isaiah (Quaerite Dominum)*. SSA, organ. Randall Egan (1992) 92-106

55:10-12   Choplin, Pepper. *This is my word*. SATB, kbd (or orchestra). GlorySound (1999) A7325

55:12   Hopson, Hal H. *Break forth into joy*. 2-part mixed, kbd. Lorenz (1981) found in *NINE BY TWO*

55:12   Schalk, Carl. *I will give you as a light to the nations* (from *Songs from Isaiah*). SATB, no acc. Concordia (2000) 98-3600

55:12-13 (based on)
Martin, Gilbert M. *You shall go out in joy*. SATB, kbd. Sacred Music Press (1997) 10/1516

56:12 (adapted)
Martin, Joseph M. *Go out in joy!* 2-part mixed, kbd. Found in *Go out in joy!* Lorenz (2001) 45/1097L

58:00 (based on)
Nelson, Ronald A. arr. *Come, leave your care* (based on a French air). 2-part mixed, kbd. AMSI (1996) 747

58:7-10 (inspired by)
Haas, David. *Share your bread with the hungry*. Unison, kbd. GIA (1997) G-4734

60:00   Boles, Frank. *Surge illuminare (The third song of Isaiah)*. SATB, organ. Paraclete (1995) PPMO 9307

60:00   Moe, Daniel. *Arise, shine*. SATB, organ. Presser (1995) 312-41678

60:1   Schalk, Carl. *You shall go out in joy* (from *Songs from Isaiah*). SATB/SATB, no acc. Concordia (2000) 98-3600

60:1-2   Goemanne, Noël. *Rise up in splendor.* SATB, organ. Mark Foster (1995) MF 2112

60:1-3   Jennings, Kenneth. *Arise, shine, for thy light has come.* SATB, kro. Augsburg (1998) 11-10817, found in *The Augsburg choirbook, Sacred choral music of the twentieth century,* ed. Kenneth Jennings

60:1-3, 11, 14, 18, 19
          Pearson, Donald. *Arise, shine.* SATB, organ. Aureole edition (Paraclete) (1994) AE70

60:1, 3, 19
          Pote, Allen. *Arise, shine, for your light has come.* SATB, kbd. Coronet (Presser) (1989) 392-41548

60:6b (based on)
          Hirten, John Karl. *For glory dawns upon you.* 2-part mixed, kbd. Augsburg (1995) 11-10650

60:6b   Hirten, John Karl. *For glory dawns upon you.* SATB, kbd. Augsburg (1998) 11-10817, found in *The Augsburg choirbook, Sacred choral music of the twentieth century,* ed. Kenneth Jennings

61:1   SEE: Psalm 95:1. Clay, Crystal Davis. *A jubilant song*

61:1   Dengler, Lee. *The spirit of the Lord is upon me.* SATB, kbd. Lorenz (1990) found in *Exaltation*

61:2 (Luke 4:18, 19; Leviticus 25:8-17; Wesley text)
          Courtney, Craig. *Blow ye the trumpet!* SATB, kbd., optional brass quintet. Beckenhorst (1995) BP 1467

62:00   Butler, Eugene. *Go through the gates.* 2-part mixed, kbd. Sacred Music Press (1988) found in *Sing a new song to the Lord,* vol. 2

62:11 (Luke 2:00)
          Beebe, Hank. *Behold, your salvation comes.* SATB, kbd. Hinshaw (1991) HPC 7068

66:1   SEE: Revelation 7:11. Mozart, W. A. *Gloria*

66:31a   SEE: Isaiah 40:1. Nelson, Ronald A. *Comfort, O comfort*

JEREMIAH

8:22   African-American spiritual (arr. Mark Shepperd). *Balm in Gilead.* SATB, kbd. Augsburg (1998) 11-10923

8:22   Fairbanks, Brian. *There is a balm.* SATB, kro. Paraclete (1995) 9507

8:22   Owens, Sam Batt. *There is a balm in Gilead.* Medium voice soloist/ SATB, no acc. Morning Star (1997) MSM-50-8832

8:22   Spiritual (arr. James Furman). *There is a balm in Gilead.* A/solo and Bar./ solo, SATB, kro. Music 70 (1988) M70-514

11:00 (Philippians 2:9-10)
          Comer, Thomas. *Anthem for Good Friday.* B/solo, S/solo, SATB, kbd. Boston Music (1992) found in *Early American sacred choral library,* vol. 2

17:7, 8, 10
          Keesecker, Thomas. *Blessed are they who trust in the Lord.* SA or TB, kbd. Concordia (1998) 98-3462

31:3   SEE: Joshua 1:5-6. Grotenhuis, Dale. *Song of commitment*

31:33-34 SEE: Ezekiel 36:25-26. Farrell, Bernadette (arr. Paul Inwood) *Give us, Lord, a new heart*

33:10-122, 14-16 (Psalm 89:1)
          Weber, Paul. *I will sing the story of your love.* SATB, organ. Augsburg (1997) 11-10839

LAMENTATIONS

1:12   Croce, Giovanni (ed. Jerald Hamilton). *O vos omnes.* SATB, kro. Aureole (MorningStar) (2000) AE 114

1:12   Pinkham, Daniel. *O vos omnes* (#3 of *Passion music*) (English/Latin). SATB, organ or string quartet. Thorpe (Presser) (1995) 392-03042

1:12   Victoria, Tomas Luis de (ed. Raymond Sprague). *O vos omnes* (Latin). SSAA, kro. Roger Dean (1998) 15/1400R

1:13   Schalk, Carl. *From above he hath sent fire* (from *Lamentations of Jeremiah*). SATB, no acc. Concordia (2000) 98-3601

1:18   Schalk, Carl. *The Lord is righteous* (from *Lamentations of Jeremiah*). SATB, no acc. Concordia (2000) 98-3601

3:22   SEE: Psalm 90:1. Ferguson, John. *A song of thanksgiving*

3:22, 23, 25
    Fritschel, James. *Steadfast love.* SATB, kbd. AMSI (1995) 501

4:13-15   Schalk, Carl. *For the sins of her prophets* (from *Lamentations of Jeremiah*). SATB, no acc. Concordia (2000) 98-3601

5:1, 7, 15, 16
    Schalk, Carl. *Remember, O Lord* (from *Lamentations of Jeremiah*). SATB, no acc. Concordia (2000) 98-3601

EZEKIEL

36:25-26 (Jeremiah 31:33-34)
    Farrell, Bernadette (arr. Paul Inwood). *Give us, Lord, a new heart.* SATB, clarinet, organ. OCP (1981) 7104

37:1-14 (inspired by)
    Dufford, Bob, S. J. *Breath of God.* SATB, 2 flutes, kbd. OCP (1997) 10506

37:26-27 Kohrs, Jonathan. *The Lord says, I will make a covenant* (Offertory: Advent III). SA/AB, or SA, or TB, organ. Concordia (1996) 98-3279

DANIEL

2:00 (based on)
    Cox, Michael. *I sought the Lord in the night.* SATB, kbd. Birnamwood (MorningStar) (2001) MSM-50-7042

3:52-90 (based on)
    Goebel-Komala, Felix. *Canticle from the flames.* SATB, guitar, kbd. GIA (1996) G-4414

HOSEA

14:1, 4-7 Farlee, Robert Buckley. *O my people, turn to me* (#3 in *Three Biblical songs*). Unison, kbd. Augsburg (1995) 11-10604

JOEL

2:12, 13 (Deuteronomy 4:29; Job 23:3)
    Mendelssohn, Felix (arr. Ellen Jane Lorenz). *If with all your hearts.* SATB, kbd. Lorenz (1949) found in *Easy standard anthems,* I

2:13 (based on) (Matthew 4:1-4; Mark 1:12-15; John 4:5-42)
    Vaughan Williams, Ralph (descant by Craig Kingsbury). *Led by the spirit* (based on tune *Kingsfold*). SATB, kbd. OCP (1996) 10621

2:13   Gerike, Henry V. *Return to the Lord.* TTBB, no acc. Concordia (1996) 98:3274

2:28 (paraphrased)
Hopson, Hal H. *I will pour out my spirit on all the earth.* SATB, organ. Concordia (1990) 97-6040 found in *Easy anthems*

2:28 Thompson, Randall *The old and the young* (#5 of *Twelve canticles*). SATB, kro. E. C. Schirmer (1986) 4103

MICAH

1:4-5 (based on)
Martin, Joseph M. *In the last days.* SATB, kbd. Purifoy (1995) 10/1290P

5:00 (adapted)
Schram, Ruth Elaine. *This will be our peace.* SATB, kbd. Hal Leonard (1997) 08741033

6:6, 7a Cherwien, David. *God has told you.* SATB, organ. Concordia (1995) 98-3180

6:6-8 Brown, Grayson Warren (arr. Val Parker and Grayson Warren Brown). *Micah's song.* Unison, kbd. OCP (1995) 10114, found in *If God is for us*

6:6-8 Bush, Gladys Blakely. *With what shall I come before the Lord.* SATB, kro. Concordia (1997) 98-3398

6:6-8 Young, Philip M. *With what shall I come before the Lord.* SATB, organ. MorningStar (1997) MS-50-9083

HABAKKUK

2:20 Hastings, Thomas. *The Lord is in his holy temple.* SATB, kbd. Boston Music (1992) found in *Early American sacred choral library,* vol. 2

2:20 SEE: Psalm 122:1-2. Pethel, Stan. *The gate of heaven*

3:17-19 SEE: Deuteronomy 8:2. Powell, Robert J. *Remember your Lord God/ Prayer of Habakkuk*

ZEPHANIAH

3:14, 17 Kohrs, Jonathan. *Sing aloud, O daughter of Zion* (Offertory: Advent IV). SA/TB, or SA, or TB, organ. Concordia (1996) 98-3279

3:14-18 (based on)
SEE: Psalm 25:3. Hurd, Bob. *Await the Lord with hope*

3:17, 20 SEE: Psalm 115:1. Busarow, Donald. *Not unto us, O Lord*

ZECHARIAH

9:9 (Matthew 21:1-11)
Taranto, A. Steven. *Into Jerusalem.* Unison, optional Orff instruments, kbd. Choristers Guild (1996) CGA 735

MALACHI

4:2 (Wesley)
Ledger, Philip. *Christ, whose glory fills the skies.* SATB, kbd. Roger Dean (Lorenz) (1988) HRD 245

The Apocrypha

JUDITH

16:1, 13-15
> Chepponis, James J. *Strike up the instruments (Canticle of Judith).* Unison, optional solo instrument, percussion, handbells, kbd. GIA (1997) G-4330

PRAYER OF AZARIAH

(Also called Song of the Three Young Children)

1:29-34
> Carmona, Paul. *A canticle of creation.* Unison, trumpet in B-flat, organ. OCP (1992) 9973.

1:29-34
> Cherwien, David. *All you works of the Lord, bless the Lord (Benedicite, omnia opera).* SATB, 2 octave handbells. Concordia (1997) 98-3330

1:29-34
> Jennings, Kenneth. *All you works of the Lord, bless the Lord.* SATB, organ or piano. Augsburg (1998) 11-10817, found in *The Augsburg choirbook, Sacred choral music of the twentieth century,* ed. Kenneth Jennings

1:29-34
> Near, Gerald. *A song of praise. (Benedictus es, Domine).* SATB, organ. Paraclete (1995) AE79

1:35-68
> Cherwien, David M. *All you works of the Lord, bless the Lord (Benedicite, omnia opera).* SATB, optional handbells, no acc. Concordia (1997) 98-3330

BARUCH

4:35 (based on)
> SEE: Baruch 5:5. DeBruyn, Randall. *Rise up, Jerusalem*

5:5 (Baruch 4:35, based on)
> DeBruyn, Randall. *Rise up, Jerusalem* (based on tune *Winchester New*). SA, flute or violin, organ. OCP (1986) 8797

The New Testament

MATTHEW

2:1-12 (based on)
SEE: Luke 2:8-20. French carol (arr. John A. Ricketts). *Sing we now of Christmas*

2:2
Blersch, Jeffrey. *The epiphany of our Lord* (*Alleluia verses*, set 2). SATB, organ. Concordia (1996) 98-3285

3:3
SEE: Isaiah 40:3. Robinson, Marc A. *Prepare ye*

3:3, 13-17
Ore, Charles W. *This is my son.* SATB, organ, optional trumpet. Concordia (1996) 98-3288

3:13-17
Plag, Johannes (ed. Richard Proulx). *Jesus went to Jordan's stream*, Op. 59, No. 10 (composed 1910). 2-part mixed, organ. Augsburg (1995) 11-10649

4:1, 2 (Sidney Lanier)
Wyton, Alec. *Into the woods my master went.* SATB, organ. Paraclete (1991) AE 31

4:1-4
SEE: Joel 2:12-13. Vaughan Williams, Ralph. *Led by the spirit*

5:1-12 (I John 5:3)
Harris, Jerry Weseley. *The Beatitudes.* SATB, kbd. Augsburg (1995) 11-10591

5:1-16
Jones, Hilton Kean. *Happy are the lowly poor.* Two-part mixed, kbd. Logia (Concordia) (1994) 98-3154

5:3-10
Billings, William. *Blessed are they.* SATB, kro. Boston Music, found in *Early American sacred choral library*, vol. 1

5:3-10
Jordan, Alice. *The Beatitudes.* SATB, organ. Randall Egan (1965, 1993) EC 204

5:3-10 (based on)
Leavitt, John. *Blessed are they.* Unison or 2-part, piano. Concordia (2000) 989-3550

5:3-10
Panchenko, Semyon (ed. Anthony Antolini). *The Beatitudes, remember us, we pray* (*Vo tastarstvii Tvoyem*) (English/Russian, Latin & Cyrillic alphabets). SSATTB, kro. Paraclete (1995) 9502

5:3-11 (Houston)
Lawrence, Stephen L. *The kingdom of God.* SATB, kbd. Lorenz (1994) 10/1174

5:3-12
Dengler, Lee. *Blessed are they.* SATB, kbd. Shawnee Press (1995) A-6973

5:4-5, 7-8, 12a
Mechem, Kirke. *Blessed are they*, Op. 66, #2. SATB, organ (piano). G. Schirmer (Hal Leonard) (1999) HL50483454

5:5, 8
SEE: Matthew 19:14. Murphy, Michael Patrick. *Let the children come*

5:12-13 (based on)
African-American spiritual (arr. Marylou India Jackson). *Done foun' my los' sheep.* SSAA, S/solo, no acc. Treble Clef Music Press (1996) TC-108

5:13
Patterson, Joy F. *You are the salt of the earth.* SATB, piano. MorningStar (1996) MSM 50-9081

5:13-16 (John 8:12)
McDonald, Mary. *You are the light.* SATB, kbd. Purifoy (1995) 10/1285P

5:14-16
Hillert, Richard. *You are the light of the world.* Any 2-part combination, oboe (or instrument in C), kbd. MorningStar (1999) MSM-2006

6:9-13   Arensky, Anton (ed. Anthony Antolini). *The Lord's prayer (Otche nash),* Op. 40, No. 3 (English/Russian, Latin & Cyrillic alphabets). SATB, kro. Paraclete (1994) 9413

6:9-13   Bell, Reta J. *Our Father, who art in heaven.* SAB, kbd. Lorenz (1963/1965) found in *Anthems for limited choirs*

6:9-13   Clausen, René. *The Lord's prayer.* SATB, kro. Mark Foster (1994) MF 2108

6:9-13   Dengler, Lee. *The Lord's prayer.* SATB, kbd. Flammer (Shawnee) (1999) A 7350

6:9-13   Larson, Lloyd. *Our Lord's prayer.* SATB, kbd. Beckenhorst (1998) BP 1524

6:9-13   Schütz, Heinrich (ed. George Guest). *The Lord's prayer.* SATB, no acc. Paraclete (1995) 9233

6:9-13   Walker, Christopher. *The Lord's prayer.* SATB, kbd. OCP (1996) 10575

6:9-13   Walker, Gwyneth. *"For Ever and Ever" – The Lord's prayer.* S/Solo, SATB, no acc. E. C. Schirmer (1994) 4316

6:13   SEE: Psalm 100:4. Bish, Diane. *Introit and prayer*

6:16 (based on)
    Shields, Valerie. *Let your light so brightly shine.* 2-part, organ, optional handbells. MorningStar (1997) MSM-50-8410

6:19-21   Frahm, Frederick. *Treasure in heaven.* SAB, piano. Concordia (1996) 98-3253

6:19-21   Graham, Michael. *Treasure.* SATB, piano (organ), cello or bassoon. Concordia (1999) 98-3541

6:19-34   Choplin, Pepper. *Lay up your treasures in heaven.* Medium voice solo, SATB, no acc. Monarch Music (Lorenz) (1996) 10/1461M

6:25-34   Dengler, Lee. *Look at the birds of the air.* SATB, optional flute, kbd. Logia (Concordia) (1994) 98-3125

6:25-34   Schutte, Dan. *See the lilies.* SATB, kbd. OCP (1995) 10760

6:26, 28-29, 34 (and attributed to the Sanskrit)
    Wetzler, Robert. *Look to this day.* SSAATTBB, optional narrator, kro. AMSI (1987) 525

6:28   Sleeth, Natalie (arr. Jane Marshall). *Consider the lilies.* 2-part mixed, flute or violin, kbd. Choristers Guild (1996) CGA 738

6:30-34   Kreutz, Robert E. *Shepherd and teacher.* 2-part, kbd. OCP (1993) 10015

6:33   Lau, Robert. *Seek ye first* (found in *Choral responses for worship*). SATB, kbd. Coronet (Presser) (1995) 392-41857

6:33 (Matthew 7:7)
    Pachelbel, Johann and Karen Lafferty (arr. Douglas E. Wagner). *Seek ye first.* 2-part mixed, handbells or kbd. Hope (1999) C5052, handbell parts published separately

7:7   SEE: Luke 11:9. Barta, Daniel. *Ask and seek and knock*

7:7   SEE: Matthew 6:33. Pachelbel, Johann and Karen Lafferty. *Seek ye first*

7:24-25   SEE: Matthew 16:18. Locklair, Dan. *St. Peter's rock*

8:8   Franck, Melchior (ed. and arr. Henry V. Gerike). *O Lord, I am not worthy.* TTBB, kro. Concordia (1998) 98-3485

8:8   Haan, Raymond H. *Supplication* (alternate text: *Alleluia! Jesus, alleluia!*) SATB, organ. MorningStar (1996) MSM-50-9076

11:4-5, 28
SEE: Luke 24:5-6. Haas, David (arr. Jeanne Cotter). *Song of the risen one*

11:28   Handel, George F. (freely arranged by Ellen Jane Lorenz). *Come unto Him (Messiah).* SATB, kbd. Lorenz (1949) found in *Easy standard anthems,* I

11:28   SEE: I Corinthians 10:17. Proulx, Richard. *Though we are many, in Christ we are one*

11:28-29 SEE: Isaiah 53:3-5. Dubois, Theodore (arr. Hal H. Hopson). *He was despised*

11:28-29 (John 14:27)
Murphy, Michael Patrick (arr. Robert J. Powell). *Come to me, all who labor.* SAB, kbd. Coronet (Presser) (1995) 392-41865

11:28-30 Killman, Daniel. *Come unto me.* SATB, organ. MorningStar (2000) MSM-50-9116

11:28-30 Mozart, W. A. (arr. Hal H. Hopson). *Come to me, all who are weary* (from *Missa Brevis*, K. 317). SATB, kbd. Flammer (Shawnee) (1999) A 7343

11:28-30 SEE: Psalm 147:3. Scott, K. Lee. *God shall the broken heart repair*

13:00 (based on)
Bolt, Conway A., Jr. *The kingdom of God.* 2-part, kbd. Choristers Guild (1994) CGA 677

13:4-8   SEE: Ecclesiastes 3:1-9. Ridge, M. E. (arr. Patrick Loomis). *Parable*

13:44-45 Hopson, Hal H. *The treasure and the pearl.* 2-part or unison, kbd. AMSI (1984) 462

14:16   Bauer, Marie Rubis. *Tu es Petrus.* SSATBB, kro. MorningStar (2000) MSM-80-854

16:13-16 Courtney, Craig. *Who do people say that I am?* SATB, organ and optional brass quartet. Sacred Music Press (1996) 10/1238

16:13-20 Angerman, David. *You are the Christ.* SATB, kbd. Shawnee (1994) A 6883

16:18 (Matthew 7:24-25; Genesis 28:17; Psalm 122:1)
Locklair, Dan. *St. Peter's rock.* SATB, organ, optional trumpet in C. Subito Music (Presser) (2000) 492-00062

18:20   Colgan, Tobias (arr. Craig Kingsbury). *Where two or three are gathered.* SATB, kbd. OCP (1996) 10703

19:14 (Matthew 5:5, 8)
Murphy, Michael Patrick (arr. John R. Murtha). *Let the children come.* SATB, optional flute or violin, kbd. Coronet (Presser) (1998) 392-42138

20:26-28 Hughes, Robert J. *Whoever would be great.* SAB, guitar or kbd. Lorenz (1993) 10/1349L

20:26-28 (based on)
Nelson, Ronald A. *Whoever would be great among you.* SAB, guitars or kbd. Augsburg (1998) 11-10817, found in *The Augsburg choirbook, Sacred choral music of the twentieth century,* ed. Kenneth Jennings

21:1-11   SEE: Zechariah 9:9. Taranto, A. Steven. *Into Jerusalem*

21:9   Archer, Malcolm. *Hosanna to the son of David.* SATB, kbd. Hinshaw (1993) HMC 1261

21:9   Armstrong, Matthew. *Hosanna.* SATB, kbd. Logia (Concordia) (1998) 98-3486

21:9 (Mark 11:9; John 12:13)
Birkley, Michael M. *Hosanna, hosanna.* 2-part mixed, kbd., and optional instruments. Concordia (2000) 98-3584

21:9 (Mark 11:9)
Burkhardt, Michael. *Hosanna* (based on melody by Christian Gregor). 2 equal voices, handbells, bass instrument. MorningStar (2000) MSM-50-3754

21:9 Johnston, Randolph. *Hosanna! Blessed is He!* (quoting tune *Ellacombe*). SATB, kbd. Lorenz (1961) found in *Easy hymn tune anthems,* I

21:9 Laubengayer, Paul. *Hosanna in the highest.* 2-part mixed, flute, kbd. Birnamwood (MorningStar) (2001) MSM-50-3755

21:9 Moe, Daniel. *Hosanna to the Son of David.* SAB, organ. Mercury (Presser) (1956, 1995) 352-00498

21:9 Moe, Daniel. *Hosanna to the Son of David.* SATB, organ. Mercury (Presser) (1956, 1995) 352-00212

21:15 Keldermans, R. *Hosanna filio David.* SSAA, kbd. Mark Foster (1997) MF 928

25:1-13 (based on)
Honoré, Jeffrey. *Rejoice, rejoice, believers.* 2-part mixed, recorder or flute, optional tambourine, kbd. Choristers Guild (1997) CGA 746

25:1-13 (based on)
Swedish folk tune (arr. Theodore Beck). *Rejoice, rejoice, believers* (uses tune *Haf trones lampa färdig*). SATB, organ. Augsburg (1992) 11-10136

25:4-6 Handl, Jacob (ed. Mary Lycan). *Virgines prudentes (O, ye wise maidens).* SSAA/SSAA, no acc. Treble Clef Music Press (1996) TC-120

25:23 (based on)
Martin, Joseph M. *Well done, faithful servant(s).* SATB, kbd. Shawnee Press (1995) A-6958

25:34 Franck, Melchior (ed. Carl Schalk). *Come, O blessed of my father.* SATB, kro. Concordia (1995) 98-3220

25:35-40 SEE: Revelation 19:00. Dufford, Bob. *The reign of God*

25:35-40 SEE: John 13:34-35. Hopson, Hal H. *Love one another*

25:40 O'Sheil, Judy (arr. John Purifoy). *Whenever you do this.* SATB, kbd. Unity (1995) 10/1270U

26:30, 41-42
Pinkham, Daniel. *In Monte Oliveti* (#1 of *Passion music*) (English/Latin). SATB, organ or string quartet. Thorpe (Presser) (1995) 392-03040

26:36-66 Anderson, Norma Sateren. *The walk to Calvary.* Unison, kbd. Choristers Guild (1996) CGA 739

26:38 (Mark 14:34; Matthew 26:45; Mark 14:41)
Pinkham, Daniel. *Tristis est anima mea* (#2 of *Passion music*) (English/Latin). SATB, organ or string quartet. Thorpe (Presser) (1995) 392-03041

26:45 SEE: Matthew 26:38. Pinkham, Daniel. *Tristis est anima mea*

27:27-37, 51, 54 (based on)
Larson, Lloyd. *A scarlet robe.* SATB, kbd. Beckenhorst (1996) BP 1494

28:1-10 (based on)
Larson, Sonia. *Sing allelu, alleluia!* 2-part or unison, kbd. AMSI (1991) 617

28:5, 7 SEE: Luke 24:4-7. Nelson, Ronald A. *Risen! Go and tell*

28:6 SEE: Mark 16:1. Kihlken, Henry, arr. *See the place where Jesus lay*

28:6-7 (Hebrews 2:7; Psalm 8:5-6)
Kosche, Kenneth T. *Alleluia! Christ has risen.* SATB, kbd. AMSI (1996) 740

28:6-7, 19
SEE: Luke 24:5-6. Haas, David (arr. Jeanne Cotter). *Song of the risen one.*

28:19-20 Bedford, Michael. *Go, therefore and make disciples.* Unison, kbd. Concordia (1996) 98-3270

28:19-20 SEE: Romans 10:13-15. Burroughs, Bob. *Whosoever*

28:19-20 McDonald, Mary. *Go ye therefore.* SAB, kbd. Found in *Go out in joy!* Lorenz (2001) 45/1097L

28:19-20 (based on) Schweizer, Mark. *Go, make of all disciples.* SATB, kbd. Logia (Concordia) (1996) 98-3276

28:20 SEE: Romans 6:9. Blersch, Jeffrey. *The ascension of our Lord (Alleluia Verses)*

MARK

1.3 SEE: Isaiah 40:3-4. Bach, J. S. (setting Hal H. Hopson). *The Lord will soon appear*

1:9 Neswick, Bruce. *Jesus came from Nazareth.* 2-part, organ. Augsburg (1995) 11-10643

1:12-15 SEE: Joel 2:12-13. Vaughan Williams, Ralph. *Led by the spirit*

1:30 SEE: Isaiah 40:3. Robinson, Marc A. *Prepare ye*

10:14-16 Armstrong, Matthew. *Suffer the little children (based on hymn tune Salzburg).* SATB, instrument in C, kbd. Concordia (1996) 98-3302

10:45 Hyslop, Scott M. *Verse for Sundays in Lent.* SATB, organ. Concordia (1999) 98-3538

11:9 SEE: Matthew 21:9. Birkley, Michael M. *Hosanna, hosanna*

11:9 SEE: Matthew 21:9. Burkhardt, Michael. *Hosanna*

14:34 SEE: Matthew 26:38. Pinkham, Daniel. *Tristis est anima mea*

14:41 SEE: Matthew 26:38. Pinkham, Daniel. *Tristis est anima mea*

16:00 (John 20:00, based on) James, Layton. *They rolled the stone away.* SAB, kbd. MorningStar (1999) MSM-50-4036

16:6 (Matthew 28:6, based on) Kihlken, Henry, arr. *See the place where Jesus lay.* SATB, optional trumpet, organ. Coronet (Presser) (1997) 392-42137

16:15 Wetzler, Robert. *Go ye into all the world.* 2-part mixed, kbd. Concordia (1999) 98-3530

LUKE

1:00 Bach, J. S. (adapted Charles Gounod; arr. Colin Mawby). *Ave Maria* (English/Latin). T/solo, SATB, organ. Mayhew (Brodt) (1994) 5101034

1:26-38 (based on) Williams, Amy Tate. *Mary.* SATB, kbd. Beckenhorst (1998) BP 1527

1:45 (based on) SEE: Psalm 25:3. Hurd, Bob. *Await the Lord with hope*

1:45-55 Roberts, Leon C. *Mary's canticle.* Unison, kbd. GIA (1993) G 3826

1:46, 47 Baker, Richard C. *My soul doth magnify the Lord (Magnificat).* SATB, kro. Randall Egan (1974, 1991) n.#.

1:46, 47 Near, Gerald. *Magnificat anima mea* (Latin). SATB, organ (organ and strings). Paraclete (1994) 9416

1:46-50 Murphy, Michael Patrick (arr. Robert J. Powell). *Holy is the Lord.* SATB, kbd. Coronet (Presser) (1995) 392-41939

1:46-55 Adlgasser, Anton Cajetan (ed. David Stein). *Magnificat in C major.* SATB, kbd. Theodore Presser (1997) 312-41689

1:46-55 Brown, M. Susan. *Mary's song.* SATB, flute, kbd., or handbells. Concordia (1996) 98-3287

1:46-55 SEE: I Samuel 2:1-10. Jennings, Carolyn. *A new magnificat*

1:46-55 (based on)
Manalo, Ricky. *Holy is the name of God (A Marian processional).* SATB, kbd. OCP (1996) 10871

1:46-55 Porter, Steven. *Magnificat anima mea* (Latin). SATB, piano. Associated (1981) A 815

1:46-55 Rotermund, Donald, arr. *A responsorial magnificat* (based on *Puer nobis nascitus*). Unison, organ, 2 octave handbells. Concordia (2000) 989-3576

1:46-55 Rubalcava, Peter. *Magnificat.* SATB, guitar, kbd. OCP (1997) 10833

1:46-55 Schiavone, John. *Magnificat: God who is mighty.* SATB, flute, oboe, kbd. OCP (1987) 8969

1:46-55 Toolan, Suzanne. *My soul proclaims.* SATB, 2 treble instruments, other. OCP (1995) 10580

1:46-55 Willcock, Christopher. *Song of the Virgin Mary.* SATB, organ. OCP (1977) 10540

1:46b-55 Zacharia, Cesare de. *Magnificat.* SATB, no acc. Augsburg (1995) 11-10508

1:46-58 Irish traditional (arr. Rory Cooney). *Canticle of the turning.* SAB, 2 instruments in C, guitar, kbd. GIA (1990) G3407

1:46-69 (adapted)
Martin, Gilbert M. *The song of Mary.* S/solo, SSA, kbd. Triune Music (Lorenz) (1994) 10/1427T

1:54 Pergolesi, G. B. (arr. Gregory M. Pysh). *Suscepit Israel (God has helped Israel)* (from *Magnificat*) (Latin/English). SA, 2-part mixed, or TB, kbd. Coronet (Presser) (1996) 392-42002

1:63,76-79
Proulx, Richard. *His name is John.* 2-part mixed, handbells (uses 8 handbells from a 3 octave set). Augsburg Fortress (1997) 11-1977

1:67-79 (Ruth Duck)
Haugen, Marty. *Now bless the God of Israel* (setting of the canticle *Benedictus*). 2-part, kbd. GIA (1992) G-4134

1:68-79 (paraphrase)
Carter, John. *Benedictus (Blessed be the God of Israel).* SATB, organ. Augsburg Fortress (2000) 0-8006-5914-7

1:68-79 Farlee, Robert Buckley. *Song of Zechariah (#2 in Three Biblical songs).* Unison, kbd. Augsburg (1995) 11-10604

1:68-79 Wood, Dale (setting by Donald Rotermund). *Blessed be the Lord.* Unison or 2-part, organ, optional 2-3 octave handbells. Concordia (1973, 1984) 98-3380

1:68-30 Jeffrey, Richard (arr. Mark Kellner). *Canticle of Zechariah.* SATB, organ with optional trumpet, timpani and guitar. MorningStar (2000) MSM-50-1087

2:00 SEE: Isaiah 62:11. Beebe, Hank. *Behold, your salvation comes*

2:00 Hastings, Thomas. *Nativity.* S/solo, B/solo, SATB, kbd. Boston Music (1991) found in *Early American sacred choral library,* vol. 1

2:8-12 (based on)
Dufford, Bob. *Children, run joyfully.* Unison, children's chorus, guitar, kbd. OCP (1993) 9936

2:8-15 (based on)
Larson, Lloyd. *Glory to God!* 2-part choir, optional percussion, kbd. Beckenhorst (1996) BP 1482

2:8-20 (Matthew 2:1-12, based on)
French carol (arr. John A. Ricketts). *Sing we now of Christmas.* SATB, optional percussion. Choristers Guild (1997) CGA

2:9-14 SEE: Psalm 91:11, 12. Nelson, Ronald A. *Angels*

2:10, 11   Beyer, Johann Samuel (arr. Ronald A. Nelson). *Fürchtet euch nicht (Be not afraid)* (German/English). Unison, string quartet, continuo. Concordia (1998) 98-3458; full score and parts 97-6735

2:11 (and other)
Averre, Dick. *Christmas fanfare.* SATB, kbd., optional brass quartet. Coronet (Presser) (1998) 392-41267

2:11   Blersch, Jeffrey. *The nativity of our Lord* (from *Alleluia verses,* Set 2). SATB, organ. Concordia (1996) 98-3285

2:11   Byrd, William (ed. Lawrence Doebler). *Hodie Christus natus est.* (Latin only). SATB, kro. Roger Dean (1996). 10/1422R

2:11   Phillips, Craig. *Hodie Christus natus est.* SATB, organ. OCP (1995) 10145

2:13, 14   Hobby, Robert. *Glory to God in the highest* (found in *Six scripture anthems,* set 2, ed. Don Rotermund). Unison, organ. Concordia (1994) 97-6462

2:14   Bell, John L. *Glory to God in the highest.* SATB, organ. GIA (1995) G-4296

2:14   Biery, James. *Glory to God.* SATB, 2 trumpets, kbd. OCP (1993) 9237

2:14   Crandal, Scot. *Gloria in excelsis Deo.* SAB, kbd. OCP (1996) 10511

2:14   Dewey, Dennis Hart. *Gloria in excelsis Deo.* SATB, kbd. GIA (1994) G-3895

2:14   Estes, Jerry. *Gloria in excelsis Deo* (found in *Three contemporary Latin settings*). 3-part mixed, piano. Shawnee (1992) D-450

2:14   Fisher, Bobby. *Glory to God.* SATB, kbd. GIA (1992) G-3727

2:14   Greer, Bruce. *Gloria in excelsis Deo.* SATB, kbd. Benson (1995) 25986-0697-7

2:14   Harlan, Benjamin. *Processional for Christmas* (incorporates carol *O come, all ye faithful*). SATB, kbd. Hal Leonard (1996) 08741029

2:14   Jones, Peter. *Glory to God.* SATB, organ. OCP (1986) 7148

2:14   Kesselman, Lee R. *Mbiri Kuna Mwari (Shona Gloria)* (in Shona). 4-part treble, percussion. Boosey & Hawkes (1995) OctB6792

2:14 (and other)
Kirk, Theron. *He came so still.* SATB, kbd., or brass quintet and cymbals. AMSI (1997) 755; instrumental parts 755-B

2:14   McIver, Robert H. *Glory to God in the highest.* SATB, unison children, kbd., with optional 2 treble instruments and tambourine. Choristers Guild (1996) CGA 722

2:14   Patton, Beverly A. *Exaudi! Laudate!* SSA, piano. Roger Dean (1998) 15/1401R

2:14   Pergolesi, G. B. (arr. Robert DeWell). *Glory to God in the highest.* SATB, kbd. Coronet (Presser) (1989) 392-41524

2:14   Roth, John. *Gloria in excelsis Deo (Holy, sing hosanna)* (melody is *All the pretty little horses*). Unison, optional instrument in C, kbd., or harp, or Orff instruments. Logia (Concordia) (1996) 98-3262

2:14   Soper, Scott. *Glory to God.* SATB, kbd. OCP (1991) 9589

2:14   Vierdanck, Johann (ed. & arr. Michael Burkhardt). *Gloria.* SA, 2 treble instruments, continuo. MorningStar (1994) MSM-50-1452

2:14   Vivaldi, Antonio (ed. S. Drummond Wolff). *Gloria in excelsis Deo.* SATB, organ, trumpet. Augsburg (1995) 11-10582

2:14   Walker, Christopher. *Glastonbury gloria.* 3-part choir, trumpet, kbd. OCP (1989) 7164

2:14   Willcock, Christopher. *Glory to God.* SATB, kbd. OCP (1991) 10154

2:29-32   Archangelsky, Alexander. *Nunc dimittis* (English). SATB, kro. J. Fischer, found in *Twenty-five anthems from the Russian liturgy*

2:29-32   Archangel'sky, Alexander (ed. Hal H. Hopson). *The Song of Simeon (Nunc dimittis).* SATB, kbd. MorningStar (1998) MSM-50-7032

2:29-32   Brown, Grayson Warren. *Lord, now let thy servant go in peace.* SATB, kbd. OCP (1992) 10008

2:29-32 (based on)   Choplin, Pepper. *Simeon's blessing (Nunc dimittis).* SATB, kbd. Flammer (1999) A 7298

2:29-32   Walker, Christopher. *Nunc dimittis.* SATB, solo instrument, kbd. OCP (1989) 9234

2:41-52   Horman, John D. *When Jesus was a growing lad.* Unison or 2-part, optional flute and handbells, kbd. Choristers Guild (1997) CGA 772

2:41-52 (based on)   Kemp, Helen. *The lost boy.* Unison, string bass or cello, kbd. MorningStar (1997) MSM-50-9454

3:4   SEE: John 1:29-34. Purifoy, John. *Like a dove*

3:40   SEE: Isaiah 40:3. Robinson, Marc A. *Prepare ye*

4:18-19   Canedo, Ken (arr. John Purifoy). *The spirit of God.* SATB, kbd. Lorenz (1998) 10/1739

4:18, 19   SEE: Isaiah 61:2. Courtney, Craig. *Blow ye the trumpet!*

6:20   SEE: Isaiah 43:1-4. Dufford, Bob (arr. Douglas Wagner). *Be not afraid*

6:48 (Luke 8:6; I Corinthians 10:4, based on)   Lord, Suzanne. *Faith that's sure.* Unison, kbd. Choristers Guild (1995) CGA 695

7:11-17   Bach, J. S. (ed. James Mansfield). *Wenn es meines Gottes Wille (If my God today shall will it)* (from Cantata 161, *Komm du Süsse Todesstunde*). SATB, organ, 2 flutes. Roger Dean (1992) HRD 351

8:6   SEE: Luke 6:48. Lord, Suzanne. *Faith that's sure*

11:1-13 (Luke 17:5, paraphrased)   Haas, David. *Increase our faith.* SATB, kbd. GIA (1997) G-4736

11:3-8 (based on)   Larson, Lloyd. *Dear heavenly father.* SATB, kbd. Fred Bock (1994) BG 2194.

11:3-8 (based on)   Larson, Lloyd. *Dear heavenly father.* 2-part, kbd. Fred Bock (1994) BG 2248

11:9 (Luke 12:31; Matthew 7:7)   Barta, Daniel. *Ask and seek and knock.* Two voices, optional instrument in C, kbd. Choristers Guild (1996) GCA683

12:31   SEE: Luke 11:9. Barta, Daniel. *Ask and seek and knock*

12:34-35 (Luke 17:20-21; Luke 23:34-35, paraphrased)   Haas, David. *O Jerusalem.* SATB, kbd. GIA (1997) G-4733

13:29 (Luke 14:15)   Kohrs, Jonathan. *And many will come from east and west* (Offertory: Advent II). ST/AB, or SA, or TB, organ. Concordia (1996) 98-3279

14:15   SEE: Luke 13:29. Kohrs, Jonathan. *And many will come from east and west*

15:00   SEE: John 4:00. Bourgeois, Louis (arr. Wayne L. Wold). *New beginnings*

15:1-32   SEE: Joshua 5:9-12. Thompson, J. Michael. *Taste and see the Lord is good*

17:5 (paraphrased)
          SEE: Luke 11:1-13. Haas, David. *Increase our faith*

17:20-21 (paraphrased)
          SEE: Luke 12:34-35. Haas, David. *O Jerusalem*

19:38   Rudolph, Glenn L. *Hosanna.* SATB, kro. GIA (1994) G-3980

19:38 (and other)
          Taylor, Jim. *Hosanna.* SATB (divsi), organ. Hinshaw (1989) HMC 1067

22:19, 20 (based on)
          Atkins, Jean and J. W. Snyder (arr. John Purifoy). *In remembrance of me.* SATB, kbd., optional flute. Lorenz (1995) 10/1400U

23:34-35 (paraphrased)
          SEE: Luke 12:34-35. Haas, David. *O Jerusalem*

23:39, 42-43
          Rossini, Gioacchino (ed. Robert Sumner). *Are you not the Christ?* SATB, no acc. Coronet (Presser) (1989) 392-41501

23:42 (Revelation 7:12)
          Fleming, Larry L. *Blessed are they.* SATB divsi, 3 octave handbells (optional instruments, organ). MorningStar (1996) MSM-50-8106

23:46 (John 17:00, taken from)
          Brown, Charles F. *Into thy hands.* SATB, kbd. Hinshaw (1998) HMC 1609

24:1-5   SEE: Psalm 91:11, 12. Nelson, Ronald A. *Angels*

24:1, 5   Wetzler, Robert. *Easter dawning at the tomb.* SATB, kro. AMSI (1995) 708

24:1-9 (based on)
          Horman, John D. *Easter song.* 3-part treble or mixed, kbd. Optional flute and 3 octave handbells. Choristers Guild (1997) CGA768

24:4-7 (Matthew 28:5, 7)
          Nelson, Ronald A. *Risen! Go and tell.* SATB, organ. AMSI (1996) 743

24:5-6 (Matthew 11:4-5, 28; Matthew 28:6-7, 19; Revelation 21:4-5)
          Haas, David (arr. Jeanne Cotter). *Song of the risen one.* SATB, kbd. GIA (1988) G-3337

24:13-15 (based on)
          Haugen, Marty. *On the journey to Emmaus.* SATB, kbd. GIA (1995) G-4278

24:32 (Psalm 119:00, based on)
          Englert, Eugene. *Make our hearts burn with love.* SATB, solo instrument, guitar, piano. OCP (1992) 9799

24:34   SEE: Psalm 118:24. Shields, Valerie. *Easter acclamation*

24:34-35 Petrich, Roger. *Alleluia! Risen indeed.* 2-part mixed, kbd. MorningStar (1998) 80-401

JOHN

1:1-5, 14 Roberts, Paul. *The word became flesh.* SATB, flute, no acc. Augsburg (1998) 11-10817, found in *The Augsburg choirbook, Sacred choral music of the twentieth century,* ed. Kenneth Jennings

1:4   SEE: I Corinthians 10:17. Proulx, Richard. *Though we are many, in Christ we are one*

1:14, 16   Bouman, Paul. *And the word became flesh.* SATB, kro. MorningStar (1999) MSM-50-1073

1:19-23   Hurd, David. *The record of John.* Bar. solo/2-part mixed, organ. Augsburg (1995) 12-400006

1:29   Bell, John L. *Agnus Dei.* SATB, no acc. GIA (1987) G-4539

1:29   Blersch, Jeffrey N. *Lamb of God.* SATB, instrument in C, organ. Concordia (1996) 98-3182

1:29   Galbraith, Nancy. *Agnus Dei.* SATB, kro. Subito (Presser) (1999) 392-01046

1:29   Kern, Philip. *Agnus Dei.* SATB, kbd. Coronet (Presser) (1995) 392-41848

1:29   Mengel, Dana. *Agnus Dei* (English). SATB, kbd. Concordia (2000) 98-3608

1:29   Mitchell, Tom. *Lamb of God.* 2-part, kbd. Coronet (Presser) (1995) 392-41852

1:29   Morley, Thomas (ed. Leonard Van Camp). *Agnus Dei.* SATB, kro. Presser (1995) 312-41656

1:29   Mozart, W. A. (ed. Nancy Telfer). *Agnus Dei* (from *Mass in C, the Coronation*). Unison, kbd. Kjos (1992) 8736

1:29   Pettit, David H. *Agnus Dei* (Latin). SATB, B/solo, flute, piano. Presser (1999) 312-42749. Accompaniment for flute, strings, organ rental available from publisher

1:29   Roth, John. *Agnus Dei* (Latin). SATB, piano. Concordia (1996) 98-3261

1:29   Starr, David. *O Lamb of God.* SATB, kbd. Coronet (Presser) (1997) 392-42114

1:29   Stroope, Z. Randall. *Lamb of God, grant us peace.* SATB, organ. Mark Foster (1994) MF 2101

1:29   Thayer, Fred. *Qui tollis peccata mundi* (from *Gloria*). SATB, kro. Music 70 (1990) M70-584

1:29-34 (Luke 3:4)
        Purifoy, John. *Like a dove.* SATB, optional congregation, kbd. Unity (1995) 10/1272U

1:36-39 (based on)
        SEE: Genesis 12:1-4. Haas, David. *I am the voice of God*

3:7-8   Martin, Joseph M. *Who knows where the wind blows?* SATB, kbd., optional narrator. Triune (Lorenz) (1995) 10/1313T

3:8   Proulx, Richard. *Wind, fire and heat, bless the Lord* (Pentecost introit). SAB, 4 handbells. AMSI (1999) 813

3:14, 15 Hyslop, Scott M. *Verse for Sundays in Lent* (Verse for Lent 3). SATB, organ. Concordia (1999) 98-3538

3:14-17 Grotenhuis, Dale. *For God so loved the world* (uses tune *O Waly Waly*). SATB, kbd. MorningStar (1998) 50-9021

3:16 (and other)
        Choplin, Pepper. *Timeless song* (from *Psalms of the wood*). SATB, kbd., and synthesizer. GlorySound (1999) A 7327

3:16   Hyslop, Scott M. *Verse for Sundays in Lent* (Verse for Lent 4). SATB, organ. Concordia (1999) 98-3538

3:16   Leaf, Robert. *Sing praise to God.* Unison, kbd. Choristers Guild (1995) CGA 712

3:16   SEE: John 13:34. Murphy, Michael Patrick (arr. Dick Averre). *A new commandment*

3:16   Stainer, John (arr. Ellen Jane Lorenz). *God so loved the world* (from *Creation*). SATB, kbd. Lorenz (1949) found in *Easy standard anthems* I

3:16-17 Larson, Lloyd. *God so loved the world.* SATB, kbd. Triune Music (1995) 10/1360T

3:16-17 Sadowski, Kevin J. *God so loved the world* (found in *Three motets from the Gospel of St. John*). SATB, no acc. Concordia (1998) 98-3472

3:16-17 Stainer, John (arr. Ellen Jane Lorenz). *God so loved the world.* SAB, kbd. Lorenz (1970) found in *Anthems for limited choirs*

3:16-17 Stainer, John (arr. Gregg Sewell). *God so loved the world.* SATB, organ, handbells. Lorenz (1985) found in *Festive bells 'n' choir*

4:00 (Luke 15:00)
         Bourgeois, Louis (setting by Wayne L. Wold). *New beginnings* (based on tune *Rendez à Dieu*). SATB, organ. Augsburg (1997) 11-10849

4:5-42   SEE: Joel 2:12-13. Vaughan Williams, Ralph. *Led by the spirit*

4:7-16 (based on)
         Page, Paul F. *Share this covenant of love.* SAB, solo instrument, kbd. OCP (1991) 9318

4:13, 14 Busch, Richard. *Qui biberit aquam.* SATB, no acc. Paraclete (1995) PPMO 9314

4:14   SEE: Isaiah 55:1. Malmin, Olaf. *Come, drink of the water*

4:24   Thompson, Randall. *God is a spirit.* SATB, kro. E. C. Schirmer (1986) 4101

6:1-5 (based on)
         Haugen, Marty. *Bread to share.* Solo voice, SATB, kbd. GIA (1995) G-4279

6:32-51 Sherman, Arnold B. *I am the bread of life.* 2-part mixed, kbd. (optional instrument in C, guitar and bass). Sacred Music Press (1988) found in *Sing a new song to the Lord,* vol 2

6:35-35 SEE: I Corinthians 11:25-26 (based on). Canedo, Ken (arr. Mark Barnard). *Every time we eat this bread*

6:51 (John 14:23)
         Brown, Grayson Warren. *Jesus, the bread of life.* SATB, organ. OCP (1981) 10490

6:51   McCabe, Michael. *I am the living bread.* SATB, no acc. Randall M. Egan (1995) EC 338

6:68 (Psalm 19:8-11)
         Joncas, Michael. *Lord, you have the words.* SATB, kbd. OCP (1990) 10193

7:37-38 SEE: I Corinthians 10:17. Proulx, Richard. *Though we are many, in Christ we are one*

8:12   Bouman, Paul. *I am the light of the world* (found in *Alleluia, I will sing*). Unison, kbd. Augsburg (1986) 11-5115

8:12   SEE: Matthew 5:13. McDonald, Mary. *You are the light*

10:11-14 Nolan, Douglas. *The good shepherd.* SATB, kbd. Flammer (Shawnee) (1999) A 7347

10:14   SEE: Romans 6:9. Wetzler, Robert. *I am the good shepherd*

11:1-44 Drennan, Patti. *I am the resurrection.* SATB, kbd., optional bass. Shawnee Press (1995) A 7001

11:25   Scheidt, Samuel (ed. Larry Cook). *I am the resurrection (Ich bin die Auferstehung)* (English/German). SSB, organ. Concordia (1996) 98-3254

11:25-26 Hildebrand, Kevin. *I am the resurrection.* SATB, kro. MorningStar (1998) MSM-50-4032

11:25-26 Rotermund, Melvin. *I am the resurrection and the life.* Unison, optional instrument in C, organ. Concordia (1996) 98-3271

12:00   Powell, Kathy. *Never the blade shall rise.* SATB, instrument in C, kbd. GIA (1994) G-3817

12:12-15 (Milman)
Darst, W. Glen. *Ride on! Ride on in majesty.* SAB, kbd. H. W. Gray (1953) 2245 (also available in SATB version)

12:12-15 (Milman)
Gippenbusch, J. *Ride on! Ride on in majesty.* SATB, kro. GIA (1987) G-2937

12:12-15 (Milman)
Norris, Kevin. *Ride on! Ride on in majesty!* 2-part mixed, kbd. Augsburg (1985) 11-2296

12:12-15 (Milman)
Stocker, David. *Ride on! Ride on in majesty* (uses tune *Winchester new*). SATB, optional instrument, organ. Thomas House (1986) 1C368621

12:12-15 (Milman)
Titcomb, Everett. *Ride on! Ride on in majesty.* SATB, kbd. Carl Fischer (1959) CM 6468

12:12-15 (Milman)
Young, Gordon. *Ride on! Ride on in majesty.* SATB, organ. Galaxy (1963) 1.2277

12:13   SEE: Matthew 21:9. Birkley, Michael M. *Hosanna, hosanna*

12:13   SEE: Psalm 118:26. Nystedt, Knut. *Hosanna! Blessed is he*

12:23   Blersch, Jeffrey. *Verse for Psalm Sunday* (based on *Vexilla regis*) (found in *Alleluia verses*). S/solo, SATB, organ. Concordia (1996) 98-3230

12:23   Hyslop, Scott M. *Verse for Sundays in Lent.* SATB, organ. Concordia (1999) 98-3538

12:23   Wienhorst, Richard. *The hour has come.* SA, kbd. Concordia (1997) 98-3301

12:32   McDonald, Mary. *Christ will be lifted up.* SAB, kbd. Found in *Christ will be lifted up.* Lorenz (2001) 45/1106M

13:1-15   Haas, David. *Song of the Lord's command.* Unison, instrument in C, kbd. GIA (1997) G-4682

13:1-15   Haas, David. *Song of the Lord's command.* SATB, instrument in C, kbd. GIA (1997) G-4682

13:1-15   Haugen, Marty. *So you must do.* SATB, kbd. GIA (1998) G-4841

13:14   Luckner, Brian. *If I have washed your feet.* SATB, no acc. Mark Foster (1996) MF 2123

13:34   SEE: John 14:15. Bales, Gerald. *Love*

13:34 (John 15:9-13)
Biery, James. *A new commandment I give you* (based on *Mandatum novum Deo veobis*). SATB, organ, optional handbells. MorningStar (2000) MSM-80-836

13:34 (Galatians 6:2)
Causey, C. Harry. *Love one another.* SATB, kbd. Lorenz (1994) 10/1100

13:34 (I Corinthians 13:00)
Dufford, Bob. *Love one another.* SATB, 2 flutes, kbd. OCP (1994) 10347

13:34 (John 3:16, and other)
Murphy, Michael Patrick (arr. Dick Averre). *A new commandment.* SATB, kbd. Coronet (Presser) (2000) 392-42297

13:34-35   Farlee, Robert Buckley. *Mandatum,* SATB, kro. Augsburg (1994) 11-10535

13:34-35 (Matthew 25:35-40)
Hopson, Hal H. *Love one another.* Unison or two-part, kbd. Choristers Guild (1996) CGA 741

14:00 (John 15:00, adapted, and other)
Canedo, Ken (arr. John Purifoy). *There is no greater love.* SATB, kbd., optional flute. Lorenz (1996) 10/1403U

14:00 (taken from)
> Irish traditional (arr. John Bell). *Let your restless hearts be still.* SATB, optional solo, kbd. GIA (1988) G4532

14:00 (John 15:00; Romans 3:00)
> Joy, Dawn. *You will not be left alone* (quoting *Veni creator spiritus*). SATB, kbd. Lorenz (1995) 10/1401U

14:1-3, 6-7, 10-14 (paraphrased)
> Haas, David. *Do not let your hearts be troubled.* SATB, optional trumpet, handbells, or cello, kbd. GIA (1995) G-4349

14:1-4   Armstrong, Matthew. *In my Father's house.* SATB, kbd. Concordia (1996) 98-3260

14:1-4   Murphy, Michael Patrick. *Let not troubled be your hearts.* SATB, kbd. Coronet (Presser) (1999) 392-42231

14:1-4, 6 Lau, Robert E. *I am the way, the truth and the life.* SATB, optional brass quartet, kbd. Coronet (Presser) (1999) 392-42251; brass 392-42251A

14:1-14   McDonald, Mary. *Peace be with you.* SATB, kbd. Monarch (Lorenz) (1998) 10/1909M

14:6   Mengel, Dana. *Come, my way, my truth, my life.* SATB, kbd. Coronet (Presser) (1996) 392-42019

14:6, 27 (based on)
> McChesney, Kevin. *May the peace of the Lord be with you today.* SATB, kbd. Shawnee Press (1995) A-6943

14:6, 27 Perti, Giacomo (arr. Hal H. Hopson). *Peace I leave with you.* SATB, organ. GIA (1997) G-4388

14:15 (John 13:34)
> Bales, Gerald. *Love.* SATB, organ. Randall Egan (1987) n.#.

14:18 (John 16:22ff)
> Sadowski, Kevin J. *I will not leave you desolate* (found in *Three motets from the Gospel of St. John*). SATB, no acc. Concordia (1998) 98-3472

14:23   SEE: John 6:51. Brown, Grayson Warren. *Jesus, the bread of life*

14:27   Landes, Rob. *Peace I leave with you.* SATB, organ. MorningStar (1998) MSM-50-5000

14:27   Larkin, Michael. *Peace, I give to you.* SATB, piano. Concordia (2000) 98-3607

14:27 (based on)
> Mendelssohn, Felix (arr. Hal H. Hopson). *Peace I leave with you.* SATB, kbd. Sacred Music Press (1995) 10/1188

14:27   SEE: Matthew 11:28-29. Murphy, Michael Patrick (arr. Robert J. Powell). *Come to me, all who labor*

14:27   Pelz, Walter L. *Peace I leave with you.* SATB, kro. Augsburg (1998) 11-10817, found in *The Augsburg choirbook, Sacred choral music of the twentieth century,* ed. Kenneth Jennings

14:27 (Philippians 4:6)
> Schultz, Timothy P. *Peace.* SATB, kro. Concordia (1999) 98-3534

14:34-35 Aston, Peter. *I give you a new commandment.* SATB, kbd. GIA (1995) G-4331

15:00   SEE: I Corinthians 11:25-26 (based on). Canedo, Ken (arr. Mark Barnard). *Every time we eat this bread*

15:00   SEE: John 14:00. Canedo, Ken (arr. John Purifoy). *There is no greater love*

15:00   SEE: John 14:00. Joy, Dawn. *You will not be left alone*

15:00 (based on)
> Martin, Joseph M. *You are the vine.* SATB, kbd. Malcolm Music (Shawnee) (1999) A 7305

15:00 (taken from)
Pote, Allen. *I am the vine.* 2-part, kbd., and flute. Lorenz (1977) found in *Songs of joy*

15:1, 4-5 Gehring, Philip. *I am the true vine* (from *Choral offertories*). SATB, organ. Concordia (2000) 98-3585

15:1, 4-5 Sadowski, Kevin J. *I am the true vine* (found in *Three motets from the Gospel of St. John*). SATB, no acc. Concordia (1998) 98-3472

15:1-11 Jothen, Michael. *You are the branches.* Unison, 2- or 3-part treble, or mixed, handbells, kbd. Choristers Guild (1996) CGA 755

15:5 American folk tune (arr. David M. Cherwien). *Life tree* (based on *O Waly Waly*). SAB, optional flute, organ. Concordia (1995) 98-3190

15:9-12 (based on)
Larson, Lloyd. *I have loved you* (uses tune *Wondrous love*). SATB, kbd. Beckenhorst (1997) BP 1514

15:9-13 SEE: John 13:34. Biery, James. *A new commandment I give you*

15:13 SEE: John 20:18. Hurd, Bob. *I have seen the Lord*

15:16-17 (based on)
Fedak, Alfred V. *Go and bear fruit.* SATB, organ. MorningStar (1998) MSM-50-8823

16:22 SEE: John 14:18. Sadowski, Kevin J. *I will not leave you desolate*

17:00 SEE: Luke 23:46. Brown, Charles F. *Into Thy hands*

17:1-11 Keesecker, Thomas. *I have known you.* SATB, piano. Concordia (1997) 98-3325

20:00 (and other)
Ellingboe, Bradley. *Mary at the tomb.* SATB, piano. Augsburg (1997) 11-10833

20:00 SEE: Mark 16:00. James, Layton. *They rolled the stone away*

20:13-16 (I Corinthians 15:55, 57)
Stainer, John (arr. Ellen Jane Lorenz). *They have taken away my Lord.* SATB, kbd. Lorenz (1951) found in *Simplified standard anthems,* I

20:18 (Job 19:25-27; II Timothy 2:9, 11-12; John 15:13; II Corinthians 4:10)
Hurd, Bob. *I have seen the Lord.* SATB, piano. OCP (1990) 9447

20:18, 19 Christiansen, Paul. *Easter morning (Peace be unto you).* SATB, kro. Augsburg (1998) 11-10817, found in *The Augsburg choirbook, Sacred choral music of the twentieth century,* ed. Kenneth Jennings

20:19-20 diLasso, Orlando (ed. Lawrence Doebler). *Surgens Jesus,* Latin only. SSATB, kro. Roger Dean (1995) 10/1332R

21:15-17 (Isaiah 53:6)
Hatton, Ray D. *Feed my lambs.* SATB, kbd., and optional instrument in C. Purifoy Publishing (Lorenz) (1994) 10/1234P

ACTS

2:1-2 Palestrina, G. P. (arr. Dwight E. Weldy). *When fully came the day of Pentecost (Dum complerentur dies Pentecostes).* SSATBB, kro. Concordia (1997) 98-3339

2:1-12 Hopson, Hal H. *Pentecost.* SATB, handbells (2 octave), organ. MorningStar (1998) 50-5408

2:17-21 Busarow, Donald. *In the last days.* SAB, flute, organ. MorningStar (1999) MSM-50-4407

2:17b-18, 21 Moreland, Richard. *I will pour out my spirit.* 2-part mixed, kbd. Augsburg (1994) 11-10541

13:47, 52 (Psalm 100, based on)
Canedo, Ken (arr. John Purifoy).
We are a light. SATB, kbd. Lorenz
(1995) 10/1404U

ROMANS

3:00   SEE: John 14:00. Joy, Dawn. *You
            will not be left alone*

5:1-2 (I John 4:7-21) (based on)
Atkins, Jean and J. W. Snyder (arr.
Mark Barnard). *Together we are love.*
2-part, kbd. Lorenz (1995) 10/1275U

6:9 (Matthew 28:20)
Blersch, Jeffrey. *Verse for The
ascension of our Lord* (based on
Noël nouvelet and *Lasst uns erfreuen*)
(found in *Alleluia verses*). SATB,
organ. Concordia (1996) 98-3230

6:9 (II Timothy 1:10)
Blersch, Jeffrey. *Verse for The
resurrection of our Lord* (based on
Noël nouvelet) (found in *Alleluia
verses*). SATB, organ. Concordia
(1996) 98-3230

6:9   SEE: I Corinthians 5:7b-8. Schalk,
           Carl. *Be known to us, Lord Jesus*

6:9 (John 10:14)
Wetzler, Robert. *I am the good
shepherd.* Unison, kbd. Augsburg
(1986) 11-5115, found in *Alleluia,
I will sing*

6:9-11   SEE: I Corinthians 5:7-8. Frahm,
           Frederick. *Christ, our passover*

8:28 (based on)
Harris, Ron. *All things, all things.*
SATB, piano. Ron Harris Music
(1987) RH 0226

8:28   SEE: Ecclesiastes 3:1-8. Ore, Charles
           W. *A time and a purpose*

8:28, 22, 26, 38, 39
Henderson, Ruth Watson. *The
strength of the spirit* (#1 of *Three
motets*). SATB, Bar. solo, kro.
Randall Egan (1991) n.#.

8:31-39 (based on)
Brown, Grayson Warren (arr. Val
Parker and Grayson Warren Brown).
If God is for us. Unison, kbd. OCP
(1995) 10114, found in *If God is for us*

8:31-39
Brown, Grayson Warren (arr. Val
Parker and Grayson Warren Brown).
If God is for us. SATB, kbd. OCP
(1995) 10383

8:31-39 (and other)
Ferguson, John. *What then.* SATB,
organ. Kjos (1996) 8827

8:31-39
Pote, Allen. *If God is for us.* SATB,
2 trumpets, kbd. Triune Music
(Lorenz) (1996) 10/1438T

8:35-38 (based on plus Swahili text)
Swahili song from Kenya (arr. Hal H.
Hopson). *He is mine (Ni wangu)*
(English/Swahili). SATB, kbd. Hope
(1999) C5006

8:35-39 (and other)
Lightfoot, Mary Lynn. *Crown him
Lord of all* (uses tune *Coronation*).
SATB, kbd. Triune (Lorenz) (1995)
10/1340T

8:35-39
Schütz, Heinrich (ed. Larry L.
Fleming). *Who shall separate us*
(English/German). SATB, organ
continuo. Augsburg (1997) 11-10834

8:35-39 (Psalm 84:4, 5, 12)
Young, Jeremy. *Nothing can come
between us.* SAB, piano. Augsburg
(1997) 11-10848

10:13-15 (Matthew 28:19-20)
Burroughs, Bob. *Whosoever.* SATB,
no acc. MorningStar (1999) 50-6012

10:15   SEE: Isaiah 52:7-8. Hassell, Michael.
           How beautiful

10:15 Mendelssohn, Felix (abridged and simplified by John Johnson). *How lovely are the messengers.* SATB, kbd. Lorenz (1968) found in *Easy standard anthems,* II

10:15-18 Grotenhuis, Dale. *How beautiful are the feet.* SATB, kbd. Coronet (Presser) (1999) 392-2236

12:1 (and Havergal)
Collins, Dori Erwin. *Offering – Take my life, that I may be.* SATB, piano, flute, optional handbells. Augsburg Fortress (2001) 98-5969

12:1-2 Johnson, Ralph M. *A living sacrifice.* Unison, kbd. Augsburg (1986) 11-5115, found in *Alleluia, I will sing*

12:1, 9, 10 (Romans 15:13)
Butler, Eugene. *The mercies of God.* SATB, kbd. Carl Fischer (1998) CM8503

13:00 SEE: Isaiah 35:00. Schoenbachler, Tim (arr. Patrick Loomis). *Maranatha*

14:6-8 Gehring, Philip. *Those who observe the day* (from *Choral offertories*). SATB, no acc. Concordia (2000) 98-3585

15:6 Patterson, Mark. *With one heart.* Unison, optional flute, kbd. Choristers Guild (1998) CGA 804

15:13 SEE: Romans 12:1, 9, 10. Butler, Eugene. *The mercies of God*

I CORINTHIANS

1:10 SEE: Psalm 133:1. Chepponis, James. *In unity and peace*

1:22-2:9 Dennis, Randall. *That I may know him.* SATB, kbd. J. R. Dennis (1991) OCT 00387

3:11, 16, 17
Bouman, Paul. *No other foundation can anyone lay.* SATB, no acc. GIA (1994) G3883

5:7-8 (Romans 6:9-11)
Frahm, Frederick. *Christ, our passover.* SAB, no acc. Concordia (1997) 98-3372

5:7b-8 (Psalm 34:8-9; Romans 6:9; Psalm 118:24)
Schalk, Carl. *Be known to us, Lord Jesus.* SATB, optional children's choir, organ, optional brass (2 trumpets, 2 trombones, timpani). Concordia (1995) 98-3202

10:4 SEE: Luke 6:48. Lord, Suzanne. *Faith that's sure*

10:16 (Psalm 116:12-13, 17-18)
Joncas, Michael. *Our blessing cup.* SATB, optional instrument, kbd. GIA (1995) G 4271

10:16-17 Gehring, Philip. *The cup of blessing that we bless* (from *Choral offertories*). SATB, kro. Concordia (2000) 98-3585

10:17 (Psalm 28:10-11; Psalm 144:15; Matthew 11:28; John 1:4; John 7:37-38; Revelation 3:20)
Proulx, Richard. *Though we are many in Christ we are one.* SATB, organ. MorningStar (1998) MSM-80-834

11:23-25 (adapted)
Pethel, Stan. *Remember me.* SATB, piano. Lorenz (1994) 10/1413L

11:24-25 (I Timothy 3:16)
Willcock, Christopher. *This body.* SAB, flute, kbd. OCP (1997) 10325

11:25 (and other)
Joncas, Michael. *When we eat this bread.* SATB, kbd. OCP (1982) 10252

11:25-26 (John 6:35-38; John 15, based on)
Canedo, Ken (arr. Mark Barnard). *Every time we eat this bread.* SATB, optional solo, kbd. Lorenz (1995) 10/1267U

12:4-6, 12-13
Hurd, Bob (arr. Craig Kingsbury).
O love of God (Amor de Dios).
SATB, flute, guitar, kbd. OCP (1994)
10151

12:13, 28
Houlihan, Patrick. *By one spirit.*
SATB, kbd. Purifoy (Lorenz) (1995)
10/1366P

13:00 (Wordsworth)
Bach, J. S. (arr. Dale Grotenhuis).
Love is kind. SATB, organ.
MorningStar (1998) MSM-50-9092

13:00 (based on)
Broughton, Edward. *Love is kind.*
SATB, kbd. Lorenz (1992)
10/140008U

13:00 (based on)
Clemens, James E. *Holy spirit,
gracious guest.* SATB, kbd. Harold
Flammer (1996) A 7084

13:00   SEE: John 13:34. Dufford, Bob.
Love one another

13:00 (based on)
Gieseke, Richard W. *May love be
ours, O Lord.* SAB or SATB, kbd.
Concordia (1997) 98-3349

13:1-13 (based on)
Larson, Lloyd. *Without love it will all
pass away.* SATB, kbd. Beckenhorst
(1996) BP 1483

13:8-10, 13 (based on)
Scott, K. Lee. *Love never fails.*
SATB, organ. MorningStar (1996)
MSM 50-9082 (NOTE: The score
contains a second anthem, *From life's
bright dawn,* which can be performed
separately or both together as one
unit.)

14:15   Rutter, John. *I will sing with the
spirit.* SATB, kbd. Hinshaw (1994)
HMC 1386

15:20-22, 57
SEE: Psalm 118:24. Cooke, S.
Charles. *This is the day*

15:20, 55, 57 (Psalm 81:3)
Wagner, Douglas E. *Easter Fanfare.*
SATB, organ, 3 optional trumpets.
H. W. Gray (1994) GCMR 03645

15:55 (and other)
Connolly, Michael. *Where, O death, is
your victory?* SATB, 2 woodwinds,
piano. GIA (1998) G-4772

15:55-56 Martin, Gilbert M. *The risen Christ.*
SATB, organ, optional trumpet.
Sacred Music Press (1996) 10/1389

15:55, 57 SEE: John 20:13-16. Stainer, John
(arr. Ellen Jane Lorenz). *They have
taken away my Lord*

15:57-58 Beebe, Hank. *Thanks be to God.*
SATB, kbd. Sacred Music Press
(1999) 10/1962S

II CORINTHIANS

2:14   Callaway, Susan Naylor. *A song of
triumph.* SATB, kbd. Purifoy
Publishing (Lorenz) (1994) 10/1150

4:6 (and other)
Scott, K. Lee. *Eternal light, shine in
my heart.* SATB, organ. MorningStar
(2000) MSM-50-8825

4:6   Roth, John D. *Let light shine.*
Unison, optional solos, optional
instrument in C, kbd. Logia
(Concordia) (1997) 98-3318

4:10   SEE: John 20:18. Hurd, Bob. *I have
seen the Lord*

5:17   SEE: Revelation 21:5. Callahan,
Charles. *A new creation*

5:17   SEE: Psalm 19:1-6. Courtney, Craig.
Creation hymn

5:17-21 SEE: Joshua 5:9-12. Thompson, J.
Michael. *Taste and see the Lord
is good*

11:23-27 (II Corinthians 12:9-10)
    Brazzeal, David. *Now Paul, he was a servant.* Unison/2-part, kbd. Choristers Guild (1997) CGA782

12:9-10   SEE: II Corinthians 11:23-27. Brazzeal, David. *Now Paul, he was a servant*

13:14   Brown, Uzee, Jr. *Be with us all, Lord* (*Benediction*). SATB, piano. Roger Dean (1995) 10/1265R

13:14   SEE: Genesis 31:40. Grotenhuis, Dale. *May the Lord watch over you and me*

GALATIANS

2:19-20 (Galatians 3:27; Galatians 6:17, based on)
    Hurd, Bob. *No longer I.* SATB, solo instrument, kbd. OCP (1991) 9449

3:27 (based on)
    SEE: Galatians 2:19-20. Hurd, Bob. *No longer I*

6:2   SEE: John 13:34. Causey, C. Harry. *Love one another*

6:14 (Watts)
    English folk song (arr. K. Lee Scott). *The wondrous cross* (uses tune *O Waly Waly*). SATB, kbd. AMSI (1987) 539

6:14 (Watts)
    Ferris, William. *When I survey the wondrous cross.* SATB, organ. Oxford (1998) 94.509

6:14 (Watts)
    Franck, Melchior (ed. Edward Klammer). *When I survey the wondrous cross.* SATB, organ. GIA (1986) G 2823

6:14 (Watts)
    Gustafson, Dwight *When I survey the wondrous cross.* SATB, organ. Coronet (Presser) (1991) 392-41664

6:14 (Watts)
    Hamill, Paul, arr. *Wondrous cross.* SATB, organ. Gemini Press (Presser) (1998) 392-01038

6:14 (Watts)
    Harris, Ed. *When I survey the wondrous cross.* SATB, organ. Hinshaw (1991) HMC 1202

6:14 (Watts)
    Lau, Robert. *When I survey the wondrous cross.* SATB, kbd. Coronet (Presser) (1998) 392-42214

6:14 (Watts)
    Miller, Edward (setting by Bruce Saylor). *When I survey the wondrous cross.* SATB, organ. Concordia (1987) 98-2776

6:14 (Watts)
    Murry, Lyn. *When I survey the wondrous cross.* SATB, organ. Fred Bock (1983) B-G0465

6:14 (Watts)
    Parks, Joe E. *When I survey the wondrous cross.* SATB, organ. Benson (Singspiration) (1992) 25986-0622

6:14 (Watts)
    Schoenfeld, William. *When I survey the wondrous cross.* SATB, organ. Coronet (Presser) (1992) 392-41734

6:14 (Watts)
    Young, Gordon. *When I survey the wondrous cross.* SATB, kbd. Coronet (Presser) (1995) 392-41991

6:14-16 (inspired by)
    Connolly, Michael. *May we never boast.* SATB, 2 flutes, guitar, piano. CIA (1995) G-4032

6:17 (based on)
    SEE: Galatians 6:2:19-20. Hurd, Bob. *No longer I*

EPHESIANS

2:7-10 (Ephesians 5:19-20)
Schutte, Dan. *Lover of us all.* SAB, optional instruments, kbd. OCP (1989) 9903

2:13, 14, 17, 19-21
Nicholson, Paul. *Christ is our peace.* SATB, no acc. Augsburg (1997) 11-10840

4:00 (based on, with additional text by Susan Palo Cherwien)
Welsh tune (arr. Ronald A. Nelson). *You fill all creation* (based on the tune *Ash Grove*). 2-part mixed, kbd. AMSI (1998) 800

4:1-3, 5-6
SEE: Psalm 133:1. Chepponis, James. *In unity and peace*

4:4-6   SEE: Psalm 133:00. Scott, K. Lee. *How very good and pleasant*

4:13 (based on)
Scott, K. Lee. *The pilgrim church of God* (based on tune *Marietta*). SATB, organ, optional congregation and brass quartet. MorningStar (1996) MSM-50-9088

4:25-32 (Ephesians 5:1)
Lantz III, David. *Walk in love.* SATB, kbd. Shawnee (1996) A 7094

5:1   SEE: Ephesians 4:25-32. Lantz, David, III. *Walk in love*

5:1-2a   Scott, K. Lee *Thy perfect love.* SAB or SATB, kbd. Choristers Guild (1995) CGA 704

5:18b-20 (based on)
Caldara, Antonio (arr. Michael Burkhardt). *Filled with the spirit.* 3-part canon, optional handbells or keyboard. MorningStar (1997) MSM-50-7402

5:19 (Psalm 9:1-2; Colossians 3:15-17, paraphrased)
Clemens, James E. *Sing and make music to the Lord.* 2-part, piano with optional percussion and handbells (2 octave set). Choristers Guild (1997) CGA 783

5:19-20 SEE: Ephesians 2:7-10. Schutte, Dan. *Lover of us all*

6:11   Hyslop, Scott M. *Verse for Sundays in Lent* (Verse for Lent 1). SATB, organ. Concordia (1999) 98-3538

6:23, 24 Grotenhuis, Dale. *Peace to you all* (#2 of *Two choral benedictions*). SATB, kro. Sacred Music Press (Lorenz) (1994) 10/1117

PHILIPPIANS

1:4-7   Williams, Paul and Donna. *Like a river in springtime.* SAB, kbd. Lorenz (1988) found in *Anthems for the SAB choir*

2:1-11 (adapted)
Swahili song from Kenya (arr. Hal H. Hopson). *Yes, Jesus is my savior.* SATB, kbd. Hope (1996) HH 3953

2:2-4   SEE: Psalm 133:1. Chepponis, James. *In unity and peace*

2:6-11   Gouzes, André. *Jesus Christ is the Lord.* SATB, no acc. GIA (1994) G-4981

2:8 (Isaiah 53:3-5, and Isaac Watts)
Malmin, Olaf G. *Meditations on the cross* (uses hymn *When I survey the wondrous cross*). SATB, kbd. AMSI (1995) 744

2:8b   Hyslop, Scott M. *Verse for Sundays in Lent* (Verse for Lent 2). SATB, organ. Concordia (1999) 98-3538

2:8-9   Ferguson, Michael. *Christus factus est.* Unison treble, organ. Paraclete (1995) PPMO 9323

2:8-9   Near, Gerald. *Christ for us became obedient unto death.* 2-part mixed, organ. Aureole (MorningStar) (2000) AE 112

2:8-11 (adapted and other)
Linker, Janet. *At the name of Jesus.* SATB, kbd. Lorenz (1996) 10/1383L

2:9-10 SEE: Jeremiah 11:00. Comer, Thomas. *Anthem for Good Friday*

2:15, 18 SEE: Philippians 3:7-16. Schutte, Dan. *Only this I want*

3:7-16 (Philippians 2:15, 18)
Schutte, Dan. *Only this I want.* SAB, kbd. OCP (1996) 10486

4:1-9 Haas, David. *Know that the Lord is near (Skye boat song).* SATB, kbd. GIA (1995) G4343

4:4 (Wesley)
Darwall, John (arr. Jimmy Owens). *Rejoice, the Lord is king* (uses tunes *Darwall* and *There is a fountain*). SATB, kbd. Tempo (1988) ES3022B

4:4 (Wesley)
Handel, G. F. (setting S. Drummond Wolff). *Rejoice, the Lord is king!* (uses tune *Gopsal*). SATB, 2 trumpets, organ. MorningStar (1990) MSM-50-9023

4:4 (Wesley)
Saint-Saëns, Camille (ed. George Martin). *Rejoice, the Lord is king.* SAB, kbd. Jack Spratt (1961) 575

4:4 (Wesley)
Willcocks, Jonathan. *Rejoice the Lord is king* (uses tune *Darwall's 148th*). SATB, kbd. Lorenz (1991) S-514

4:4, 6, 7 Courtney, Craig. *Rejoice!* SATB, 2 instruments in C or B-flat, kbd. Beckenhorst (1995) BP 1466

4:4-7 Hopson, Hal H. *Rejoice in the Lord always.* SATB, organ. GIA (1990) G-3323

4:4-7 Martinson, Joe. *Rejoice in the Lord always.* 2- or 3-part, organ. GIA (1998) G-4450

4:6 SEE: John 14:27. Schultz, Timothy. *Peace*

4:6-7 (and hymn text *For peace with God above*)
Scott, K. Lee. *The peace of God.* SATB, organ. Concordia (1996) 98-3289

4:7 (and other)
Spong, Jon. *The peace of God.* SATB, organ. Randall Egan (1992) EC 92-103

4:8 (and other)
Murphy, Michael Patrick (arr. John R. Murtha). *Think on these things.* SATB, kbd., with optional handbells (3 octaves). Coronet (Presser) (1999) 392-42230

4:11 SEE: Isaiah 45:23. McDonald, Mary. *Holy, true and faithful God*

COLOSSIANS

1:9-14 McDonald, Mary. *Worthy of the Lord.* SATB, kbd. Purifoy (1995) 10/1293P-1

1:27 Crawshaw, Craig (arr. John Purifoy). *Hope of glory.* SATB, kbd. Radiant Music (Lorenz) (1999) 10/2193RA

2:6-10 (and other)
Scott, K. Lee. *To see your glory.* SATB, kbd. Concordia (2000) 98-3588

3:12-17 Landes, Rob. *The peace of Christ.* SATB, organ. Sacred Music Press (1996) 10/1239

3:12-17 Powell, Kathy. *Put on love.* SATB, instrument in C, piano. GIA (1995) G-4078

3:12-17 Sowerby, Leo. *Put on therefore as the elect of God.* SATB, organ. Leo Sowerby Foundation (Randall M. Egan) (1995) ES 1001

3:15-17 (paraphrased)
SEE: Ephesians 5:19. Clemens, James E. *Sing and make music to the Lord*

I THESSALONIANS

2:19 (Psalm 65:00, based on)
McDonald, Mary. *Call forth with songs of joy.* SATB, kbd. Monarch Music (Lorenz) (1996) 10/1451M

3:12-13 Wilcock, Christopher. *A blessing.* 2-part choir, flute, piano. OCP (1988) 10348

II THESSALONIANS

4:13-18 Harbison, John. *Concerning them which are asleep* (found in *Six motets*). SATB, kro. Associated (1994) HL50482305

I TIMOTHY

1:17 Hopson, Hal H. *Immortal, invisible God only wise.* SATB, optional brass quartet, 3 handbells, organ. GIA (1989) G-3254

1:17 Peterson, Gerald. *Immortal, invisible* (uses Welsh melody *St. Denio*). SATB, organ. Lorenz (1995) 10/1318L

3:16 SEE: I Corinthians 11:24-25. Willcock, Christopher. *This body*

II TIMOTHY

1:2, 6, 7-9 Proulx, Richard. *Strong, loving, and wise.* SATB, organ. MorningStar (1996) MSM-50-8706

1:6-9 Harbison, John. *Wherefore I put thee in remembrance (Two Emmanuel motets)* (found in *Six motets*). SATB, kro. Associated (1990) HL504882305

1:10 SEE: Romans 6:9. Blersch, Jeffrey. *The resurrection of our Lord (Alleluia verses)*

1:10b Hildebrand, Kevin. *Alleluia! Christ has destroyed death.* SATB, no acc. MorningStar (1999) 50-4037

2:9, 11-12
SEE: John 20:18. Hurd, Bob. *I have seen the Lord*

PHILEMON

0:3-7 Larson, Lloyd. *May you know God's grace.* SATB, optional instrument in C, kbd. Flammer (1999) A 7223

HEBREWS

2:7 SEE: Matthew 28:6-7. Kosche, Kenneth T. *Alleluia! Christ has risen*

12:2 Kosche, Kenneth. *Come, let us fix our eyes on Jesus.* 2-part choir, 2 optional instruments in C, optional cello or bassoon, organ. Concordia (1995) 98-3198

JAMES

5:00 SEE: Isaiah 35:00. Schoenbachler, Tim (arr. Patrick Loomis). *Maranatha*

5:8 (based on)
SEE: Psalm 25:3. Hurd, Bob. *Await the Lord with hope*

I PETER

1:3-5 Guimont, Michael. *A living hope.* SATB, kbd. GIA (1993) G-3688

1:22 SEE: Psalm 133:00. Scott, K. Lee. *How very good and pleasant*

2:4-10 Helgen, John. *We are God's people.* SATB, piano, recorder (flute). Kjos (2000) 8935

2:9   Hobby, Robert A. *You are a chosen race.* SATB, kro. Concordia (1999) 98-3537

2:21-24 (Isaiah 53:4, 5)
    Dean, Stephen. *Ours were the griefs he bore.* SATB, no acc. OCP (1989) 7246

4:8-9   Burroughs, Bob. *Remember this.* SATB, optional clarinet, kbd. Hinshaw (1997) HMC 1554

I JOHN

1:5   SEE: Isaiah 26:3. Neswick, Bruce. *Thou wilt keep Him in perfect peace*

2:1-2 (I John 3:1)
    Gehring, Philip. *If anyone does sin* (from *Choral offertories*). SATB, kro. Concordia (2000) 98-3585

3:1   SEE: I John 2:1-2. Gehring, Philip. *If anyone does sin*

3:2-3   Schramm, Charles W., Jr. *When He appears.* SAB, organ. Concordia (1999) 98-3528

4:7-9   Harbison, John. *Beloved, let us love one another (Two Emmanuel motets)* (found in *Six motets*). SATB, kro. Associated (1990) HL504882305

4:7-11 (adapted)
    Harris, Ed. *Love is of God.* SAB, kbd. Coronet (Presser) (1998) 392-41236

4:7-11 (adapted)
    Schram, Ruth Elaine. *God is love.* SATB, kbd., optional flute. Belwin (1996) BSC9705

4:7-11   Sherman, Arnold B. *Let us love one another.* Unison or 2-part mixed, optional instrument in C, kbd. Found in *10 anthems for about 10 singers.* Lorenz (1990) 45/1094L

4:7-11 (based on)
    Sherman, Arnold B. *Let us love one another.* 2-part, kbd., optional instrument in C. Lorenz (1990) found in *Sing to the Lord a new song*

4:7-21   SEE: Romans 5:1-2. Atkins, Jean and J. W. Snyder. *Together we are love*

5:3   SEE: Matthew 5:1-12. Harris, Jerry Weseley. *The Beatitudes*

5:7-8   Haydn, Johann Michael (ed. David Stern). *Tres sunt, qui testimonium* (English/Latin). SATB, kbd. Presser (1998) 312-41698

REVELATION

1:18   Wilson, Roger C. *Easter sentence.* SATB, no acc. Lorenz 1953, found in *Easy hymn tune anthems*, I

3:20   SEE: I Corinthians 10:17. Proulx, Richard. *Though we are many, in Christ we are one*

3:20-21   Gehring, Philip. *I am standing at the door* (from *Choral offertories*). SATB, kro. Concordia (2000) 98-3585

4:9 (Revelation 5:9-10, 13)
    Gibbs, Allen Orton. *A song to the lamb (Dignus es).* SATB, brass quintet (2 trumpets, horn, trombone, tuba), organ. Augsburg (1994) 11-10538

4:11 (5:9-10, 13)
    White, David Ashley. *A song to the Lamb (Dignus es).* 2-part, organ. Concordia (1998) 98-3471

4:11   SEE: Psalm 47:00. Wilkinson, Sandy. *Come, celebrate our God and king*

5:9-10, 13
    SEE: Revelation 4:9. Gibbs, Allen Orton. *A song to the lamb*

5:9-10, 13
SEE: Revelation 4:11. White, David Ashley. *A song to the lamb*

5:12-13   Leavitt, John. *Worthy is Christ.* SATB, optional brass, timpani, organ or piano. Concordia (2000) 98-3609

7:11 (Isaiah 66:1)
Mozart, W. A. *Gloria* (from *Twelfth Mass*). SATB, kbd. Lorenz (1951), found in *Simplified standard anthems,* I

7:12   SEE: Luke 23:42. Fleming, Larry L. *Blessed are they*

7:12   Hamilton, Edward. *Blessing, honor, power and glory.* SATB, kbd. Boston Music (1991) found in *Early American sacred choral library,* vol. 1

7:15   Blersch, Jeffrey. *All Saints' Day* (*Alleluia verses*, set 2). SATB, organ. Concordia (1996) 98-3285

11:17-18, (Revelation 12:10b-12a)
Callahan, Charles. *Canticle of praise.* SATB, organ. Randall Egan (1995) EC 342

12:10b-12a
SEE: Revelation 11:17-18. Callahan, Charles. *Canticle of praise*

14:13   Schalk, Carl. *Blessed are the dead who die in the Lord.* SATB, kro. Concordia (1995) 98-3214

15:00 (based on)
Hoddinott, Alun. *Vespers canticle.* SSATB, organ. Paraclete (1995) 9508

15:3 (plus Te Deum).
Gaul, Alfred R. (arr. James Denton). *Great and marvelous are thy works* (from *The holy city*). SATB, organ. Lorenz (1968) found in *Easy standard anthems,* II

15:3   SEE: Psalm 135:2, 3. Spinney, Walter (arr. Roger C. Wilson). *Ye that stand in the house of the Lord*

15:3-4 (Psalm 86:9)
Callahan, Charles. *Revelation canticle.* 2-part mixed or equal voices, organ. Randall Egan (1994) EC 328

15:3-4   Neswick, Bruce. *Magna et mirabilia* (English). SSATB, organ. Paraclete (1995) 9504

19:00 (based on; Matthew 25:35-40)
Dufford, Bob. *The reign of God.* SATB, kbd. OCP (1996) 10840

19:00 (based on)
LaValley, Jeffrey (choral setting by Jack Schrader). *Revelation 19.* SATB, piano. Hope (1998) GC 997

19:6-7 (based on)
Wood, Dale. *Rejoice, be glad, give praise!* (based on *Darwall's 148th*). SATB, optional brass quartet, handbells. Sacred Music Press (1994) 10/1111

21:00   Powell, Robert J., arr. *O holy city, seen of John* (uses tune *Morning song*). SATB, organ, optional brass quartet. GIA (1997) G-4482

21:1   SEE: Revelation 21:5. Callahan, Charles. *A new creation*

21:1-4   Schalk, Carl. *I saw a new heaven and a new earth.* SATB, kro. Augsburg Fortress (1997) 11-10803.

21:1-4   Schalk, Carl. *I saw a new heaven and a new earth.* SATB, kro. Augsburg (1998) 11-10817, found in *The Augsburg choirbook, Sacred choral music of the twentieth century,* ed. Kenneth Jennings

21:1-5   Gawthrop, Daniel E. *The new Jerusalem.* SATB, organ. Dunstan House (1991) DH9102

21:3   SEE: Deuteronomy 8:2. Powell, Robert J. *Remember your Lord God/ Prayer of Habakkuk*

21:4-5   SEE: Luke 24:5-6. Haas, David (arr. Jeanne Cotter). *Song of the risen one*

21:5 (II Corinthians 5:17; Revelation 21:1)
Callahan, Charles. *A new creation.*
SATB, organ. Randall Egan (1992)
EC92-104

22:2, 3 SEE: Psalm 46:4, 5. Traditional Irish
melody. *There is a river*

22:5 (based on)
Martin, Joseph M. *We will need no candle.* SATB, kbd. Shawnee Press
(1995) A-6947

22:12-20 (based on)
Clemens, James E. *The spirit and the bride say, "Come!"* SATB,
congregation, organ. Concordia
(2000) 98-3581

22:13 Blersch, Jeffrey. *The festival of Christ the king* (based on *Wachet auf* and
Divinum mysterium) (*Alleluia verses*,
set 2). SATB, organ. Concordia
(1996) 98-3285

22:20 (adapted)
Manz, Paul. *E'en so, Lord Jesus, quickly come.* SSAA, kro.
MorningStar (1998) MSM-50-0450

Composer Index

A

African-American spiritual.
Balm in Gilead (arr. Mark Shepperd). Jeremiah 8:22.
Joshua fit de battle of Jericho. Joshua 6:00 (based on).

Aguiar, Ernani.
Salmo 150 (Psalm 150). Psalm 150:00.

Akins, John R.
Enter his gates with thanksgiving. Psalm 100:00 (based on).

Aks, Catherine.
Venite, Exultemus Domino. Psalm 95:00.

Albrecht, Ronald.
Even the sparrow. Psalm 84:00.

Aldgasser, Anton Cajetan.
Magnificat in C major. Luke 1:46-55.

Alstott, Owen.
How lovely is your dwelling place. Psalm 84:00.

American folk melody.
My shepherd will supply my need (setting by Howard Helvey). Psalm 23:00.

American folk tune.
Life tree (arr. David M. Cherwien). John 15:5.
My shepherd will supply my need (arr. Austin Lovelace). Psalm 23:00.

Anderson, Norma Sateren.
The walk to Calvary. Matthew 26:36-66.

Angerman, David.
You are the Christ. Matthew 16:13-20.

Anonymous.
By the rivers of Babylon. Psalm 137:00.
Praise God from whom all blessings flow (ed. William P. Rowan). Psalm 100:00.

Archangelsky, Alexander.
Nunc dimittis. Luke 2:29-32.

Archangel'sky, Alexander.
Nunc dimittis. Luke 2:29-32.

Archer, Malcolm.
Hosanna to the son of David. Matthew 21:9.

Arensky, Anton.
Bow down thine ear, O Lord. Psalm 86:1, 3, 5.
The Lord's prayer. Matthew 6:9-13.

Armstrong, Matthew.
Hosanna. Matthew 21:9.
In my father's house. John 14:1-4.
Suffer the little children. Mark 10:14-16.

Aston, Peter.
I give you a new commandment. John 14:34-35.

Atkins, Jean and J. W. Snyder.
In remembrance of me (arr. John Purifoy). Luke 22:19, 20.
Together we are love (arr. Mark Barnard). Romans 5:1-2.

Averre, Dick.
Christmas fanfare. Luke 2:11.

B

Bach, J. S.
Ave Maria (adapted C. Gounod; arr. Colin Mawby). Luke 1:00.
The heavens declare Thy glory. Psalm 19:1-6, 14 (arr. Michael Burkhardt).
The Lord will soon appear. Isaiah 40:3-4 (setting Hal H. Hopson).
Love is kind (arr. Dale Grotenhuis) I Corinthians 13:00.
May God bless you now. Psalm 115:14.
Wenn es meines Gottes Wille (Cantata 161). Luke 7:11-17.

Baker, Richard C.
My soul doth magnify the Lord. Luke 1:46, 47.
Sing unto the Lord. Psalm 30:4, 5, 12.

Bales, Gerald.
Deus misereatur (Psalm 67). Psalm 67:00.
I waited patiently for the Lord. Psalm 40:1.
Jubilate Deo. Psalm 100:00.
Love. John 14:15.
Quam dilecta. Psalm 84:1, 2, 4, 12.

Barnard, Mark.
Give thanks to the Lord. Psalm 118:00.
My heart is ready. Psalm 108:00.
Sing Alleluia to our king. Psalm 118:22.
Taste and see (arr. John Purifoy). Psalm 34:00.

Barrett, Michael.
Truly God is good. Psalm 93:00.

Barta, Daniel.
Ask and seek and knock. Luke 11:9.
Psalm 121. Psalm 121:00.

Bauer, Marie Rubis.
Tu es Petrus. Matthew 14:16.

Baumbach, Adolph.
Let the words of my mouth. Psalm 19:14.

Beck, Theodore.
Sing to the Lord a new song. Psalm 149:1, 3-4.

Bedford, Michael.
Go, therefore and make disciples. Matthew 28:19-20.

Beebe, Hank.
Behold, your salvation comes. Isaiah 62:11.
Thanks be to God. I Corinthians 15:57-58.

Beethoven, Ludwig van.
Give thanks to God (ed. Richard Proulx). Psalm 107:1, 9-10, 20, 22.
The heavens are praising (arr. Arthur Frackenpohl). Psalm 19:00.
My soul longs for you, O God (arr. Hal. H. Hopson). Psalm 25:00.

Behnke, John A.
I know that my redeemer lives (arr.). Job 19:25-27.
I thank you, Lord. Psalm 138:1, 8.
Listen to what the Lord is saying. Psalm 85:8-9, 13.
The Lord is king. Psalm 99:1-3.
The Lord's my shepherd. Psalm 23:00.
Sing to the Lord a new song. Psalm 96:1-4a, 7a, 8, 11-12.

Bell, John L.
  Agnus Dei. John 1:29.
  Bless, O my soul. Psalm 103:1-5, 20-22.
  Do not be vexed. Psalm 37:1-10.
  Glory to God in the highest. Luke 2:14.
  How long, O Lord. Psalm 13:00.
  I cry to God. Psalm 77:00.
  The Lord is my shepherd. Psalm 23:00.
  Lord, who may enter your house? Psalm 15:00.
  Lord, you have been our refuge. Psalm 90:00.
  Sing a new song. Psalm 96:00.
  When Israel came out of Egypt's land. Psalm 114:00.
  With grace and carefulness. Psalm 65:10-11, 14.
Bell, Reta J.
  Our Father, who art in heaven. Matthew 6:9-13.
Bender, Mark.
  I will praise you, O Lord, with all my heart.
    Psalm 138:1-3, 7-8.
Bengston, Bruce.
  Behold my servant. Isaiah 42:1, 6.
Berger, Jean.
  The eyes of all wait upon thee. Psalm 145:15, 16.
  I to the hills lift up mine eyes. Psalm 121:00.
Berry, Cindy.
  Stand up and bless the Lord. Nehemiah 9:5b-6
    (based on).
Bertalot, John.
  Alleluia, come, let us sing. Psalm 95:00.
Beyer, Johann Samuel.
  Be not afraid. Luke 2:10, 11 (arr. Ronald A. Nelson).
  Fürchtet euch nicht. Luke 2:10, 11 (arr. Ronald A.
    Nelson).
Biery, James.
  Glory to God. Luke 2:14.
Billings, William.
  Blessed are they. Matthew 5:3-10.
  Universal praise (ed. Leonard Van Camp). Psalm
    149:00.
Birkley, Michael M.
  Hosanna, hosanna. Matthew 21:9.
Bisbee, B. Wayne.
  Sing for joy to God our strength. Psalm 81:1.
  Teach me your way, O Lord. Psalm 86:11-12, 15-16a.
Bish, Diane.
  Introit and prayer. Psalm 100:4.
Blersch, Jeffrey N.
  All Saints' Day. Revelation 7:15.
  The epiphany of our Lord. Matthew 2:2.
  The Festival of Christ the King. Revelation 22:13.
  The Festival of the Reformation. Psalm 48:14.
  Lamb of God. John 1:29.
  The nativity of our Lord. Luke 2:11.
  The transfiguration of our Lord. Psalm 45:2.
  Verse for Palm Sunday. John 12:23.
  *Verse for the ascension of our Lord (Alleluia
    verses).* Romans 6:9.
  Verse for The Holy Trinity. Isaiah 6:3.
  Verse for Palm Sunday. John 12:23.
  Verse for the resurrection of our Lord. Romans 6:9.
Blow, John.
  O God, wherefore art Thou absent. Psalm 74:1-3.
  Save me, O God. Psalm 69:1, 3, 7, 10, 13, 14.

Bober, Melody.
  Praise awaits you. Psalm 65:00.
Boles, Frank.
  Surge illuminare (The third song of Isaiah). Isaiah
    60:00.
Bolt, Conway A., Jr.
  The kingdom of God. Matthew 13:00 (based on).
Bouman, Paul.
  God be merciful. Psalm 67:00.
  I am the light of the world. John 8:12.
  It is a good thing to give thanks. Psalm 92:1-5.
Bourgeois, Louis.
  New beginnings. John 4:00 (arr. Wayne L. Wold).
Bouman, Paul.
  And the word became flesh. John 1:14, 16.
  No other foundation can anyone lay. I Corinthians
    3:11, 16, 17.
Boyce, William.
  Psalm of joy (alt. and arr. Jane McFadden and
    Janet Linker). Psalm 104:00 (based on).
Brahms, Johannes (arr. Hal H. Hopson).
  Let all the gates be opened wide. Psalm 42:7-10.
Brazzeal, David.
  Now Paul, he was a servant. II Corinthians 11:23-27.
Breedlove, Jennifer.
  Throughout every age. Psalm 90:00.
Broughton, Edward.
  Love is kind. I Corinthians 13:00 (based on).
Brown, Charles F.
  I will lift up mine eyes. Psalm 121:00.
  Into Thy hands. Like 23:46.
Brown, Grayson Warren.
  I love you, O Lord. Psalm 18:00 (based on).
  If God is for us (arr. Val Parker & Grayson Warren
    Brown). Romans 8:31-39 (based on)
  Jesus, the bread of life. John 6:51.
  Lord, now let thy servant go in peace. Luke 2:29-32.
  May the Lord bless you. Numbers 6:24-26 (based on).
  Micah's song. Micah 6:6-8.
  Psalm 20. Psalm 20:00.
  Psalm 42: My soul is thirsting. Psalm 42:00.
  This is the day. Psalm 118:1, 4, 24.
Brown, Jody and Jeff McGaha.
  O give thanks to the Lord. Psalm 105:00 (based on).
Brown, M. Susan.
  Mary's song. Luke 1:46-55.
Brown, Uzee, Jr.
  Be with us all, Lord. II Corinthians 13:14.
Buck, Pery C.
  Sing to the Lord a joyful song (setting Robert
    Below). Psalm 145:1-2.
Bullard, Janice M.
  Psalm 123. Psalm 123:00.
Bunjes, Paul G.
  I know that my redeemer lives. Job 19:25-27.
Burkhardt, Michael.
  Hosanna. Matthew 21:9.
  Psalm 23. Psalm 23:00.
  Psalm 46. Psalm 46:00.
  Thy holy sings. Psalm 25:00.
Burroughs, Bob.
  Remember this. I Peter 4:8-9.
  Whosoever. Romans 10:13-15.

Burson, John Wyatt.
  The Lord is my light. Psalm 27:00.
Busarow, Donald.
  A festival Psalm. Psalm 150:00.
  He shall give his angels charge over Thee. Psalm
    91:4, 11-12.
  In the last days. Acts 2:17-21.
  It is a good thing to give thanks (Psalm 92). Psalm
    92:1-5, 12
  Proclaim with me. Psalm 34:1-9.
  Psalm 117, Praise the Lord, all you nations.
    Psalm 117:00.
  Not unto us, O Lord. Psalm 115:1.
  O Lord, You are my God and king (Parry). Psalm
    145:1-3, 8-13.
Busch, Richard.
  Qui biberit aquam. John 4:13, 14.
  Vocem jucunditatis. Isaiah 48:20.
Bush, Gladys Blakely.
  With what shall I come before the Lord. Micah
    6:6-8.
Butler, Eugene.
  Go through the gates. Isaiah 62:00.
  God has gone up with a merry shout. Psalm 47:00.
  God, our strength. Psalm 81:00.
  Let the heavens praise your wonders. Psalm 89:00.
  The Mercies of God. Romans 12:1, 9, 10.
  My heart is ready. Psalm 108:00.
  Praise him, alleluia! Psalm 107:8.
  Sing all the earth to God. Psalm 96:00.
  To render thanks. Psalm 92:00.
Byrd, William.
  Hodie Christus natus est. Luke 2:11.

C

Caceres, Abraham.
  This is the day. Psalm 118:24.
Caesar, Anthony.
  Psalm 121. Psalm 121:00.
Caldara, Antonio.
  Filled with the spirit (arr. Michael Burkhardt).
    Ephesians 5:18b-20.
Callahan, Charles.
  Canticle of praise. Revelation 11:17-18.
  How many are your works, O Lord. Psalm
    104:11-15a.
  My soul is thirsting for you, O Lord, my God.
    Psalm 63:2-6.
  A new creation. Revelation 21:5.
  O praise ye the Lord. Psalm 148:00.
  Psalm 32. Psalm 32:00.
  Revelation canticle. Revelation 15:3-4.
  The second song of Isaiah. Isaiah 55:6-11.
  Send us your strength, O God. Psalm 104:6-10.
  The spirit of the Lord. Psalm 104:1-12.
  This is the day! Psalm 118:24.
Callahan, James.
  Hark my beloved. Song of Song 2:8-13.
Callaway, Susan Naylor.
  A song of triumph. II Corinthians 2:14.

Canedo, Ken.
  Every time we eat this bread (arr. Mark Barnard).
    I Corinthians 11:25-26.
  Fly like a bird (arr. Mark Barnard). Psalm 139:00.
  The spirit of God (arr. John Purifoy). Luke 4:18-19.
  There is no greater love. John 14:00.
  We are a light. Acts 13:47, 52.
Cann, Jesse.
  Psalm 150 - Hallelujah! Psalm 150:00.
Caracciolo, Stephen.
  To everything there is a season. Ecclesiastes 3:00.
Carmona, Paul.
  A canticle of creation. Prayer of Azariah 1:29-34.
Carr, Benjamin.
  O be joyful. Psalm 100:00.
Carter, Andrew.
  God be merciful unto us and bless us. Psalm 67:00.
Carter, John.
  Benedictus (Blessed be the God of Israel). Luke
    1:68-79 (paraphrased).
  I will always give thanks. Psalm 34:1 (adapted).
Castillo, Eugene.
  Have mercy on us, Lord. Psalm 51:00.
Causey, C. Harry.
  Love one another. John 13:34.
  Prince of peace. Isaiah 9:2, 6.
  To build your kingdom. Psalm 127:1 (based on).
Chant (Gregorian).
  Laudate Dominum. Psalm 117:00.
Chassidic melody.
  I rejoice when I heard them say. Psalm 122:00
    (arr. Richard Proulx).
Chepponis, James J.
  Eastertime Psalm. Psalm 118:1-2, 16-17, 22-23.
  In unity and peace. Psalm 133:1.
  Psalm 34. Psalm 34:00.
  Psalm 146. Psalm 146:2, 6-10.
  Strike up the instruments (Canticle of Judith).
    Judith 16:1, 13-15.
Cherwien, David M.
  All you works of the Lord, bless the Lord. Prayer
    of Azariah 1:35-68.
  God has told you. Micah 6:6, 7a.
Choplin, Pepper.
  Lay up your treasures in heaven. Matthew 6:19-34.
  My shepherd is the Lord. Psalm 23:00.
  Psalm of joy. Psalm 95:00.
  Simeon's blessing. Luke 2:29-32.
  This is my word. Isaiah 55:10-12.
  Timeless song. John 3:16 (and other).
  Train up a child. Proverbs 22:6.
Christiansen, F. Melius.
  Psalm 50, Offer unto God. Psalm 50:14-15.
Christiansen, Paul.
  Easter morning. John 20:18, 19.
Christianson, Donald G. and Carrie L. Kraft.
  Lord, have mercy. Psalm 40:00.
Christopherson, Dorothy.
  Let all the peoples praise God. Psalm 150:00.
Clausen, René.
  The Lord's prayer. Matthew 6:9-13.
Clay, Crystal Davis.
  A jubilant song. Psalm 95:1.

Clemens, James E.
Holy spirit, gracious guest. I Corinthians 13:00 (based on).
Praise the Lord in the highest. Psalm 148:00.
Sing and make music to the Lord. Ephesians 5:19.
The spirit and the bride say, 'come!' Revelation 22:12-20 (based on).
With my voice I cry out to the Lord. Psalm 142:00.
Cobb, Nancy Hill.
Bless the Lord, O my soul. Psalm 103:1, 8, 11.
Colgan, Tobias.
Where two or three are gathered (arr. Craig Kingsbury). Matthew 18:20.
Collins, Dori Erwin.
Offering – Take my life, that I may be. Romans 12:1.
Comer, Thomas.
Anthem for Good Friday. Jeremiah 11:00.
Connolly, Michael.
May we never boast. Galatians 6:14-16 (inspired by).
Tell all the nations. Psalm 96:1-3, 7-8, 10 (adapted).
Where, O death, is your victory? I Corinthians 15:55.
Conte, David.
Set me as a seal. Song of Songs 8:6-7.
Cooke, S. Charles.
This is the day. Psalm 118:24.
Cooney, Rory.
Canticle of the turning. Luke 1:46-58.
Every morning in your eyes. Psalm 34:00.
Psalm 17: When your glory appears. Psalm 17:1, 5-6, 8, 15.
Psalm 51: Create me again. Psalm 51:00.
Psalm 104: Send out your spirit. Psalm 104:00.
Psalm 128: All the days of our lives. Psalm 128:00 (based on).
Psalm of the redeemed. Psalm 1:00.
Cornell, Garry A.
Hail to the Lord's annointed. Psalm 72:00.
Cortez, Jaime.
Rain down (arr. Craig Kingsbury). Psalm 33:00 (based on).
Vayan al mundo/ Go out to the world. Psalm 96:00.
Cotter, Jeanne.
I will praise your name. Psalm 145:00.
Let us go rejoicing. Psalm 122:00.
Lord, send out your spirit. Psalm 104:00.
Courtney, Craig.
Be not afraid. Isaiah 43:1-4.
Blow ye the trumpet! Isaiah 61:2.
Creation hymn. Psalm 19:1-5.
Praise the Lord who reigns above. Psalm 150:00.
Psalm 91. Psalm 91:1-7, 9-12.
Psalm 147. Psalm 147:1-11.
Rejoice! Philippians 4:4, 6, 7.
Sing to the Lord a new song. Psalm 96:00.
There is a time. Ecclesiastes 3:1-8.
Who do people say that I am? Matthew 16:13-16.
Cox, Michael.
I know that my redeemer lives. Job 19:25-27.
I sought the Lord in the night. Daniel 2:00 (based on).
The Lord is my light. Psalm 27:1, 3.
Crandal, Scot.
Gloria in excelsis Deo. Luke 2:14.
Crawshaw, Craig.
Hope of glory. Colossians 1:27.

Croce, Giovanni.
O vos omnes. Lamentations 1:12 (ed. Jerald Hamilton).
Croft, William.
Festival 'St. Anne' (arr. Hal H. Hopson). Psalm 80:00.
A song of hope (arr. John Ferguson). Psalm 84:00.
Curry, Craig.
Everlasting praise. I Chronicles 16:25-34 (adapted).

D

Dams, Julian.
If I take the wings of the morning. Psalm 139:8-9.
Dare, Carol R.
In quietness and confidence. Isaiah 30:15, 18.
Darst, W. Glen.
Ride on! Ride on in majesty. John 12:12-15.
Darwall, John.
Rejoice, the Lord is king (arr. Courtney). Psalm 33:12, 18-22.
Rejoice, the Lord is king (arr. Jimmy Owens). Philippians 4:4 (Wesley).
Day, J. R.
Search me, O God. Psalm 139:23-24.
Day, James R.
Listen, O heavens. Deuteronomy 32:1-4.
Dean, Stephen.
Ours were the griefs he bore. I Peter 2:21-24.
Peoples of earth. Psalm 100:00.
DeBruyn, Randall.
Rise up, Jerusalem. Baruch 5:5.
DeLong, Richard.
Sing to the God of Israel (Canticle of Deborah). Judges 5:1-5, 10-12.
Dengler, Lee.
Bless the Lord, O my soul. Psalm 103:00 (based on).
Blessed are they. Matthew 5:3-12.
I lift my eyes. Psalm 121:00 (paraphrased).
Look at the birds of the air. Matthew 6:25-34.
Lord, have mercy. Isaiah 53:3, 6.
The Lord's prayer. Matthew 6:9-13.
The Spirit of the Lord is upon me. Isaiah 61:1.
Dennis, Randall.
That I may know him. I Corinthians 1:22-2:9.
Dewey, Dennis Hart.
Gloria in excelsis Deo. Luke 2:14.
Diemer, Emma Lou.
Psalm 100. Psalm 100:00.
Psalm 148. Psalm 148:00.
Dietterich, Philip R.
Wilt not Thou turn again, O God? Psalm 85:6, 7.
diLasso, Orlando.
Surgens Jesus. John 20:19-20.
Dirksen, Richard.
By the Babylonian rivers. Psalm 137:00.
Donaghy, Emily.
Fear thou not. Isaiah 43:1, 2.
Drennan, Patti.
I am the resurrection. John 11:1-44.
The Lord is my light. Psalm 27:00.
With a voice of joy. Psalm 42:4-8 (based on).

Dubois, Theodore.
    He was despised (arr. Hal H. Hopson). Isaiah
      53:3-5.
Ducis, Benedictus.
    My faith is sure. Psalm 116:10-13.
Dufford, Bob.
    Be not afraid (arr. Douglas Wagner). Isaiah 43:104.
    Breath of God. Ezekiel 37:1-14 (inspired by).
    Children, run joyful. Luke 2:8-12 (based on).
    Every valley. Isaiah 40:1, 3, 4, 9.
    Love one another. John 13:34.
    The reign of God. Revelation 19:00 (based on).
Dvorák, Antonin.
    God is my shepherd. Psalm 23:00.
    I will sing new songs of gladness. Psalm 144:00.

E

Ellingboe, Bradley.
    The house of the Lord. Psalm 113:00.
    Mary at the tomb. John 20:00.
Ellis, John.
    Praise, my soul, the king of heaven. Psalm 103:00.
Emig, Louis Myers.
    Let us sing to the Lord. Psalm 149:00.
Englert, Eugene.
    Make our hearts burn with love. Luke 24:32.
English folk song.
    The wondrous cross (arr. K. Lee Scott). Galatians
      6:14.
Entsminger, Deen E.
    Rise up my love, my fair one. Song of Songs 2:10,
      11, 12.
Estes, Jerry.
    Gloria in excelsis Deo. Luke 2:14.
Evans, John E.
    Sanctus. Isaiah 6:3.

F

Fairbanks, Brian.
    There is a balm. Jeremiah 8:22.
Farlee, Robert Buckley.
    God is my strength and song. Psalm 118:14-17,
      22-24.
    Mandatum. John 13:34-35.
    O my people, turn to me. Hosea 14:1, 4-7.
    Song of Zechariah. Luke 1:68-79.
Farrant, Richard.
    Hide not thou Thy face from us, O Lord. Psalm
      27:10.
Farrell, Bernadette.
    Give us, Lord, a new heart (arr. Paul Inwood).
      Ezekiel 36:25-26.
    O God, you search me. Psalm 139:00 (based on).
    Those who sow in tears. Psalm 125:00.
Fauré, Gabriel.
    Sanctus from *Messe basse* (ed. Nancy Telfer).
      Isaiah 6:3.
    Sanctus from *Requiem* (ed. Robert Roth). Isaiah 6:3.

Fedak, Alfred V.
    Go and bear fruit. John 15:16-17 (based on).
    This is the day. Psalm 118:1, 17, 24.
Fellows, Donald Kramer.
    Behold, our God. Isaiah 35:4.
Ferguson, John.
    Psalm 130, Out of the depths. Psalm 130:00
      (based on).
    A song of thanksgiving. Psalm 90:1.
    What then. Romans 8:31-39.
Ferguson, Michael.
    Christus factus est. Philippians 2:8-9.
Ferris, William.
    Be merciful, O God. Psalm 51:00.
    When I survey the wondrous cross. Galatians 6:14.
Fischer, Dave.
    Sing praise and celebrate. Psalm 118:24.
Fisher, Bobby.
    Glory to God. Luke 2:14.
Fleming, Larry L.
    Blessed are they. Luke 23:42.
Foley, John, S. J.
    Our God has done great things for us. Psalm
      125:00.
    Your works, O God. Psalm 104:00 (based on).
Ford, Sandra T.
    O Lord, you know my heart. Psalm 139:00.
Fortunato, Frank.
    Praise the Lord in song. Isaiah 12:2-6.
Foundry Collection.
    Praise the Lord who reigns above (arr. Alice
      Parker). Psalm 150:00.
Frahm, Frederick.
    Christ, our passover. I Corinthians 5:7-8.
    Treasure in heaven. Matthew 6:19-21.
Franck, César.
    Holy, holy, holy (Sanctus) (arr. Donald Moore).
      Isaiah 6:3.
Franck, Melchior.
    Come, O blessed of my father (arr. Carl Schalk).
      Matthew 25:34.
    O Lord, I am not worthy (ed. and arr. Henry V.
      Gerike). Matthew 8:8.
    When I survey the wondrous cross (ed. Edward
      Klammer). Galatians 6:14 (Watts).
French carol.
    Sing we now of Christmas (arr. John A. Ricketts).
      Luke 2:8-20.
Friedman, Mark.
    Make a joyful noise. Psalm 150:00 (based on).
Fritschel, James.
    Into your hands. Psalm 31:5.
    Steadfast love. Lamentations 3:22, 23, 25.

G

Galbraith, Nancy.
    Agnus Dei. John 1:29.
Gastoldi, Giovanni.
    Deus in adjutorium. Psalm 69:00.
    Dixit Dominus. Psalm 109:00
    In convertendo. Psalm 125:00.

Gaul, Alfred R.
Great and marvelous are thy works. Revelation 15:3.
Gawthrop, Daniel E.
The new Jerusalem. Revelation 21:1-5.
Gerike, Henry V.
Return to the Lord. Joel 2:13.
Gering, Philip.
I am standing at the door. Revelation 3:20-21.
I am the true vine. John 15:1, 4-5.
If anyone does sin. I John 2:1-2.
Taste and see that the Lord is good. Psalm 34:8-10.
The cup of blessing that we bless. I Corinthians
10:16-17.
Those who observe the day. Romans 14:6-8.
Gibbs, Allen Orton.
A song to the lamb. Revelation 4:11.
Gieseke, Richard W.
May love be ours, O Lord. I Corinthians 13:00
(based on).
Gippenbusch, J.
Ride on! Ride on in majesty. John 12:12-15.
Glaser, Carl.
O for a thousand tongues (arr. Theron Kirk).
Psalm 98:00.
O for a thousand tongues to sing (arr. David W.
Music). Psalm 98:00.
O for a thousand tongues to sing (arr. Walter
Pelz). Psalm 98:00.
Goebel-Komala, Felix.
Canticle from the flames. Daniel 3:52-92 (based on).
How lovely is your dwelling place. Psalm 84:00.
Goemanne, Noël.
Rise up in splendor. Isaiah 60:1-2.
Goss, John.
O taste and see. Psalm 34:6-10.
Gounod, Charles.
Send out thy light. Psalm 43:3, 4.
Gouzes, André.
Jesus Christ is the Lord. Philippians 2:6-11.
Graham, Michael.
Treasure. Matthew 6:19-21.
Graun, Karl.
He was despised (arr. Dale Grotenhuis). Isaiah 53:3.
Greer, Bruce.
Gloria in excelsis Deo. Luke 2:14.
Gregorian Chant.
The Asperges (setting by Richard Keys Biggs).
Psalm 51:3-4, 9.
Grier, Gene and Lowell Everson.
The Lord is my shepherd. Psalm 23:00.
Grotenhuis, Dale.
For God so loved the world. John 3:14-17.
How beautiful are the feet. Romans 10:15-18.
How long, O Lord? Psalm 13:00.
I will exalt you, my God and king. Psalm 45:00.
May the Lord watch over you and me. Genesis 31:40.
Peace to you all. Ephesians 6:23, 24.
Set me as a seal. Song of Songs 8:6-7.
Song of commitment. Joshua 1:5-6.
The time for singing. Song of Songs 2:10-12.
Grown, Grayson Warren.
Don't be worried. Psalm 37:00 (based on).

Guimont, Michael.
Blessed are you. Psalm 128:00.
A living hope. I Peter 1:3-5.
Gustafson, Dwight.
When I survey the wondrous cross. Galatians 6:14
(Watts).

H

Haan, Raymond H.
Acquaint now thyself with Him. Job 22:21, 26, 28b.
Alleluia! Jesus, alleluia! (see *Supplication*)
As Jacob with travel. Genesis 28:10-22 (based on).
Like as a father. Psalm 103:13.
The shepherd song. Psalm 23:1.
Supplication. Matthew 8:8.
Haas, David.
Do not let your hearts be troubled. John 14:1-3,
6-7, 10-14.
God shepherds the poor. Psalm 107:00.
I am the voice of God. Genesis 12:1-4.
I put my life in your hands. Psalm 31:00
(paraphrased).
I was glad. Psalm 122:00.
Increase our faith. Luke 11:1-13.
Know that the Lord is near. Philippians 4:1-9.
O Jerusalem. Luke 12:34-35 (paraphrased).
Share your bread with the hungry. Isaiah 58:7-10
(inspired by).
Show me the path. Psalm 16:00 (adapted).
Song of the Lord's command. John 13:1-15.
Song of the risen one (arr. Jeanne Cotter). Luke
24:5-6.
Your wonderful name. Psalm 8:00.
Hailstork, Adolphus.
How long? Psalm 113:00.
I will lift up mine eyes. Psalm 121:00.
Hallquist, Gary.
I was glad. Psalm 122:1.
Hallquist, Gary and Benjamin Harland.
Holy Lord of hosts. Isaiah 6:00.
Halmos, László.
Jubilate deo. Psalm 100:00.
Hamil, Paul.
Wondrous cross. Galatians 6:14.
Hamilton, Edward.
Blessing, honor, power and glory. Revelation 7:12.
Hampton, Keith.
My God is an awesome God. Psalm 24:00 (based on).
Hancock, Gerre.
O Lord our governor. Psalm 8:1, 4-7, 10.
Handel, George F.
And the glory of the Lord (Messiah) (ed. James
Denton). Isaiah 40:5.
Arise, O God, and judge the nations (arr. Walter
Ehret). Psalm 82:8.
Bow down and hear me (adapted from *Rinaldo*)
(arr. Geoffrey Allen). Psalm 86:00.
Come unto Him (Messiah) (arr. Ellen Jane
Lorenz). Matthew 11:28.

For unto us a child is born (Messiah).
  arr. Lynn S. Lund. Isaiah 9:6.
  arr. Sharon Elergy Rogers. Isaiah 9:6.
  arr. Roger C. Wilson. Isaiah 9:6.
He is the king of glory (setting by Hal H. Hopson).
  Psalm 24:7-10.
The heav'ns declare God's mighty power (arr. Hal
  H. Hopson). Psalm 19:00.
How excellent thy name (ed. Robert S. Hines).
  Psalm 8:1.
Lift up your voice and sing (arr. Hal H. Hopson)
  (from *Joshua*). Psalm 100:00.
O exult yourself above the heavens (from *Judas
  Maccabaeus*). Psalm 57:5, 7-8.
O praise the Lord with one accord (arr. Walter
  Rodby). Psalm 135:00.
O sing unto the Lord (arr. Robert N. Roth). Psalm
  96:1.
Rejoice, the Lord is King! (setting S. Drummond
  Wolff). Philippians 4:4 (Wesley).
The sacrifice of God (arr. Richard Langdon).
  Psalm 51:17, 19.
Sing his praise! (arr. Theron Kirk). Psalm 100:2.
Handl, Jacob.
  Psalm 47:00 (Omnes gentes plaudite manibus).
    Psalm 47:00.
  Virgines prudentes (O, ye wise maidens). Matthew
    25:4-6.
Hanon, Ray D.
  Feed my lambs. John 21:15-17.
Harbison, John.
  *Beloved, let us love one another (Two Emmanuel
    motets).* I John 4:7-9.
  Concerning them which are asleep.
    I Thessalonians 4:13-18.
  *Wherefore I put thee in remembrance (Two
    Emmanuel motets).* II Timothy 1:6-9.
Harlan, Benjamin.
  Make a joyful noise. Psalm 100:00.
  Noah. Genesis 7:00.
  Processional for Christmas. Luke 2:14.
Harris, Ed.
  I will lift my eyes. Psalm 121:00.
  Love is of God. I John 4:7-11.
  When I survey the wondrous cross. Galatians 6:14
    (Watts).
Harris, Jerry Weseley.
  The Beatitudes. Matthew 5:1-12.
Harris, Ron.
  All things, all things. Romans 8:28 (based on).
Hassell, Michael.
  How beautiful. Isaiah 52:7-8.
  How exalted is your name. Psalm 8:00.
Hassler, Hans Leo.
  Cantate Domino (ed. John Hooper). Psalm 96:1-3.
Hastings, Thomas.
  The Lord is in his holy temple. Habakkuk 2:20.
  Nativity. Luke 2:00.
Haugen, Marty.
  Bread to share. John 6:1-5 (based on).
  Come, O come, let us sing. Psalm 95:00 (based on).
  I will walk in the presence of God. Psalm 116:1-8,
    12-13.

In the morning I will sing. Psalm 63:2-9.
Now bless the God of Israel. Luke 1:67-79.
On the journey to Emmaus. Luke 24:13-15.
  (based on).
So you must do. John 13:1-15.
To you, O Lord. Psalm 25:00.
Haydn, Franz Joseph.
  Fields are dancing with ripened corn (ed. Walter
    Ehret). Psalm 65:00.
  Sanctus (ed. Rod Walker). Isaiah 6:3.
  Sing to the Lord a new song (ed. Hal H. Hopson).
    Psalm 96:00.
Haydn, Johann Michael.
  Eripe me, Domine (ed. David Stein). Psalm
    143:9-10.
  Tres sunt, qui testimonium. I John 5:7-8.
  Tribulationes cordis mei (ed. David Stein). Psalm
    25:17-18.
Hayes, Mark.
  The God of love my shepherd is. Psalm 23:00
    (adapted).
  Psalm 150. Psalm 150:00 (based on).
  Rejoice and sing out his praises. Psalm 104:33-34.
  This is the day the Lord has made. Psalm 118:24
    (adapted).
  To love our God. Ecclesiastes 1:00.
Heck, Lyle.
  Make a joyful noise unto the Lord. Psalm 100:00.
Helgen, John.
  We are God's people. I Peter 2:4-10.
Helvey, Howard. See American folk melody.
Henderson, Ruth Watson.
  The strength of the spirit (Three motets). Romans
    8:28, 22, 26, 38, 39.
Hildebrand, Kevin.
  Alleluia! Christ has destroyed death.
    II Timothy 1:10b.
  I am the resurrection. John 11:25-26.
  Psalm 121. Psalm 121:00.
Hillert, Richard.
  He shall give his angels charge over you. Psalm
    91:9-12, 15-16.
  You are the light of the world. Matthew 5:14-16.
Hilton, John.
  Sing a round of praise (arr. Hal H. Hopson).
    Psalm 150:00.
Himmel, F. H.
  Incline thine ear. Psalm 70:1.
Hirten, John Karl.
  Blest be God. Isaiah 43:1, 2, 10.
  For glory dawns upon you. Isaiah 60:6b.
Hobby, Robert.
  Glory to God. Luke 2:13, 14.
  Have you not known? Isaiah 40:28-31.
  Lord, you have searched me. Psalm 139:00
    (based on).
  Thy holy wings. Psalm 25:00.
  You are a chosen race. I Peter 2:9.
Hoddinott, Alun.
  Set me as a seal upon thine heart. Song of Songs
    2:10-12.
  Vespers canticle. Revelation 15:00.

Hodges, Edward.
O praise the Lord. Psalm 100:00.
Hoekstra, Thomas.
Psalm 8. Psalm 8:00.
Psalm 138. Psalm 138:00.
Holden-Holloway, Deborah.
Lift up your heads. Psalm 24:7-10.
Holyoke, Samuel.
Hear our prayer. Psalm 143:00.
Honoré, Jeffrey.
Psalm 27: The Lord is my light. Psalm 27:00.
Psalm 103: The Lord is compassionate. Psalm 103:00.
Psalm 126: The Lord has done great things for us. Psalm 126:00.
Rejoice, rejoice, believers. Matthew 25:1-13 (based on).
Hopson, Hal H.
Antiphonal praise. Psalm 47:00.
Break forth into joy. Isaiah 55:112.
Hallelujah! Sing praise to the Lord. Psalm 150:00.
I will pour out my spirit on all the earth. Joel 2:28.
Immortal, invisible God only wise. I Timothy 1:17.
Jubilate Deo (Be joyful you people). Psalm 100:00.
Let us, with a gladsome mind. Psalm 136:1, 7, 25.
Lord, O Lord, your name is wonderful. Psalm 8:00.
Love one another. John 13:34-35.
O Lord from the depths I cry. Psalm 130:00.
O Lord, hear me. Psalm 143:00 (paraphrased).
Pentecost. Acts 2:1-12.
Praise the Lord! O heavens adore him. Psalm 148:00.
A Psalm of confession. Psalm 51:1-4, 7-9.
Rejoice in the Lord always. Philippians 4:4-7.
The treasure and the pearl. Matthew 13:44-45.
Horman, John D.
Easter song. Luke 24:1-9 (based on).
Oh, how beautiful! Psalm 84:00.
When Jesus was a growing lad. Luke 2:41-52.
Houlihan, Patrick.
By one spirit. I Corinthians 12:13, 28.
Hovland, Egil.
Laudate Dominum. Psalm 150:00.
Hughes, Howard.
I know that my redeemer lives. Job 19:25-27.
Hughes, Robert J.
Praise to the Lord, the almighty. Psalm 103:1-6.
Whoever would be great. Matthew 20:26-28.
Hurd, Bob.
Await the Lord with hope. Psalm 25:3.
I have seen the Lord. John 20:18.
Let us go rejoicing. Psalm 122:1-9.
My soul is thirsting. Psalm 63:1-8.
No longer I. Galatians 2:19-20.
O love of God (arr. Craig Kingsbury). I Corinthians 12:4-6, 12-13.
Psalm 51: Create in me. Psalm 51:3-4, 12, 14, 17, 19.
Psalm 85: Show us your kindness. Psalm 85:00.
Psalm 91: Be with me. Psalm 91:00.
Hurd, Bob and Joe Bellamy.
Psalm 95: If today (arr. Craig Kingsbury). Psalm 95:00.

Hurd, David.
The record of John. John 1:19-23.
Hyslop, Scott M.
Verses for Sundays in Lent. Mark 10:45; John 3:14, 15; John 3:16; John 12:23; Ephesians 6:11; Philippians 2:8b.

I

Innwood, Paul.
God mounts his throne. Psalm 47:1-2, 5-8.
I will sing for ever of your love, O Lord. Psalm 89:2, 21-22, 25, 27, 29, 34.
Let my prayer rise before you. Psalm 141:00.
Ippolitov-Ivanov, Michael.
Bless the Lord, O my soul (arr. Ellen Jane Lorenz). Psalm 103:1, 2, 8, 11.
Incline thine ear. Psalm 31:1-4
Irish melody.
There is a river (arr. Richard Dickinson). Psalm 46:4, 5.
Irish traditional.
Canticle of the turning (arr. Rory Cooney). Luke 1:46-58.
Let your restless hearts be still (arr. John Bell). John 14:00 (taken from).
Ivanov, P.
Psalm of praise (arr. Ellen Jane Lorenz). Psalm 135:1, 21.
Ives, Charles (ed. John Kirkpatrick and Gregg Smith).
Psalm 14. Psalm 14:00.

J

Jackson, Marylou India.
Done foun' my los' sheep. Matthew 5:12-13 (based on).
Joshua fit de battle of Jericho. Joshua 6:00 (based on).
James, Donald.
O be joyful in the Lord. Psalm 100:00.
James, Gary.
Bless the Lord, O my soul. Psalm 103:1-4, 15-16.
James, Layton.
Create in me. Psalm 51:10-13.
Make a joyful noise unto the Lord. Psalm 100:00.
They rolled the stone away. Mark 16:00 (based on).
Janco, Steven R.
God has put the angels in charge of you. Psalm 91:1-6, 10-11.
Jeffrey, Richard
Canticle of Zechariah. Luke 1:68-80.
Jenkins, Steve.
Create in me. Psalm 51:00.
Jennings, Carol arr.
Praise, my soul, the God of heaven. Psalm 103:00.
Jennings, Carolyn.
Bless the Lord, O my soul. Psalm 103:00.
A new magnificat. I Samuel 2:1-10.

Jennings, Kenneth.
All you works of the Lord, bless the Lord. Prayer of Azariah 1:29-34.
Arise, shine, for thy light has come. Isaiah 60:1-3.
When we eat this bread. I Corinthians 11:25.
With a voice of singing. Isaiah 48:20b.
Johengen, Carl.
How wonderful is your name. Psalm 8:00.
In the land of the living. Psalm 27:00.
Let all the peoples praise you! Psalm 67:00.
Johnson, Ralph M.
A living sacrifice. Romans 12:1-2.
Johnson, Randolph.
Hosanna! Blessed is He! Matthew 21:9.
Johnson, Stephen P.
Psalm 130: Out of the depths. Psalm 130:00.
Joncas, Michael.
As the deer. Psalm 42:2.
As morning breaks. Psalm 63:00.
Lord, you have the words. John 6:68.
On eagles' wings (arr. Edwin Earle Ferguson). Psalm 91:00.
Our blessing cup. I Corinthians 10:16.
This is the day. Psalm 118:1-2, 16-17, 22-23, 24.
A voice cries out. Isaiah 40:1-11.
Jones, Hilton Kean.
Happy are the lowly poor. Matthew 5:1-16.
Jones, Peter.
Glory to God. Luke 2:14.
Jordan, Alice.
The Beatitudes. Matthew 5:3-10.
Sing with joy. Psalm 95:00.
Jothen, Michael.
You are the branches. John 15:1-11.
Joy, Dawn.
You will not be left alone. John 14:00.

K

Kalbach, Don.
Make a joyful noise. Psalm 100:00.
Kalinnikoff, P.
To thee, O Lord, do I lift up my soul. Psalm 25:1-2.
Kauffmann, Ronald.
Let the people praise Thee, O God. Psalm 67:00.
Keesecker, Thomas.
Blessed are they who trust in the Lord. Jeremiah 17:7, 8, 10.
I have known you. John 17:1-11.
Return, Lord. Isaiah 40:3.
Keil, Kevin.
Guide us, Lord. Psalm 90:00.
Keldermans, R.
Hosanna filio David. Matthew 21:15.
Kemp, Helen.
The lost boy. Luke 2:41-52 (based on).
Kern, Philip.
Agnus Dei. John 1:29.
Kerrick, Mary Ellen.
Shout for joy. Psalm 100:00.
Kesselman, Lee R.
Mbiri Kuna Mwari (Shona Gloria). Luke 2:14.

Kihlken, Henry, arr.
See the place where Jesus lay. Mark 16:6.
Killman, Daniel.
Come unto me. Matthew 11:28-30.
You shall be as the tree. Psalm 1:00 (adapted).
Kimberling, Clark.
The king of love my shepherd is. Psalm 23:00.
Kirk, Theron.
He came so still. Luke 2:14.
Kirkland, Terry.
Cast your burden upon the Lord. Psalm 55:22.
This is the day! Psalm 118:24.
Kohrs, Jonathan.
And many will come from east and west (Offertory: Advent II). Luke 13:29.
The Lord says, I will make a covenant (Offertory: Advent III). Ezekiel 37:26-27.
Sing aloud, O daughter of Zion (Offertory: Advent IV). Zephaniah 3:14, 17.
Surely his salvation is at hand (Offertory: Advent I). Psalm 85:9, 12-13.
Kosche, Kenneth T.
Alleluia! Christ has risen. Matthew 28:6-7.
Canticle of praise. Psalm 111:1-3.
Come, let us fix our eyes on Jesus. Hebrews 12:2.
I know that my redeemer lives. Job 19:25.
It is a good thing. Psalm 92:1-3.
The Lord is my light and my salvation. Psalm 27:1, 7, 11.
The Lord's my shepherd. Psalm 23:00.
O taste and see. Psalm 34:1-8.
Psalm 46. Psalm 46:00.
Psalm 63. Psalm 63:00.
Psalm 103. Psalm 103:00.
Psalm 110. Psalm 110:00.
Psalm 118. Psalm 118:00.
Psalm 143. Psalm 143.00.
Unless the Lord builds the house. Psalm 127:1-2.
Unto us a child is born. Isaiah 9:6.
You will keep in perfect peace. Isaiah 26:3-4.
Kreutz, Robert E.
Shepherd and teacher. Matthew 6:30-34.

L

Lafferty, Karen and Johann Pachelbel.
Seek ye first (arr. Douglas E. Wagner). Matthew 6:33.
Landes, Rob.
Lord, Thou hast been our dwelling place. Psalm 90:1-6, 12, 17.
Peace I leave with you. John 14:27.
The peace of Christ. Colossians 3:12-17.
Lantz, David, III.
May God be gracious. Psalm 67:1-2.
O come, let us sing unto the Lord. Psalm 95:00.
Walk in love. Ephesians 4:25-32.
Larkin, Michael.
Comfort, comfort now my people. Isaiah 40:1-4.
Crucifixus. Isaiah 53:4-5.
The eyes of all. Psalm 145:15-16.

O taste and see. Psalm 34:00.
Peace, I give to you. John 14:27.

Larson, Lloyd.
Dear heavenly Father. Luke 11:3-8.
Declare the glory among the nations! Psalm 96:00.
Glory to God! Luke 2:8-15 (based on).
God so loved the world. John 3:16-17.
I have loved you. John 15:9-12 (based on).
I will praise you, O Lord, with all my heart.
    Psalm 9:1-10 (based on).
Lift up your heads. Psalm 24:7-10.
May you know God's grace. Philemon 0:3-7.
O God we do exalt your name. Psalm 95:00
    (adapted).
Our Lord's prayer. Matthew 6:9-13.
A scarlet robe. Matthew 27:27-37, 51, 54.
Surely he has borne our griefs. Isaiah 53:4-6.
Take up the tambourine. Psalm 117:00.
A voice cries out, 'Prepare the way of the Lord.'
    Isaiah 40:1, 3-5.
Without love it will all pass away.
    I Corinthians 13:1-13 (based on).

Larson, Sonia.
Psalm 103. Psalm 103:1-4.
Sing Allelu, Alleluia! Matthew 28:1-10.

Lassus, Rudolf de.
Stars in the sky proclaim. Psalm 19:1-6.

Latvian folk melody/tune.
By the Babylonian rivers. Psalm 136:00.
By the Babylonian rivers. Psalm 137:00.

Lau, Robert.
Bless the Lord, O my soul. Psalm 103:3.
Come bless the Lord. Psalm 134:1.
Come bless the Lord. Psalm 143:00.
I am the way, the truth, the life. John 14:1-4, 6.
The Lord bless you and keep you. Numbers 6:24-26.
O clap your hands. Psalm 47:00.
Seek ye first. Matthew 6:33.
Surely the Lord is in this place. Genesis 28:16, 17.
To thy pastures. Psalm 23:00.
When I survey the wondrous cross. Galatians 6:14.

Laubengayer, Paul.
Hosanna in the highest. Matthew 21:9.
Rise up, my love. Song of Songs 2:10-12.

LaValley, Jeffrey.
Revelation 19. Revelation 19:00 (based on).

Lawrence, Stephen L.
The kingdom of God. Matthew 5:3-11.

Lawson, Gordon.
God is gone up. Psalm 47:5-6.
Psalm 23. Psalm 23:00.

Leaf, Robert.
All praise. Psalm 148:00.
My heart is ready to sing. Psalm 108:1-5.
Sing praise to God. John 3:16.

Leavitt, John.
Blessed are they. Matthew 5:3-10 (based on).
The Lord is my light and my salvation (from
    Requiem). Psalm 27:00.
The Lord is my shepherd (from *Requiem*). Psalm
    23:00.

Oh, clap your hands (from *Requiem*). Psalm 47:00.
Worthy is Christ. Revelation 5:12-13.

Ledger, Philip.
Christ, whose glory fills the skies. Malachi 4:2.

Lentz, Roger.
A Lord-built house. Psalm 127:00 (based on).

Levi, Michael.
Canticle. Psalm 89:1, 2.

Levine, Elliot Z.
Psalm 8 (O Lord our God). Psalm 8:1, 3-9.

Lewis, Eric.
Glorify the Lord with me. Psalm 34:3.

Lias, Stephen.
Come glorify the Lord! Psalm 34:00.

Liddle, Samuel (arr. William Livingston).
The Lord is my shepherd. Psalm 23:00.

Liebergen, Patrick M.
Laudate! Psalm 150:00.

Lightfoot, Mary Lynn.
Crown him Lord of all. Romans 8:35-39.

Lindh, Jody W.
Behold, God is my salvation. Isaiah 12:2, 4.
Israel, awake! Judges 5:2-3, 12.

Lindley, Simon.
O God, my heart is ready. Psalm 108:00.

Linker, Janet.
At the name of Jesus. Philippians 2:8-11.

Lisicky, Paul.
Filling me with joy. Psalm 139:00.
Shelter. Psalm 91:00 (based on).

Locke, Matthew.
Turn thy face from my sins. Psalm 51:9-13.

Locklair, Dan.
St. Peter's rock. Matthew 16:18.

Loeffler, Charles M.
By the rivers of Babylon. Psalm 137:00.

Lord, Suzanne.
Faith that's sure. Luke 6:48.
I will praise my God. Psalm 40:00.

Lotti, Antonio.
Sing a song of joy (ed. and arr. Hal H. Hopson).
    Isaiah 55:1, 2.

Lovelace, Austin C.
Bless thou the Lord, O my soul. Psalm 103.00.
May God bless and keep you. Numbers 6:24-26.
Surely God is in this place. Genesis 28:16b, 17b.
The universal praises. Psalm 148:00.

Löwenthal, Tom.
These words. Deuteronomy 6:4.

Luckner, Brian.
If I have washed your feet. John 13:14.

Lund, Lynn S.
Surely, He hath borne our griefs. Isaiah 53:4-5.

Lung, Richard Ho.
When I look at the heavens. Psalm 8:00 (based on).

Luther, Martin.
I shall not die (Non moriar) (ed. William Braun).
    Psalm 118:17.
Psalm XLVI (setting by John Ness Beck). Psalm
    46:00.

M

MacAller, Dominic.
I know that my redeemer lives. Job 19:25-27.
Mackie, Ruth E.
Psalm 84. Psalm 84:00.
Malmin, Olaf G.
Advent proclamation. Isaiah 9:2.
Come, drink of the water. Isaiah 55:1.
Meditations on the cross. Philippians 2:8.
Malone, Matthew.
Bless the Lord, O my soul. Psalm 103:1-5, 22.
Manalo, Ricky.
Be glad in the Lord. Psalm 97:00.
Holy is the name of God. Luke 1:46-55 (based on).
Manz, Paul.
E'en so, Lord Jesus, quickly come. Revelation 22:20 (adapted).
Marcello, Benedetto.
O God, creator (ed. and arr. Dale Grotenhuis). Psalm 8:00.
Teach me now, O Lord (ed. and arr. Dale Grotenhuis). Psalm 119:00.
Marshall, Jane.
How lovely is your dwelling place. Psalm 84:00.
Martin, Gilbert M.
Canticle of praise (Venite exultemus). Psalm 95:1.
The risen Christ. I Corinthians 15:55-56.
The song of Mary. Luke 1:46-49 (adapted).
True builder of the house. Psalm 90:1, 2.
You shall go out in joy. Isaiah 55:12-13 (based on).
Martin, Joseph M.
All we like sheep. Isaiah 53:6.
Canticle of hope. Isaiah 25:00.
Come, sing unto the Lord. Psalm 96:00 (based on).
Go out in joy! Isaiah 56:12 (adapted).
I will awaken the dawn. Psalm 108:1-5.
In the last days. Micah 1:4-5.
My friend, do not forget. Proverbs 6:20-22 (based on).
Trust in the Lord. Proverbs 3:5.
We will need no candle. Revelation 22:5.
Well done, faithful servant(s). Matthew 25:23.
Who knows where the wind blows? John 3:7-8.
You are the vine. John 15:00 (based on).
Martinson, Joel.
Locus iste. Isaiah 40:1.
O sing to the Lord a new song. Psalm 96:1-4.
Psalm 85. Psalm 85:00.
Psalm 98. Psalm 98:00.
Rejoice in the Lord always. Philippians 4:4-7.
Mason, Lowell.
Holy is the Lord. Isaiah 6:3.
O praise God in his holiness. Psalm 150:00.
Matthews, Thomas.
Sing, sing to the Lord. Psalm 96:00.
Maunder, J. H.
Praise the Lord, O Jerusalem (Wilson). Psalm 147:12-13.
McCabe, Michael.
God is gone up! Psalm 47:5.
I am the living bread. John 6:51.
A Psalm of the redeemed. Psalm 1:00.

McChesney, Kevin.
May the peace of the Lord be with you today. John 14:6, 27.
O clap your hands. Psalm 47:1, 2, 6.
McClellan, Michael.
A new song of praise. Psalm 98:00.
McConnell, David A.
Rise up, my love, my fair one. Song of Songs 2:10-12.
McCray, James.
Lift up your heads. Psalm 24:00.
Orietur stella. Numbers 24:17-18.
Rise up, my love, my fair one. Song of Songs 2:10-12.
McDonald, Mary.
Blessed be our Lord. Psalm 72:18-19.
Call forth with songs of joy. 1 Thessalonians 2:19.
Christ will be lifted up. John 12:32.
Go ye therefore. Matthew 28:19-20.
Holy, true and faithful God. Isaiah 45:23.
Like eagles, you will fly! Psalm 103:1-5.
Peace be with you. John 14:1-14.
Praise the Lord in a song. Psalm 69:30.
Trust in the Lord. Proverbs 3:5-6.
Unto God be glory. Psalm 100:00.
We will serve the Lord. Joshua 24:15.
Worthy of the Lord. Colossians 1:9-14.
You are the light. Matthew 5:13-16.
McHugh, Charles R.
Psalm 100. Psalm 100:00.
McIver, Robert H.
Glory to God in the highest. Luke 2:14.
McKinney, Richard.
The heavens are telling. Psalm 19:00 (paraphrased).
McLarry, Beverly.
Send your bread forth. Ecclesiastes 11:1, 2, 7, 8.
McRae, Shirley.
Carol of prophecy. Isaiah 11:00.
Mechem, Kirke.
Blessed are they. Matthew 5:4-5, 7-8, 12a.
Medema, Ken and Ron Harris.
In the shadow of your wings. Psalm 63:00 (based on).
Mendelssohn, Felix.
But the Lord is mindful of his own (St. Paul). Psalm 115:12.
Cast your burden upon the Lord (Elijah). Psalm 55:22.
He watching over Israel (arr. Gene Grier and Lowell Everson). Psalm 121:4.
Hear, O Lord (Christus). Psalm 51:00.
How lovely are the messengers. Romans 10:15.
Hymne – Hear my prayer. Psalm 55:1-7.
I waited for the Lord. Psalm 40:1.
I waited for the Lord. Psalm 40:1, 4.
If with all your heart. Joel 2:12, 13.
The Lord is mindful of his own. Psalm 115:00.
O rest in the Lord (Elijah) (arr. Jonathan Willcocks). Psalm 37:7.
Peace I leave with you (arr. Hal H. Hopson). John 14:27.
There shall a star (ed. Ken Fleet). Numbers 24:17.

Mengel, Dana.
  Agnus Dei. John 1:29.
  As pants the hart for cooling streams. Psalm 42:00.
  Come, my way, my truth, my life. John 14:6.
  How can I repay the Lord. Psalm 116:00.
  I to the hills will lift my eyes. Psalm 121:00 (and other).
  Kyrie eleison. Isaiah 53:4-5.
  Let creation raise the strain. Psalm 148:00.
  My shepherd will supply my need. Psalm 23:00.
  Sing to the Lord a new song. Psalm 149:00.
Mennicke, David L.
  Come, O thou traveler unknown. Genesis 32:23-30 (based on).
Micheltree, John.
  Set me as a seal upon your heart. Song of Songs 8:6-7.
Miller, Edward.
  When I survey the wondrous cross (setting by Bruce Saylor). Galatians 6:14 (Watts).
Mitchell, Tom.
  Lamb of God. John 1:29.
  Teach me, O Lord, the way of your statutes. Psalm 119:00.
Moe, Daniel.
  Arise, shine. Isaiah 60:00.
  Hosanna to the Son of David. Matthew 21:9.
Molique, Wilhelm B.
  Lead me, O Lord (arr. Lani Smith). Psalm 5:8.
Moore, Bob.
  Psalm 103: Our God is rich in love. Psalm 103:00.
Moreland, Richard.
  I will pour out my spirit. Acts 2:17b-18, 21.
Morley, Thomas.
  Agnus Dei (ed. Leonard Van Camp). John 1:29.
Monteverdi, Claudio
  Cantate Domino (ed. Karl-Heinz Schnee). Psalm 98:00.
Mozart, W. A.
  Agnus Dei (ed. Nancy Telfer). John 1:29.
  Come be joyful (arr. Hal H. Hopson). Psalm 100:1, 2.
  Come to me, all who are weary (arr. Hal H. Hopson). Matthew 11:28-30.
  Gloria. Revelation 7:11.
  Holy be Thy glorious name (arr. Jay Daniels). Psalm 72:00.
  Jubilate Deo (O be joyful). Psalm 100:00.
  Laudate Dominum (ed. Nancy Telfer). Psalm 117:00.
  The Lord is my shepherd (ed. Ellen Jane Lorenz). Psalm 23:00.
  Mercy, God have mercy (arr. Theron Kirk). Psalm 51:00
  Not unto us, O Lord (arr. William Livingston). Psalm 115:1, 2.
  Sanctus (ed. Anthony Howells). Isaiah 5:3.
  Sanctus (ed. Henry Kihlken). Isaiah 5:3.
  Sing to the Lord a new song (ed. Henry Kihlken). Psalm 96:1, 3.
  To God be joyful (arr. Hal H. Hopson). Psalm 100:00.

Mulet, Henri.
  Laudate Dominum. Psalm 117.
Mulholland, James Quitman.
  Canticle of Psalms. Psalm 27:00, Psalm 103:00, Psalm 23:00.
  Psalm 23. Psalm 23:00.
  Psalm 27. Psalm 27:00.
  Psalm 84. Psalm 84:00.
  Psalm 103. Psalm 103:00.
Murphy, Michael Patrick.
  Come to me, all who labor. Matthew 11:28-29.
  Holy is the Lord. Luke 1:46-50.
  If with all your hearts. Deuteronomy 4:29.
  In the arms of my shepherd. Psalm 23:00.
  Let not troubled be your hearts. John 14:1-4.
  Let the children come. Matthew 19:14.
  The Lord is my light and my salvation. Psalm 27:00.
  A new commandment. John 13:34.
  Think on these things. Philippians 4:8.
Murry, Lyn.
  When I survey the wondrous cross. Galatians 6:14 (Watts).

N

Near, Gerald.
  Arise, my love, my fair one. Song of Songs 2:10-12.
  Christ for us became obedient unto death. Philippians 2:8-9.
  The king of love my shepherd is. Psalm 23:00.
  Magnificat anima mea. Luke 1:46, 47.
  A song of praise. Prayer of Azariah 1:29-34.
Neaveill, Ryan.
  Let everything that has breath praise the Lord. Psalm 150:00.
Nelson, Daniel.
  I will lift my eyes unto the hills. Psalm 121:00.
Nelson, Ronald A.
  Angels. Psalm 91:11, 12.
  Be still and know. Psalm 46:10, 11.
  Come, leave your care. Isaiah 58:00.
  Comfort, O comfort. Isaiah 40:1.
  Higher than the heavens. Psalm 108:1-6.
  Risen! Go and tell. Luke 24:4-7.
  Whoever would be great among you. Matthew 20:26-28 (based on).
  With my whole heart. Psalm 9:1, 2, 10.
  You fill all creation. Ephesians 4:00 (based on).
Nesheim, Paul.
  I will sing of Thy might. Psalm 59:16-17.
Neswick, Bruce.
  Hearken to my voice, O Lord, when I call. Psalm 27:10-13.
  I will set His dominion in the sea. Psalm 89:26-28, 51.
  Jesus came from Nazareth. Mark 1:9.
  Magna et mirabilia. Revelation 15:3-4.
  O taste and see. Psalm 34:8.
  Thou wilt keep him in perfect peace. Isaiah 26:3.
Nicholson, Paul.
  Christ is our peace. Ephesians 2:13, 14, 17, 19-21.

Nickson, John.
A festive alleluia. Psalm 100:4-5.
Niedmann, Peter.
Praise the Lord, his glories show. Psalm 150:00.
Nikolsky, A.
O taste and see how gracious is the Lord. Psalm 34:8.
Nolan, Douglas.
The good shepherd. John 10:11-14.
Norris, Kevin.
Ride on! Ride on in majesty! John 12:12-15.
North, Jack.
Holy, holy, holy. Isaiah 6:3.
Nystedt, Knut.
Hosanna! Blessed is he. Psalm 118:26.

O

O'Hearn, Arletta.
Psalm 27 – Trust in God. Psalm 27:00.
Ore, Charles W.
This is my son. Matthew 3:3, 13-17.
A time and a purpose. Ecclesiastes 3:1-8.
O'Sheil, Judy.
Whenever you do this (arr. John Purifoy).
Matthew 25:40.
Owens, Sam Batt.
He shall come down. Psalm 72:6, 8, 11a.
He shall come down like rain. Psalm 72:00.
Hide me under the shadow of your wings. Psalm 17:6, 8.
Lift up your heads, O gates. Psalm 24:7-10.
Out of the depths. Psalm 130:1, 4.
There is a balm in Gilead. Jeremiah 8:22.
This is the day. Psalm 118:24.

P/Q

Pachelbel, Johann.
Sing to the Lord a new song (ed. Donald Rotermund). Psalm 98:1-3, 8.
Pachelbel, Johann and Karen Lafferty.
Seek ye first (arr. Douglas E. Wagner). Matthew 6:33.
Page, Anna Laura.
The Lord is my keeper. Psalm 121:5, 7.
Page, Paul F.
Share this covenant of love. John 4:7-16 (based on).
Palestrina, G. P.
When fully came the day of Pentecost (Dum complerentur dies Pentecostes) (ed. Dwight E. Weldy). Acts 2:1-2.
Palmer, Nicholas.
Psalm 47: God mounts his throne. Psalm 47:00.
Panchenko, Semyon.
The Beatitudes (Remember us, we pray) (Vo tsarstvii Tvoyem). Matthew 5:3-10.
Parks, Joe E.
When I survey the wondrous cross. Galatians 6:14 (Watts).

Parry, C. Hubert.
O Lord, you are my God and King (arr. Donald Busarow). Psalm 145:1-3, 8-13.
O praise ye the Lord (arr. Mark White). Psalm 150:00.
O praise ye the Lord (arr. S. Drummond Wolff). Psalm 148:00.
Pasatieri, Thomas (with George Herbert).
Canticle of praise. Psalm 67:00.
Patterson, Joy F.
Be joyful in the Lord. Psalm 100:00.
You are the salt of the earth. Matthew 5:13.
Patterson, Mark.
With one heart. Romans 15:6.
Patton, Beverly A.
Exaudi! Laudate! Luke 2:14.
Pearson, Donald.
Arise, shine. Isaiah 60:1-3, 11, 14, 18, 10.
Pelz, Walter L.
O give thanks to the Lord. I Chronicles 16:00.
Peace I leave with you. John 14:27.
Praise the almighty, my soul adore him. Psalm 146:00.
A Psalm of celebration. Psalm 96:00.
Show me thy ways. Psalm 25:4, 5.
Pergolesi, G. B.
Glory to God in the highest (arr. Robert DeWell). Luke 2:14.
O bless the Lord, O my soul (arr. Hal H. Hopson). Psalm 100:00 (paraphrase).
Suscepit Israel (Magnificat). Luke 1:54.
Perti, Giacomo.
Peace I leave with you (arr. Hal H. Hopson). John 14: 6, 27.
Peter, Johann Friedrich.
Das Land ist voll Erkenntnis des Herrn. Isaiah 11:9.
Peterson, Gerald.
Immortal, invisible. I Timothy 1:17.
Pethel, Stan.
The gate of heaven. Psalm 122:1-2.
I shall yet praise him. Psalm 42:00.
Remember me. I Corinthians 11:23-25.
We come rejoicing. Psalm 63:00 (based on).
Petrich, Roger.
Alleluia! Risen indeed. Luke 24:34-35.
Pettit, David H.
Agnus Dei. John 1:29.
Pflueger, Carl.
Consider and hear me. Psalm 13:1, 3, 5.
Phillips, Craig.
Hodie Christus natus est. Luke 2:11.
Pinkham, Daniel.
In Monte Oliveti. Matthew 26:30, 41-42.
O vos omnes. Lamentations 1:12.
Tristis est anima mea. Matthew 26:38.
Vinea mea electa. Isaiah 5:1-7.
Pitoni, Giuseppi O.
Laudate Dominum (Sing praise to God above) (ed. Patrick M. Liebergen). Psalm 117:00.
Plag, Johannes.
Jesus went to Jordan's stream. Matthew 3:13-17.

Pollock, Gail Leven.
  I will sing to the Lord. Psalm 16:00.
Pooler, Marie.
  Truly blest. Psalm 23:00 (based on).
Porter, Steven.
  Magnificat anima mea. Luke 1:46-55.
Pote, Allen.
  Arise, shine, for your light has come. Isaiah 60:1, 3, 19.
  I am the vine. John 15:00.
  I wanted patiently for the Lord. Psalm 40:00.
  If God is for us. Romans 8:31-39.
  In this house of worship. Psalm 122:1.
  Lord, for the years. Psalm 134:00.
  A new song. Psalm 96:00 (based on).
  Praise the goodness of God. Psalm 145:00 (based on).
Powell, Kathy.
  Never the blade shall rise. John 12:00.
  Put on love. Colossians 3:12-17.
Powell, Robert J.
  Be joyful in the Lord. Psalm 100:00.
  Give ear, O shepherd of Israel. Psalm 80:00.
  He hath triumphed gloriously. Exodus 15:1-2.
  I will magnify Thee. Psalm 145:1-2, 8-10, 21-22.
  My heart is steadfast, O God. Psalm 57:7-11.
  O holy city, seen of John. Revelation 21:00.
  O Lord, our Lord. Psalm 8:1-6, 9.
  Remember your Lord God/Prayer of Habakkuk. Deuteronomy 8:2.
  Sing to the Lord a joyful song. Psalm 145:1-2.
  Surely he hath borne our griefs. Isaiah 53:4-5.
Praetorius, Hieronymus.
  Gaudete omnes. Psalm 100:00.
Proulx, Richard.
  The eyes of all. Psalm 145:14-17.
  His name is John. Luke 1:63, 76-79.
  How good it is to sing praise. Psalm 147:00.
  In te speravi, Domine. Psalm 31:2.
  My heart is full today. Psalm 111:00.
  Of the kindness of the Lord. Psalm 33:1, 51, 6, 9 (based on).
  One thing I seek. Psalm 27:5.
  A radiant light. Isaiah 9:5, 6, 9.
  Rorate caeli. Isaiah 45:8.
  Strong, loving, and wise. II Timothy 1:2, 6, 7-9.
  Taste and see. Psalm 34:2-11.
  Though we are many, in Christ we are one. I Corinthians 10:17.
  Thy law is within my heart. Psalm 40:4-8.
  Trust. Psalm 31:14-15.
  Wind, fire and heat, bless the Lord. John 3:8.
Purcell, Henry.
  O give thanks! Psalm 136:00.
  O God, have mercy (arr. Hal H. Hopson). Psalm 51:00.
Purifoy, John.
  Like a dove. John 1:29-34.
  They that wait upon the Lord. Isaiah 40:1-2, 11-31.

R

Rachmaninoff, Sergi.
  To thee, O Lord do I lift up my soul. Psalm 25:1, 2.
Raminsh, Imant.
  Cantate Domino. Psalm 149:1-3.
Renick, Charles R.
  This is the day the Lord has made. Psalm 118:00.
Ridge, M. E.
  In the day of the Lord. Isaiah 2:00.
  Parable (arr. Patrick Loomis). Ecclesiastes 3:1-9.
Roberts, J. Varley.
  Seek ye the Lord. Isaiah 55:6, 7.
Roberts, Leon C.
  Cry out with joy and gladness. Isaiah 12:2-6.
  He shall be called wonderful. Isaiah 9:6, 40.
  Let us go rejoicing. Psalm 121:00.
  Lord, make us turn to you. Psalm 80:2-3, 15-16, 18-19.
  Mary's canticle. Luke 1:45-55.
  This is the day. Psalm 118:00.
  To you, O Lord, I lift my soul. Psalm 25:00.
Roberts, Paul.
  The word became flesh. John 1:1-5, 14.
Robinson, Marc A.
  Prepare ye. Isaiah 40:3.
Rogers, Sharon Elery, arr.
  A song of faith. Genesis 28:10-22.
Rogner, James A.
  Give ear, O Lord, and visit me. Psalm 86:00 (based on).
Rollins, Joan E.
  Whence then comes wisdom. Job 28:20-21, 23-24, 28.
Romer, Charles B.
  Come, let us sing to the Lord! Psalm 95:1-7.
Rossini, Gioacchino.
  Are you not the Christ? Luke 23:39, 42-43.
Rotermund, Donald.
  A responsorial magnificat. Luke 1:46-55.
Rotermund, Melvin.
  I am the resurrection and the life. John 11:25-26.
Roth, John.
  Agnus Dei. John 1:29.
  Create in me. Psalm 51:10-12.
  David's song. Psalm 23:00.
  From all who dwell below the skies. Psalm 117:00.
  Gloria in excelsis Deo. Luke 2:14.
  Let light shine. II Corinthians 4:6.
  O give thanks unto the Lord. Psalm 118:00 (paraphrased).
Routley, Erik.
  The music of earth (arr. Austin C. Lovelace). Psalm 147:00.
Rowan, William P.
  Psalm 150. Psalm 150:00.
Rubalcava, Peter.
  Magnificat. Luke 1:46-55.
Rudolph, Glenn L.
  Hosanna. Luke 19:38.
  One thing I ask of the Lord. Psalm 27:1, 4, 6.
Rutter, John.
  I will sing with the spirit. I Corinthians 14:15.
  O how amiable are thy dwellings. Psalm 84:00.

S

Sadowski, Kevin J.
God so loved the world. John 3:16, 17.
I am the true vine. John 15:1, 4-5.
I will not leave you desolate. John 14:18.

Saint-Saëns, Camille.
Rejoice, the Lord is king (ed. George Martin).
Philippians 4:4 (Wesley).

Sanders, John.
The creator. Isaiah 40:31.

Sartor, David.
Thy light is come. Isaiah 40:00 (adapted).

Scandinavian folk melody.
Give thanks to God. Psalm 136:1-9, 23-24 (arr.
Dale Grotenhuis).

Schalk, Carl.
All the ends of the earth. Psalm 22:27.
And the ransomed of the Lord shall return. Isaiah
51:11.
Arise, shine; for your light has come. Isaiah 60:1.
Be known to use, Lord Jesus. I Corinthians 5:7b-8.
Blessed are the dead who die in the Lord.
Revelation 14:13.
From above he hath sent fire. Lamentations 1:13.
For the sins of her prophets. Lamentations 4:13-15a.
The God of Love my shepherd is. Psalm 23:00
(Herbert).
Have mercy on me, O God. Psalm 51:1a, 2, 7, 9, 13.
I saw a new heaven and a new earth. Revelation
21:1-4.
I will give you as a light to the nations. Isaiah 49:6.
I will sing to the Lord as long as I live. Psalm
104:25, 31, 32, 34.
The Lord is righteous. Lamentations 1:18.
Our soul waits for the Lord. Psalm 33:20-22.
Out of the depths. Psalm 130:00.
Remember, O Lord. Lamentations 5:1, 7, 15, 16.
Show me your ways, O Lord. Psalm 25:1-21, 4.
You shall go out in joy. Isaiah 49:6.

Scheidt, Samuel.
I am the resurrection (ed. Larry Cook). John 11:25.

Schiavone, John.
Cry out with joy. Psalm 100:1-2a.
Magnificat: God who is mighty. Luke 1:46-55.
Surely he has borne our griefs. Isaiah 53:4-5.

Schoenbachler, Tim.
Maranatha (arr. Patrick Loomis). Isaiah 35:00.

Schoenfeld, William.
When I survey the wondrous cross. Galatians 6:14
(Watts).

Schram, Ruth Elaine.
God is love. I John 4:7-11 (adapted).
This one will be our peace. Micah 5:00.

Schramm, Charles W., Jr.
I will exalt you, O Lord. Psalm 30:1-5, 12-13.
When He appears. I John 3:2-3.
You are my son. Psalm 2:7-8.

Schröter, Leonhart.
Hail to the Lord's annointed (setting by Mark
Bender). Psalm 72:00.

Schubert, Franz.
The Lord is my shepherd (arr. Walter Ehret).
Psalm 23:00.
O be joyful, joyful in the Lord. Psalm 100:00.
Strike the cymbal (arr. Dale Grotenhuis). Psalm
150:00.

Schultz, Larry E.
Let us rejoice and sing. Psalm 118:24.

Schultz, Ralph C.
Create in me. Psalm 51:11-13.
Sing for joy. Psalm 66:1.

Schultz, Timothy P.
God is our refuge and strength. Psalm 46:00.
Peace. John 14:27.

Schulz-Widmar, Russell.
Through all the changing scenes of life. Psalm
34:00 (based on).

Schurr, Walter W.
Fix these words. Deuteronomy 11:18.

Schutte, Dan.
How long, O Lord. Psalm 13:00.
Let us go to the altar. Psalm 42:00.
Like cedars (arr. Randall DeBruyn). Psalm 92:00.
Lover of us all. Ephesians 2:7-10.
Only this I want. Philippians 3:7-16.

Schutte, Rory.
Every morning in your eyes. Psalm 34:00.

Schütz, Heinrich.
Give glory all creation (arr. John Leavitt). Psalm
103:00.
I ask one thing of the Lord (ed. David W. Music).
Psalm 27:4.
Lord, hear my prayer (Erhöre mich) (arr. David W.
Music). Psalm 4:1.
The Lord's prayer (ed. George Guest). Matthew
6:9-13.
*O be joyful, all ye nations (Jubilate Deo omnia
terra)* (ed. Leonard Van Camp). Psalm 100:00.
Praise God in heaven. Psalm 9:11-12.
Psalm 150. Psalm 150:00.
Who shall separate us (ed. Larry L. Fleming).
Romans 8:35-39.

Schweizer, Mark.
Go, make of all disciples. Matthew 28:19-20.
Let all the rivers clap their hands. Psalm 98:00.

Schwoebel, David.
The Lord is my strength and my song. Exodus
15:2, 11.

Scott, K. Lee.
All the day long. Psalm 25:4-8.
Declare God's glory. Psalm 96:00.
Eternal light, shine in my heart. II Corinthians 4:6.
Festive Jubilate. Psalm 100:00.
God shall the broken heart repair. Psalm 147:3.
How very good and pleasant. Psalm 133:00.
Let all the world. Psalm 67:3-5.
Love never fails. I Corinthians 13:8-10, 13.
O God of font and altar. Psalm 29:1-2.
Open to me the gates of righteousness. Psalm
118:19-22, 24.
The peace of God. Philippians 4:6-7.
The pilgrim church of God. Ephesians 4:13.

Sing aloud to God our strength. Psalm 81:1-3.
Sing to the Lord a new song. Psalm 96:00
(paraphrased).
Thy perfect love. Ephesians 5:1-2a.
To see your glory. Colossians 2:6-10 (and other)
When the morning stars together. Job 38:7.
Sedio, Mark.
By the Babylonian rivers. Psalm 136:00.
Raise a joyful sound. Psalm 95:00.
Sing Alleluia! Jesus lives! Psalm 95:00.
Teach me your way, O Lord. Psalm 86:00.
Selby, William.
O be joyful in the Lord. Psalm 100:00.
Sensmeier, Randall.
The Lord is my shepherd. Psalm 23:00.
Sharpe, Carlyle.
Sing unto the Lord a new song. Psalm 96:1-10.
Shelley, Harry Rowe.
The king of love my shepherd is. Psalm 23:00.
Shepperd, Mark.
Balm in Gilead. Jeremiah 8:22.
I will yet praise him. Psalm 42:00.
Sherman, Arnold B.
I am the bread of life. John 6:32-51.
Let us love one another. I John 4:7-11.
Shields, Valerie.
Easter acclamation. Psalm 118:24.
Let your light so brightly shine. Matthew 5:16.
Shoemaker-Lohmeyer, Lisa.
This is the day the Lord has made. Psalm 118:24,
27-29.
Showalter, Anthony J.
Leaning. Deuteronomy 33:27.
Shute, Linda Cable.
This is the day. Psalm 118:00.
Sleeth, Natalie.
Consider the lilies (arr. Jane Marshall). Matthew 6:28.
Let all the people praise thee. Psalm 67:3 (based on).
Smith, Lani.
Jacob's vision. Genesis 28:10-22.
Smith, Timothy R.
The Lord is my shepherd. Psalm 23:00.
Taste and see. Psalm 34:1-7, 9.
Snyder, Audrey.
The time of singing. Song of Songs 2:11-12.
Soper, Scott.
Glory to God. Luke 2:14.
The goodness of the Lord. Psalm 27:00 (based on).
I will always thank the Lord. Psalm 34:1.
Loving and forgiving. Psalm 103:00 (based on).
My life is in your hands. Psalm 31:00.
Song of Moses. Exodus 15:00 (adapted).
What shall I give. Psalm 116:00.
South African freedom song.
We are singing for the Lord is our light (arr. Hal
H. Hopson). Psalm 27:1-4 (based on).
Sowerby, Leo.
Put on therefore as the elect of God. Colossians
3:12-17.
Spanish folktune.
Flee as a bird (arr. Leland B. Sateren). Psalm 11:1b.
Spencer, Linda.
Wings of the dawn. Psalm 139:00.

Spevacek, Linda Steen.
The blessing of Aaron. Numbers 6:24-26.
Spinney, Walter.
Ye that stand in the house of the Lord. Psalm
135:2, 3.
Spiritual.
Jacob's ladder (arr. Roger C. Wilson). Genesis
28:10-22.
Jacob's ladder/Hold on (arr. Marc Robinson).
Genesis 28:10-22.
There is a balm in Gilead (arr. James Furman).
Jeremiah 8:22.
Spong, Jon.
The peace of God. Philippians 4:7.
Sr. Maria of the Cross.
Like the deer. Psalm 41:1-2.
Stainer, John.
God so loved the world. John 3:16.
God so loved the world. John 3:16-17.
How beautiful upon the mountains. Isaiah 52:7.
They have taken away my Lord. John 20:13-16.
Stanford, C. Villiers.
How beauteous are their feet. Isaiah 52:7.
Staplin, Carl.
O clap your hands, all ye people! Psalm 47:00.
Starr, David.
It is a good thing to sing. Psalm 92:00.
O Lamb of God. John 1:29.
Shout for joy. Psalm 100:00.
Stand up and bless the Lord. Nehemiah 9:5, 6.
Stearns, Peter Pindar.
The Lord is my shepherd. Psalm 23:00.
Thou wilt keep him in perfect peace. Isaiah 25:3, 4, 8.
Steffy, Thurlow T.
Praise to the Lord, the almighty. Psalm 103:1-6.
Stocker, David.
Ride on! Ride on in majesty. John 12:12-15.
Story, Donald J.
Sing to the Lord a joyful song. Psalm 145:1-2.
Stroope, Z. Randall.
Lamb of God, grant us peace. John 1:29.
Swahili song from Kenya.
He is mine (arr. Hal H. Hopson). Romans 8:35, 38.
Yes, Jesus is my savior (arr. Hal H. Hopson).
Philippians 2:1-11 (adapted).
Swedish folk tune.
Oh, sing to God a new song. Psalm 96:1-4.
Rejoice, rejoice, believers (arr. Theodore Beck).
Matthew 25:1-13 (based on).
Sweelinck, Jan P.
Gaudete omnes (Rejoice, ye people) (ed. Leonard
Van Camp). Psalm 100:00.
Sing to the Lord (ed. and arr. Robert S. Hines).
Psalm 96:1.

T

Talbot, John Michael.
Father, I put my life in your hands. Psalm 31:2, 6,
12-13, 15-17, 25.
Taranto, A. Steven.
Into Jerusalem. Zechariah 9:9.

Taulè, Alberto.
 Toda la Tierra (All earth is waiting) (arr. Jerry
  Gunderson). Isaiah 40:3-5.
Taylor, Jim.
 Hosanna. Luke 19:38 (and other).
Telemann, George Philipp.
 I want to praise the Lord all of my life (arr. Susan
  Palo Cherwien). Psalm 34:1.
Thayer, Fred.
 Qui tollis peccata mundi. Luke 1:29.
Thompson, J. Michael.
 Taste and see the Lord is good. Joshua 5:9-12.
Thompson, Randall.
 God is a spirit. John 4:24.
 The old and the young. Joel 2:28.
Tiefenbach, Peter.
 What shall I render to the Lord? Psalm 116:12-
  14, 17-19.
Titcomb, Everett.
 Ride on! Ride on in majesty. John 12:12-15.
Toolan, Suzanne.
 My soul proclaims. Luke 1:46-55.
Tschaikovsky, P. I.
 Lord, I cry unto thee. Psalm 141:1, 2, 3, 8.
 Praise ye the Lord. Psalm 150:2, 3.
 Praise ye the name of the Lord. Psalm 135:1, 3, 21.

U

Ure, James.
 Psalm 4. Psalm 4:00.

V

Vantine, Bruce.
 Your word is a candle. Psalm 119:105.
Vaughan Williams, Ralph.
 Led by the spirit. Joel 2:12-13.
Vedel, Artemiy.
 By the banks of Babylon's streams. Psalm 137:1-
  5, 7-9.
Victoria, Tomás Luis de.
 Ecce nunc benedicite Dominum (arr. Robert J.
  Powell). Psalm 134:1-3.
 Hearken, bless ye the Lord. Psalm 134:1-3.
 O vos omnes (ed. Raymond Sprague).
  Lamentations 1:12.
 *Vere languores nostros (Truly our Lord has
  suffered).* Isaiah 53:4.
Vierdanck, Johann.
 Gloria (ed. Michael Burkhardt). Luke 2:14.
Vivaldi, Antonio.
 Beatus Vir. Psalm 112:00.
 Gloria in excelsis Deo (ed. S. Drummond Wolff).
  Luke 2:14.
 Sing to the Lord (arr. Hal H. Hopson). Psalm
  148:00.
Voorhaar, Richard E.
 Sing out to God. Psalm 126:00.

W

Wagner, Douglas E.
 A time for all things. Ecclesiastes 3:1 (adapted).
 Create in me a clean heart. Psalm 51:20-15.
 Easter fanfare. I Corinthians 15:20, 55, 57.
 O be joyful. Psalm 5:00.
Walker, Christopher.
 Glastonbury gloria. Luke 2:14.
 Let my prayer rise. Psalm 141:2.
 Lord is my light. Psalm 27:00.
 The Lord's prayer. Matthew 6:9-13.
 May God bless and keep you. Numbers 6:22-27.
 Nunc dimittis. Luke 2:29-32.
 Song of the Virgin Mary. Luke 1:46-55.
Walker, Gwyneth.
 "For ever and ever" – The Lord's Prayer.
  Matthew 6:9-13.
Weber, Paul.
 I will sing the story of your love. Jeremiah 33:10-
  11, 14-16.
Welsh tune.
 You fill all creation. Ephesians 4:00 (based on).
Wesley, Samuel S.
 Lead me, Lord. Psalm 5:8.
West, John E.
 Hide me under the shadow of thy wings. Psalm 17:8.
 The Lord is exalted. Isaiah 33:5, 9, 10.
Westra, Evert.
 The Lord, your God, will come. Isaiah 35:4c-6a.
Wetzler, Robert.
 Always, only, for my king. Psalm 19:14.
 As the hart. Psalm 42:00.
 Easter dawning at the tomb. Luke 24:1, 5.
 Go ye into all the world. Mark 16:15.
 He shall direct your paths. Proverbs 3:5-6.
 I am the good shepherd. Romans 6:9.
 Look to this day. Matthew 6:26, 28-29, 34.
 Oh, for a thousand tongues. Psalm 98:00.
 Oh, for a thousand tongues to sing. Isaiah 43:1, 3.
White, David Ashley.
 Cantate Domino. Psalm 96:1-4.
 Have mercy on me, O God. Psalm 51:1-8, 10-12.
 The Lord is king. Psalm 99:1-3, 9.
 Miserere mei. Psalm 51:1.
 A song to the lamb. Revelation 4:11.
Wienhorst, Richard.
 Give praise, you servants of the Lord. Psalm 113:00.
 The hour has come. John 12:23.
Wilcock, Christopher.
 A blessing. I Thessalonians 3:12-13.
 Glory to God. Luke 2:14.
 The Lord now rules. Psalm 92:1-5, 12.
 This body. I Corinthians 11:24-25.
Wilkinson, Sandy.
 Come, celebrate our God and King. Psalm 47:00.
 Take my heart. Psalm 51:9-13.
Willan, Healey.
 Create in me a clean heart, O God. Psalm 51:10-12.
Willcocks, Jonathan.
 Rejoice the Lord is King. Philippians 4:4 (Wesley).

Williams, Amy Tate.
    Mary. Luke 1:26-38 (based on).
Williams, David H.
    I know that my redeemer lives. Job 19:25.
Williams, Paul and Donna.
    Like a river in springtime. Philippians 1:4-7.
Williams, Thomas J.
    Lift up your heads (arr. Stan Pethel). Psalm 24:7-10.
Wilson, Roger C.
    Easter sentence. Revelation 1:18.
Wilson, Russell.
    They that wait upon the Lord. Isaiah 40:31.
Wold, Wayne L.
    Alleluia, I have chosen. II Chronicles 7:16.
    O sovereign God. Psalm 8:00.
Wood, Dale.
    Blessed be the Lord. Luke 1:68-79.
    Rejoice, be glad, give praise. Revelation 19:6-7.
Wright, Paul Leddington.
    I will sing to the Lord. Exodus 15:1, 2, 11, 13, 17.
    This is the day. Psalm 118:24.
Wright, Vicki Hancock.
    I will praise God. Psalm 145:00 (based on).
Wyrtzen, Don.
    Fanfare of praise. Psalm 98:4-6 (based on).
Wyton, Alec.
    Into the woods my master went. Matthew 4:1, 2.

XYZ

Young, Gordon.
    Glorious and everlasting God. Psalm 104:24.
    The king of love. Psalm 23:00 (Baker).
    O for a thousand tongues to sing. Psalm 98:00.
    Ride on! Ride on in majesty. John 12:12-15.
    This is the day the Lord hath made. Psalm 118:24.
    The trumpeters and the singers were as one.
       II Chronicles 5:13.
    When I survey the wondrous cross. Galatians 6:14.
Young, Jeremy.
    Nothing can come between us. Romans 8:35-39.
    Praise God with the trumpet. Psalm 150:00.
Young, Philip M.
    As a hart longs for flowing streams. Psalm 42:1-5.
    I will extol you, O Lord. Psalm 30:00 (adapted).
    I will lift up my eyes. Psalm 121:1-3, 5, 8.
    My heart is steadfast, O God. Psalm 57:7-11.
    With what shall I come before the Lord. Micah
       6:6-8.
Zabel, Albert.
    Come, joy! Leviticus 19:9.
Zacharia, Cesare de.
    Magnificat. Luke 1:46b-55.
Zaimont, Judith Lang.
    Psalm 97 (from *Sacred service*). Psalm 97:00.
Zimmermann, Heinz Werner.
    Psalm 23 (The Lord is my shepherd). Psalm 23:00.
Zulu traditional song.
    We are singing for the Lord is our light (arr. Hal
       H. Hopson). Psalm 27:1-4.

Title Index

A

Acquaint now thyself with Him. Job 22:21, 26, 28b. Haan, Raymond H.

Advent proclamation. Isaiah 9:2. Malmin, Olaf G.

Agnus Dei.
    Bell, John L. John 1:29.
    Galbraith, Nancy. John 1:29.
    Kern, Philip. John 1:29.
    Mengel, Dana. John 1:29.
    Morley, Thomas (ed. Leonard Van Camp). John 1:29.
    Mozart, W. A. (ed. Nancy Telfer). John 1:29.
    Pettit, David H. John 1:29.
    Roth, John. John 1:29.

All earth is waiting. Isaiah 40:3-5. Taulè, Alberto (arr. Jerry Gunderson).

All praise. Psalm 148:00. Leaf, Robert.

All Saints' Day. Revelation 7:15. Blersch, Jeffrey.

All the day long. Psalm 25:4-8. Scott, K. Lee.

All the ends of the earth. Psalm 22:27. Schalk, Carl.

All things, all things. Romans 8:28 (based on). Harris, Ron.

All we like sheep. Isaiah 53:6. Martin, Joseph M.

All you works of the Lord, bless the Lord.
    Cherwin, David M. Prayer of Azariah 1:35-68.
    Jennings, Kenneth. Prayer of Azariah 1:29-34.

Alleluia! Christ has destroyed death.
    II Timothy 1:10b. Hildebrand, Kevin.

Alleluia! Christ has risen. Matthew 28:6-7. Kosche, Kenneth T.

Alleluia, come, let us sing. Psalm 95:00. Bertalot, John.

Alleluia, I have chosen. II Chronicles 7:16. Wold, Wayne L.

Alleluia! Risen indeed. Luke 24:34-35. Petrich, Roger.

Always, only, for my king. Psalm 19:14. Wetzler, Robert.

And many shall come from east and west (Offertory: Advent II). Luke 13:29. Kohrs, Jonathan.

And the glory of the Lord (Messiah). Isaiah 40:5. Handel, George F.

And the ransomed of the Lord shall return. Isaiah 51:11. Schalk, Carl.

And the word became flesh. John 1:14, 16. Bourman, Paul.

Angels. Psalm 91:11, 12. Nelson, Ronald A.

Anthem for Good Friday. Jeremiah 11:00. Comer, Thomas.

Antiphonal praise. Psalm 47:00. Hopson, Hal H.

Are you not the Christ? Luke 23:39, 42-43. Rossini, Gioacchino (ed. Robert Sumner).

Arise, my love, my fair one. Song of Songs 2:10-12. Near, Gerald.

Arise, O God, and judge the nations. Psalm 82:8. Handel, G. F. (arr. Walter Ehret).

Arise, shine.
    Moe, Daniel. Isaiah 60:00.
    Pearson, Donald. Isaiah 60:1-3, 11, 14, 18, 19.

Arise, shine, for your light has come.
    Jennings, Kenneth. Isaiah 60:1-3.
    Pote, Allen. Isaiah 60:1, 3, 19.
    Schalk, Carl. Isaiah 60:1.

As a hart longs for flowing streams. Psalm 42:1-5. Young, Philip M.

As Jacob with travel. Genesis 28:10-22 (based on). Haan, Raymond H.

As morning breaks. Psalm 63:00. Joncas, Michael.

As pants the hart for cooling streams. Psalm 42:00. Mengel, Dana.

As the deer. Psalm 42.2. Joncas, Michael.

As the hart. Psalm 42:00. Wetzler, Robert.

Ask and seek and knock. Luke 11:9. Barta, Daniel.

The Asperges. Psalm 51:3-4, 9. Gregorian chant (setting by Richard Keys Biggs).

At the name of Jesus. Philippians 2:8-11. Linker, Janet.

Ave Maria. Luke 1:00. Bach, J. S. (adapted Charles Gounod, arr. Colin Mawby).

Await the Lord with hope. Psalm 25:3. Hurd, Bob.

B

Balm in Gilead. Jeremiah 8:22. African-American spiritual (arr. Mark Shepperd).

Be glad in the Lord. Psalm 97:00. Manalo, Ricky.

Be joyful in the Lord.
    Patterson, Joy F. Psalm 100:00.
    Powell, Robert J. Psalm 100:00.

Be known to use, Lord Jesus. I Corinthians 5:7b-8. Schalk, Carl.

Be merciful, O God. Psalm 51:00. Ferris, William.

Be not afraid.
    Beyer, Johann Samuel (arr. Ronald A. Nelson). Luke 2:10, 11.
    Courtney, Craig. Isaiah 43:1-4.
    Dufford, Bob (arr. Douglas Wagner). Isaiah 43:1-4.

Be still and know. Psalm 46:10. Nelson, Ronald A.

Be with us all, Lord. II Corinthians 13:14. Brown, Uzee, Jr.

The Beatitudes.
    Harris, John Weseley. Matthew 5:1-12.
    Jordan, Alice. Matthew 5:3-10.

The Beatitudes (Remember us, we pray) (Votsarstvii tvoyem). Matthew 5:3-10. Panchenko, Semyon.

Beatus vir.
    Psalm 112:00. Vivaldi, Antonio (ed. Joan Whittemore).

Behold, God is my salvation. Isaiah 12:2, 4. Lindh, Jody W.

Behold my servant. Isaiah 42:1, 6. Bengston, Bruce.

Behold, our God. Isaiah 35:4. Fellows, Donald Kramer.

Behold, your salvation comes. Isaiah 62:11. Beebe, Hank.

Beloved, let us love one another (Two Emmanuel motets). I John 4:7-9. Harbison, John.

Benedictus. Luke 1:68-79 (paraphrase). Carter, John.

Bless, O my soul. Psalm 103:1-5, 20-22. Bell, John L.

Bless the Lord, O my soul.

    Cobb, Nancy Hill. Psalm 103:1, 8, 11.

    Dengler, Lee. Psalm 103:00 (based on).

    Ippolitov-Ivanov, Michael (arr. Ellen Jane Lorenz). Psalm 103:1, 2, 8, 11.

    James, Gary. Psalm 103:1-4, 15-16.

    Jennings, Carolyn. Psalm 103:00.

    Lau, Robert. Psalm 103:1.

    Malone, Matthew. Psalm 103:1-5, 22.

Bless thou the Lord, O my soul. Psalm 103:00. Lovelace, Austin C.

Blessed are the dead who die in the Lord. Revelation 14:13. Schalk, Carl.

Blessed are they.

    Billings, William. Matthew 5:3-12.

    Dengler, Lee. Matthew 5:3-12.

    Fleming, Larry L. Luke 23:42.

    Leavitt, John. Matthew 5:3-10 (based on).

    Mechem, Kirke. Matthew 5:4-5, 7-8, 12a.

Blessed are they who trust in the Lord. Jeremiah 17:7, 8, 10. Keesecker, Thomas.

Blessed are you. Psalm 128:00. Guimont, Michael.

Blessed be our Lord. Psalm 72:18-19. McDonald, Mary.

Blessed be the Lord. Luke 1:68-79. Wood, Dale (setting Donald Rotermund).

A blessing. I Thessalonians 3:12-13. Wilcock, Christopher.

Blessing, honor, power and glory. Revelation 7:12. Hamilton, Edward.

The blessing of Aaron. Numbers 6:24-26. Spevacek, Linda Steen.

Blest be God. Isaiah 43:1, 2, 10. Hirten, John Karl.

Blow ye the trumpet! Isaiah 61:2. Courtney, Craig.

Bow down and hear me. Psalm 86:00. Handel, G. F. (arr. Geoffrey Allen).

Bow down thine ear, O Lord. Psalm 86:1, 3, 5. Arensky, Anton.

Bread to share. John 6:1-5 (based on). Haugen, Marty.

Break forth into joy. Isaiah 55:12. Hopson, Hal H.

Breath of God. Ezekiel 37:1-14. Dufford, Bob.

But the Lord is mindful of His own (St. Paul). Psalm 115:12. Mendelssohn, Felix.

By one spirit. I Corinthians 12:13, 28. Houlihan, Patrick.

By the Babylonian rivers.

    Latvian folk melody (arr. Mark Sedio). Psalm 136:00.

    Latvian folk tune (arr. Richard Erickson). Psalm 137:00.

By the banks of Babylon's streams. Psalm 137:1-5, 7-9. Vedel, Artemiy.

By the rivers of Babylon.

    Anonymous. Psalm 137:00.

    Loeffler, Charles M. Psalm 137:00.

C

Call forth with songs of joy. I Thessalonians 2:19. McDonald, Mary.

Cantate Domino.

    Hassler, Hans Leo. (ed. John Hooper). Psalm 96:1-3.

    Monteverdi, Claudio. Psalm 98:00.

    Raminsh, Imant. Psalm 149:1-3.

    White, David Ashley. Psalm 96:1-4.

Canticle. Psalm 89:1, 2. Levi, Michael.

Canticle from the flames. Daniel 3:52-90 (based on). Goebel-Komala, Felix.

A canticle of creation. Prayer of Azariah 1:29-34. Carmona, Paul.

Canticle of hope. Isaiah 25:00. Martin, Joseph M.

Canticle of praise.

    Callahan, Charles. Revelation 11:17-18.

    Kosche, Kenneth T. Psalm 111:1-3.

    Pasatieri, Thomas (with George Herbert). Psalm 67:00.

Canticle of praise (Venite exultemus). Psalm 95:1. Martin, Gilbert M.

Canticle of Psalms. Psalms 27:00, 103:00, 23:00. Mulholland, James Quitman.

Canticle of the turning. Luke 1:46-58. Irish traditional (arr. Rory Cooney).

Canticle of Zechariah. Luke 1:68-80. Jeffrey, Richard.

Carol of prophecy. Isaiah 11:00. McRae, Shirley.

Cast your burden upon the Lord.

    Kirkland, Terry. Psalm 55:22.

    Mendelssohn, Felix (ed. Telfer). Psalm 55:22.

Children, run joyfull. Luke 2:8-12. Dufford, Bob.

Christ for us became obedient unto death. Philippians 2:8-9. Near, Gerald.

Christ is our peace. Ephesians 2:13, 14, 17, 19-21. Nicholson, Paul.

Christ, our passover.

    Frahm, Frederick. I Corinthians 5:7-8.

Christ, whose glory fills the skies. (Wesley) Ledger, Philip. Malachi 4:2.

Christ will be lifted up. John 12:32. McDonald, Mary.

Christmas fanfare. Luke 2:11. Averre, Dick.

Christus factus est. Philippians 2:8-9. Ferguson, Michael.

Come, be joyful. Psalm 100:1, 2. Mozart, W. A. (arr. Hal H. Hopson).

Come bless the Lord.

    Lau, Robert. Psalm 134:00.

    Lau, Robert. Psalm 143:00.

Come, celebrate our God and king. Psalm 47:00. Wilkinson, Sandy.

Come, drink of the water. Isaiah 55:1. Malmin, Olaf G.

Come glorify the Lord! Psalm 34:00. Lias, Stephen.

Come, joy! Leviticus 19:9. Zabel, Albert.

Come, leave your care. Isaiah 58:00. arr. Nelson, Ronald A.

Come, let us fix our eyes on Jesus. Hebrews 12:2. Kosche, Kenneth.

Come, let us sing to the Lord! Psalm 95:1-7. Romer, Charles B.

Come, my way, my truth, my life. John 14:6. Mengel, Dana.

Come, O blessed of my father. Matthew 25:34. Franck, Melchior (ed. Carl Schalk).

Come, O come, let us sing. Psalm 95:00 (based on). Haugen, Marty.

Come, O thou traveler unknown. Genesis 32:23-30 (based on). Mennicke, David L.

Come, sing unto the Lord.
> Martin, Joseph M. Psalm 96:00.
> Martin, Joseph M. Psalm 96:00 (based on).

Come to me, all who are weary. Matthew 11:28-30. Mozart, W. A. (arr. Hal H. Hopson).

Come to me, all who labor. Matthew 11:28-29. Murphy, Michael Patrick (arr. Robert J. Powell).

Come unto Him (Messiah). Matthew 11:28. Handel, George F. (freely arranged by Ellen Jane Lorenz).

Come unto me. Matthew 11:28-30. Killman, Daniel.

Comfort, comfort now my people. Isaiah 40:1-4. Larkin, Michael.

Comfort, O comfort. Isaiah 40:1. Nelson, Ronald A.

Concerning them which are asleep. I Thessalonians 4:13-18. Harbison, John.

Consider and hear me. Psalm 13:1, 3, 5. Pflueger, Carl.

Consider the lilies. Matthew 6:28. Sleeth, Natalie (arr. Jane Marshall).

Create in me.
> James, Layton. Psalm 51:10-13.
> Jenkins, Steve. Psalm 51:00.
> Roth, John. Psalm 51:10-12.
> Schultz, Ralph C. Psalm 51:11-13.

Create in me a clean heart. Psalm 51:20-15. Wagner, Douglas E.

Create in me a clean heart, O God. Psalm 51:10-12. Willan, Healey.

Creation hymn. Psalm 19:1-6. Courtney, Craig.

The creator. Isaiah 40:31. Sanders, John.

Crown him Lord of all. Romans 8:35-39. Lightfoot, Mary Lynn.

Crucifixus. Isaiah 53:4-5, Larkin, Michael.

Cry out with joy. Psalm 100:1-2a. Schiavone, John.

Cry out with joy and gladness. Isaiah 12:2-6. Roberts, Leon C.

The cup of blessing that we bless. I Corinthians 10:16-17. Gehring, Philip

D

David's song. Psalm 23:00. Ruth, John.

Dear heavenly Father. Luke 11:3-8. Larson, Lloyd.

Declare God's glory. Psalm 96:00. Scott, K. Lee.

Declare the glory among the nations! Psalm 96:00 (adapted). Larson, Lloyd.

Deus in adjutorium. Psalm 69:00. Gastoldi, Giovanni.

Deus misereatur (Psalm 67). Psalm 67:00. Bales, Gerald.

Dixit Dominus. Psalm 109:00. Gastoldi, Giovanni.

Do not be vexed. Psalm 37:1-10. Bell, John L.

Do not let your hearts be troubled. John 14:1-3, 6-7, 10-14. Haas, David.

Done foun' my los' sheep. Matthew 5:12-13, based on. African-American spiritual (arr. Marylou India Jackson).

Don't be worried. Psalm 37:00 (based on). Grown, Grayson Warren.

Dum complerentur dies Pentecostes. Palestrina (See *When fully came the day of Pentecost*)

E

The earth is full of the knowledge of God. Isaiah 11:9. Peter, Johann Friedrich.

Easter acclamation. Psalm 118:24. Shields, Valerie.

Easter dawning at the tomb. Luke 24:1, 5. Robert Wetzler.

Easter fanfare. I Corinthians 15:20, 55, 57. Wagner, Douglas.

Easter morning. John 20:18, 19. Christiansen, Paul.

Easter sentence. Revelation 1:18. Wilson, Roger C.

Easter song. Luke 24:1-9 (based on). Horman, John D.

Eastertime Psalm. Psalm 118:1-2, 16-17, 22-23. Chepponis, James J.

Ecce nunc benedicite Dominum. Psalm 134:1-3. Victoria, Tomás (arr. Robert Powell)

E'en so, Lord Jesus, quickly come. Revelation 22:20 (adapted). Manz, Paul.

Enter his gates with thanksgiving. Psalm 100:00 (based on). Akins, John R.

The Epiphany of our Lord. Matthew 2:2. Blersch, Jeffrey.

Eripe me, Domine. Psalm 143:9-10. Haydn, Johann Michael (ed. David Stein).

Eternal light, shine in my heart. II Corinthians 4:6. Scott, K. Lee.

Even the sparrow. Psalm 84:00. Albrecht, Ronald.

Everlasting praise. I Chronicles 16:25-34. Curry, Craig.

Every morning in your eyes. Psalm 34:00. Cooney, Rory.

Every time we eat this bread. I Corinthians 11:25-26 (based on). Canedo, Ken.

Every valley. Isaiah 40:1, 3, 4, 9. Dufford, Bob.

Exaudi! Laudate! Luke 2:14. Patton, Beverly A.

The eyes of all.
> Larkin, Michael. Psalm 145:15-16.
> Proulx, Richard. Psalm 145:14-17.

The eyes of all wait upon thee. Psalm 145:15, 16. Berger, Jean.

F

Faith that's sure. Luke 6:48. Lord, Suzanne.

Fanfare of praise. Psalm 98:4-6 (based on). Wyrtzen, Don.

Father, I put my life in your hands. Psalm 31:2, 6, 12-13, 15-17, 25. Talbot, John Michael.

Fear thou not. Isaiah 43:1, 2. Donaghy, Emily.

Feed my lambs. John 21:15-17. Hanon, Ray D.

The Festival of Christ the King. Revelation 22:13. Blersch, Jeffrey.

The Festival of the Reformation. Psalm 48:14. Blersch, Jeffrey.

A festival Psalm. Psalm 150:00. Busarow, Donald.

A festive Alleluia. Psalm 100:4-5. Nickson, John.

Festive Jubilate. Psalm 100:00. Scott, K. Lee.

Festival 'St. Anne.' Psalm 80:00. Croft, William (arr. Hal H. Hopson).

Fields are dancing with ripened corn. Psalm 65:00 (paraphrased). Haydn, Franz Joseph (arr. Walter Ehret).

Filled with the spirit. Ephesians 5:18b-20. Caldara, Antonio (arr. Michael Burkhardt).

Filling me with joy. Psalm 139:00. Lisicky, Paul.

Fix these words. Deuteronomy 11:18. Schurr, Walter W.

Flee as a bird. Psalm 11:1b. Spanish folk tune.

Fly like a bird. Psalm 139:00. Canedo, Ken (arr. Mark Barnard).

"For ever and ever" – The Lord's Prayer. Matthew 6:9-13. Walker, Gwyneth.

For glory dawns upon you. Isaiah 60:6b. Hilton, John Karl.

For God so loved the world. John 3:14-17. Grotenhuis, Dale.

For the sins of her prophets. Lamentations 4:13-15a. Schalk, Carl.

For unto us a child is born (Messiah). Isaiah 9:6. Handel, George F.

From above he hath sent fire. Lamentations 1:13. Schalk, Carl.

From all who dwell below the skies. Psalm 117:00. Roth, John.

Fürchtet euch nicht. Luke 2:10, 122. Beyer, Johann Samuel (arr. Ronald A. Nelson).

G

The gate of heaven. Psalm 122:1-2. Pethel, Stan.

Gaudete omnes. Psalm 100:00. Praetorius, Hieronymus.

Gaudete omnes (Rejoice, ye people). Psalm 100:00. Sweelinck, Jan P.

Give ear, O Lord, and visit me. Psalm 86:00 (based on). Rogner, James A.

Give ear, O shepherd of Israel. Psalm 80:00. Powell, Robert J.

Give glory all creation. Psalm 103:00. Schütz, Heinrich (arr. John Leavitt).

Give praise, you servants of the Lord. Psalm 113:00. Wienhorst, Richard.

Give thanks to God.
    Beethoven, Ludwig van. Psalm 107:1, 9-10, 20, 22.
    Scandinavian folk melody. Psalm 136:1-9, 23-24 (arr. Dale Grotenhuis).

Give thanks to the Lord. Psalm 118:00. Barnard, Mark.

Give us, Lord, a new heart. Ezekiel 36:25-26. Farrell, Bernadette (arr. Paul Inwood).

Glastonbury gloria. Luke 2:14. Walker, Christopher.

Gloria.
    Mozart, W. A. Revelation 7:11.
    Vierdanck, Johann (ed. Michael Burkhardt). Luke 2:14.

Gloria in excelsis Deo.
    Crandal, Scot. Luke 2:14.
    Dewey, Dennis Hart. Luke 2:14.
    Estes, Jerry. Luke 2:14.
    Greer, Bruce. Luke 2:14.
    Roth, John. Luke 2:14.
    Vivaldi, A. (ed. S. Drummond Wolff). Luke 2:14.

Glorify the Lord with me. Psalm 34:3. Lewis, Eric.

Glorious and everlasting God. Psalm 104:24. Young, Gordon.

Glory to God.
    Biery, James. Luke 2:14.
    Fisher, Bobby. Luke 2:14.
    Hobby, Robert. Luke 2:13, 14.
    Jones, Peter. Luke 2:14.
    Larson, Lloyd. Luke 2:8-15.
    Soper, Scott. Luke 2:14.
    Willcock, Christopher. Luke 2:14.

Glory to God in the highest.
    Bell, John L. Luke 2:14.
    McIver, Robert H. Luke 2:14.
    Pergolesi, G. B. (arr. Robert DeWell). Luke 2:14.

Go and bear fruit. John 15:16-17. Fedak, Alfred V.

Go, make of all disciples. Matthew 28:19-20. Schweizer, Mark.

Go out in joy! Isaiah 56:12 (adapted). Martin, Joseph M.

Go, therefore, and make disciples. Matthew 28:19-20. Bedford, Michael.

Go through the gates. Isaiah 62:00. Butler, Eugene.

Go ye into all the world. Mark 16:15. Wetzler, Robert.

Go ye therefore. Matthew 28:19-20. McDonald, Mary.

God be merciful. Psalm 67:00. Bouman, Paul.

God be merciful unto us and bless us. Psalm 67:00. Carter, Andrew.

God has gone up with a merry shout. Psalm 47:00. Butler, Eugene.

God has put the angels in charge of you. Psalm 91:1-6, 10-11. Janco, Steven R.

God has told you. Micah 6:6, 7a. Cherwien, David.

God is a spirit. John 4:24. Thompson, Randall.

God is gone up!
    Lawson, Gordon. Psalm 47:5-6.
    McCabe, Michael. Psalm 47:5.

God is love. I John 4:7-11. Schram, Ruth Elaine.

God is my shepherd. Psalm 23:00. Dvořák, Antonin.

God is my strength and song. Psalm 118:14-17, 22-24. Farlee, Robert Buckley.

God is our refuge and strength. Psalm 46:00. Schultz, Timothy P.

God mounts his throne. Psalm 47:1-2, 5-8. Innwood, Paul.

The God of love my shepherd is.
    Hayes, Mark. Psalm 23:00 (adapted).
    Schalk, Carl. Psalm 23:00.

God, our strength. Psalm 81:00. Butler, Eugene.

God shall the broken heart repair. Psalm 147:3. Scott, K. Lee.

God shepherds the poor. Psalm 107:00. Haas, David.

God so loved the world.
    Larson, Lloyd. John 3:16-17.
    Sadowski, Kevin J. John 3:16, 17.
    Stainer, John (arr. Ellen Jane Lorenz). John 3:16.
    Stainer, John (arr. Ellen Jane Lorenz). John 3:16-17.
    Stainer, John (arr. Gregg Sewell). John 3:16-17.

The good shepherd. John 10:11-14. Nolan, Douglas.

The goodness of the Lord. Psalm 27:00 (based on). Soper, Scott.

Great and marvelous are Thy works. Revelation 15:3. Gaul, Alfred R.

Guide us, Lord. Psalm 90:00. Keil, Kevin.

H

Hail to the Lord's annointed.
    Cornell, Garry A. Psalm 72:00.
    Schröter, Leonhart (setting by Mark Bender).
      Psalm 72:00.
Hallelujah! Sing praise to the Lord. Psalm 150:00.
    Hopson, Hal H.
Happy are the lowly poor. Matthew 5:1-16. Jones,
    Hilton Kean.
Hark my beloved. Song of Songs 2:8-13. Callahan,
    James.
Have mercy on me, O God.
    Schalk, Carl. Psalm 51:1a, 2, 7, 9, 13.
    White, David Ashley. Psalm 51.1-8, 10-12.
Have mercy on us, Lord. Psalm 51:00. Castillo,
    Eugene.
Have you not known? Isaiah 40:28-31. Hobby,
    Robert A.
He came so still. Luke 2:14. Kirk, Theron.
He hath triumphed gloriously. Exodus 15:1-2.
    Powell, Robert J.
He is mine. Romans 8:35, 38. Swahili song from
    Kenya (arr. Hal H. Hopson).
He is the king of glory. Psalm 24:7-10. Handel,
    George F. (setting by Hal H. Hopson).
He shall be called wonderful. Isaiah 9:6, 40.
    Roberts, Leon C.
He shall come down. Psalm 72:6, 8, 11a. Owens,
    Sam Batt.
He shall come down like rain. Psalm 72:00. Owens,
    Sam Batt.
He shall direct your paths. Proverbs 3:5-6. Wetzler,
    Robert.
He shall give his angels charge over thee. Psalm
    91:4, 11-12. Busarow, Donald.
He was despised.
    Dubois, Theodore (arr. Hal H. Hopson). Isaiah 53:3-5.
    Graun, Karl (arr. Dale Grotenhuis). Isaiah 53:3.
He watching over Israel. Psalm 121:4 (arr. Gene
    Grier and Lowell Everson).
Hear, O Lord (Christus). Psalm 51:00. Mendelssohn,
    Felix (arr. Hal H. Hopson).
Hear our prayer. Psalm 143:00. Holyoke, Samuel.
*Hearken, bless ye the Lord (Ecce nunc benedicite
    Dominum).* Psalm 134:1-3. Victoria, Tomás (arr.
    Robert J. Powell).
Hearken to my voice, O Lord, when I call. Psalm
    27:10-13. Neswick, Bruce.
The heavens are praising. Psalm 19:00. Beethoven,
    Ludwig van (arr. Arthur Frackenpohl).
The heavens are telling. Psalm 19:00 (paraphrased).
    McKinney, Richard.
The heavens declare Thy glory. Psalm 19:1-6, 14.
    Bach, J. S. (arr. Michael Burkhardt)
The heav'ns declare God's mighty power. Psalm
    19:00. Handel, G. F. (arr. Hal H. Hopson).
Hide me under the shadow of thy wings. Psalm 17:8.
    West, John E.
Hide me under the shadow of your wings. Psalm
    17:6, 8. Owens, Sam Batt.
Hide not thou Thy face from us, O Lord. Psalm
    27:10. Farrant, Richard (arr. Kenneth Kosche).

Higher than the heavens. Psalm 108:1-6. Nelson,
    Ronald A.
His name is John. Luke 1:63, 76-79. Proulx, Richard.
Hodie Christus natus est.
    Byrd, William (ed. Lawrence Doebler). Luke 2:11.
    Phillips, Craig. Luke 2:11.
Holy be Thy glorious name. Psalm 72:00. Mozart,
    W. A. (arr. Jay Daniels).
Holy, holy, holy. Isaiah 6:3. North, Jack.
Holy, holy, holy (Sanctus). Isaiah 6:3. Franck, César
    (arr. Donald Moore).
Holy is the Lord.
    Mason, Lowell. Isaiah 6:3.
    Murphy, Michael Patrick. Luke 1:46-50.
Holy is the name of God. Manalo, Ricky. Luke 1:46-
    55 (based on).
Holy Lord of hosts.
    Isaiah 6:00. Hallquist, Gary and Benjamin Harlan.
Holy spirit, gracious guest. I Corinthians 13:00
    (based on). Clemens, James E.
Holy, true and faithful God. Isaiah 45:23.
    McDonald, Mary.
Hope of glory. Colossians 1:27. Crawshaw, Craig.
Hosanna.
    Armstrong, Matthew. Matthew 21:9.
    Burkhardt, Michael. Matthew 21:9.
    Rudolph, Glenn L. Luke 19:38.
    Taylor, Jim. Luke 19:38 (and other).
Hosanna! Blessed Is He!
    Johnston, Randolph. Matthew 21:9.
    Nystedt, Knut. Psalm 118:26.
Hosanna filio David. Matthew 21:15. Keldermans, R
Hosanna, hosanna. Matthew 21:9. Birkley, Michael M.
Hosanna in the highest. Matthew 21:9. Laubengayer,
    Paul.
Hosanna to the Son of David.
    Archer, Malcolm. Matthew 21:9.
    Moe, Daniel. Matthew 21:9.
The hour has come. John 12:23. Wienhorst, Richard.
The house of the Lord. Psalm 113:00. Ellingboe, Bradley.
How beauteous are their feet. Isaiah 52:7. Stanford,
    C. Villiers.
How beautiful. Isaiah 52:7-8. Hassell, Michael.
How beautiful are the feet. Romans 10:15-18.
    Grotenhuis, Dale.
How beautiful upon the mountains. Isaiah 52:7.
    Stainer, John (ed. John Carlton).
How can I repay the Lord. Psalm 116:00. Mengel, Dana.
How exalted is your name. Psalm 8:00. Hassell, Michael.
How excellent thy name. Psalm 8:1. Handel, G. F.
    (ed. Robert S. Hines).
How good it is to sing praise. Psalm 147:00. Proulx,
    Richard.
How long? Psalm 113:00. Hailstork, Adolphus.
How long, O Lord?
    Bell, John L. Psalm 13:00.
    Grotenhuis, Dale. Psalm 13:00.
    Schutte, Dan. Psalm 13:00.
How lovely is your dwelling place.
    Alstott, Owen. Psalm 84:00.
    Goebel-Komala, Felix. Psalm 84:00.
    Marshall, Jane. Psalm 84:00.
How lovely are the messengers. Romans 10:15.
    Mendelssohn, Felix (ed. John Johnson).

How many are your works, O Lord. Psalm 104:11-15a.
Callahan, Charles.

How very good and pleasant. Psalm 133:00. Scott,
K. Lee.

How wonderful is your name. Psalm 8:00. Johengen,
Carl.

Hymne - Hear my prayer. Psalm 55:1-7.
Mendelssohn, Felix (ed. & arr. Robert S. Hines).

I

I am standing at the door. Revelation 3:20-21.
Gehring, Philip.

I am the bread of life. John 6:32-51. Sherman,
Arnold B.

I am the good shepherd. Romans 6:9. Wetzler, Robert.

I am the light of the world. John 8:12. Bouman, Paul.

I am the living bread. John 6:51. McCabe, Michael.

I am the resurrection.
Drenna, Patti. John 11:1-44.
Hildebrand, Kevin. John 11:25-26.
Scheidt, Samuel. John 11:25

I am the resurrection and the life. John 22:25-26.
Rotermund, John.

I am the true vine. John 15:1, 4-5. Sadowski, Kevin J.

I am the vine.
Gehring, Philip. John 15:1, 4-5.
Pote, John. John 15:00.

I am the voice of God. Genesis 12:1-4. Haas, David.

I am the way, the truth, the life. John 14:1-6. Lau,
Robert C.

I ask one thing of the Lord. Psalm 27:4. Schütz,
Heinrich.

I cry to God. Psalm 77:00. Bell, John L.

I give you a new commandment. John 14:34-35.
Aston, Peter.

I have known you. John 17:1-11. Keesecker, Thomas.

I have loved you. John 15:9-12 (based on). Larson,
Lloyd.

I have seen the Lord. John 20:18. Hurd, Bob.

I know that my redeemer lives.
Behnke, John (arr.). Job 19:25-27.
Bunjes, Paul G. Job 19:25-27.
Cox, Michael (arr.). Job 19:25-27.
Hughes, Howard. Job 19:25-27.
Kosche, Kenneth T. Job 19:25.
MacAller, Dominic. Job 19:25-27.
Williams, David H. Job 19:25.

I lift my eyes. Psalm 121:00 (paraphrased). Dengler, Lee.

I love you, O Lord. Psalm 18:00 (based on). Brown,
Grayson Warren.

I put my life in your hands. Psalm 31:00
(paraphrased). Haas, David.

I rejoice when I heard them say. Psalm 122:00.
Chassidic melody (arr. Richard Proulx).

I saw a new heaven and a new earth. Revelation
21:1-4. Schalk, Carl.

I shall yet praise him. Psalm 42:00. Pethel, Stan.

I sought the Lord in the night. Daniel 2:00 (based
on). Cox, Michael.

I thank you, Lord. Psalm 138:1-3. Behnke, John A.

I to the hills will lift my eyes.
Berger, Jean. Psalm 121:00.
Mengel, Dana. Psalm 121:00.

I waited for the Lord.
Mendelssohn, Felix (arr. Walter Ehret). Psalm 40:1.
Mendelssohn, Felix (arr. James Denton).
Psalm 40:1, 4.

I waited patiently for the Lord.
Bales, Gerald. Psalm 40:1.
Pote, Allen. Psalm 40:00.

I want to praise the Lord all of my life. Psalm 34:1.
Telemann, Georg Philipp (arr. Susan Palo Cherwien).

I was glad.
Haas, David. Psalm 122:00.
Hallquist, Gary. Psalm 122:1.

I will always give thanks. Carter, John. Psalm 34:1
(adapted).

I will always thank the Lord. Soper, Scott. Psalm 34:1.

I will awaken the dawn. Psalm 108:1-5. Martin,
Joseph M.

I will exalt you, my God and King. Psalm 45:00.
Grotenhuis, Dale.

I will extol you, O Lord.
Schramm, Charles W., Jr. Psalm 30:11-5, 12-13.
Young, Philip M. Psalm 30:00 (adapted).

I will give you as a light to the nations. Isaiah 49:6.
Schalk, Carl.

I will lift my eyes. Psalm 121:00. Harris, Ed.

I will lift my eyes unto the hills. Psalm 121:00.
Nelson, Daniel.

I will lift up mine eyes.
Brown, Charles F. Psalm 121:00.
Hailstork, Adolphus. Psalm 121:00.

I will lift up my eyes. Psalm 121:1-3, 5, 8. Young,
Philip M.

I will magnify Thee. Psalm 145:1-2, 8-10, 21-22.
Powell, Robert J.

I will not leave you desolate. John 14:18. Sadowski,
Kevin J.

I will pour my spirit. Acts 1:17b-18. Moreland,
Richard.

I will pour out my spirit on all the earth. Joel 2:28.
Hopson, Hal H.

I will praise God. Psalm 145:00 (based on). Wright,
Vicki Hancock.

I will praise my God. Psalm 40:00. Lord, Suzanne.

I will praise you, O Lord, with all my heart.
Bender, Mark. Psalm 138:1-3, 7-8.
Larson, Lloyd. Psalm 9:1-10.

I will praise your name. Psalm 145:00. Cotter, Jeanne.

I will set his dominion in the sea. Psalm 89:26-28, 51.
Neswick, Bruce.

I will sing for ever of your love, O Lord. Psalm 89:2,
21-22, 25, 27, 29, 34. Inwood, Paul.

I will sing new songs of gladness. Psalm 144:00.
Dvořák, Antonin.

I will sing of thy might. Psalm 59:16-17. Nesheim, Paul.

I will sing the story of your love. Jeremiah 33:10-11,
14-16. Weber, Paul.

I will sing to the Lord.
>   Pollock, Gail Leven. Psalm 16:00.
>   Wright, Paul Leddington. Exodus 15:1, 2, 11, 13, 17.

I will sing to the Lord as long as I live. Psalm
104:25, 31, 32, 34. Schalk, Carl.

I will sing with the spirit. I Corinthians 14:15.
Rutter, John.

I will walk in the presence of God. Psalm 116:1-8,
12-13. Haugen, Marty.

I will yet praise him. Psalm 42:00. Shepperd, Mark.

Ich bin die Auferstehung. John 11:25-26. Scheidt,
Samuel (ed. Larry D. Cook).

If anyone does sin. I John 2:1-2. Gehring, Philip.

If God is for us.
>   Brown, Grayson Warren. Romans 8:31-39 (based on).
>   Pote, Allen. Romans 8:31-39.

If I have washed your feet. John 13:14. Luckner, Brian.

If I take the wings of the morning. Psalm 139:8-9.
Dams, Julian.

If with all your heart. Joel 2:12, 13. Mendelssohn,
Felix.

Immortal, invisible. I Timothy 1:17. Peterson, Gerald.

Immortal, invisible God only wise. I Timothy 1:17.
Hopson, Hal H.

In convertendo. Psalm 125:00. Gastoldi, Giovanni.

In Monte Oliveti. Matthew 26:30, 41-42. Pinkham,
Daniel.

In my father's house. John 14:1-4. Armstrong, Matthew.

In quietness and confidence. Isaiah 30:15, 18. Dare,
Carol R.

In remembrance of me. Luke 22:19, 20. Atkins, Jean
and J. W. Snyder (arr. John Purifoy).

In te speravi, Domine. Psalm 31:1-2. Proulx, Richard.

In the arms of my shepherd. Psalm 23:00. Murphy,
Michael Patrick (arr. Dick Averre).

In the day of the Lord. Isaiah 2:00. Ridge, M. E.

In the land of the living. Psalm 27:00. Johengen, Carl.

In the last days.
>   Busarow, Donald. Acts 2:17-21.
>   Martin, Joseph M. Micah 1:4-5.

In the morning I will sing. Psalm 63:2-9. Haugen, Marty.

In the shadow of your wings. Psalm 63:00 (based
on). Medema, Ken and Ron Harris.

In this house of worship. Psalm 122:1. Pote, Allen.

In unity and peace. Psalm 133:1. Chepponis, James.

Incline thine ear.
>   Himmel, F. H. Psalm 70:1.
>   Ippolitoff-Ivanoff. M. Psalm 31:1-4.

Increase our faith. Luke 11:1-13. Haas, David.

Into Jerusalem. Zechariah 9:9. Taranto, A. Steven.

Into the woods my master went. Matthew 4:1, 2.
Wyton, Alec.

Into Thy hands. Luke 23:46. Brown, Charles F.

Into your hands. Psalm 31:5. Fritschel, James.

Introit and prayer. Psalm 100:4. Bish, Diane.

Israel awake! Judges 5:2-3, 12. Lindh, Jody W.

It is a good thing. Psalm 92:1-3. Kosche, Kenneth T.

It is a good thing to give thanks.
>   Bouman, Paul. Psalm 92:1-5.
>   Busarow, Donald. *(Psalm 92).* Psalm 92:1-5, 12.

It is a good thing to sing. Psalm 92:00. Starr, David.

J

Jacob's ladder. Genesis 28:10-22. Spiritual (arr.
Roger C. Wilson).

Jacob's ladder/Hold on. Genesis 28:10-22. Spiritual
(arr. Marc Robinson).

Jacob's vision. Genesis 28:10-22. Smith, Lani.

Jesus came from Nazareth. Mark 1:9. Neswick, Bruce.

Jesus Christ is the Lord. Philippians 2:6-11. Gouzes,
André.

Jesus, the bread of life. John 6:51. Brown, Grayson
Warren.

Jesus went to Jordan's stream. Matthew 3:13-17.
Plag, Johannes.

Joshua fit de battle of Jericho. Joshua 6:00 (based on).
Jackson, Marylou India.

A jubilant song. Psalm 95:1. Clay, Crystal Davis.

Jubilate Deo.
>   Bales, Gerald. Psalm 100:00.
>   Halmos, László. Psalm 100:00.
>   Hopson, Hal H. Psalm 100:00.
>   Mozart, W. A. (ed. Robert Kendall). Psalm 100:00.

K

The king of love. Psalm 23:00 (Baker). Young, Gordon.

The king of love my shepherd is.
>   Kimberling, Clark. Psalm 23:00.
>   Near, Gerald. Psalm 23:00.
>   Shelley, Harry Rowe. Psalm 23:00.

The kingdom of God.
>   Bolt, Conway A., Jr. Matthew 13:00 (based on).
>   Lawrence, Stephen L. Matthew 5:3-11.

Know that the Lord is near. Philippians 4:1-9. Haas,
David.

Kyrie eleison. Isaiah 53:4-5. Mengel, Dana.

L

Lamb of God.
>   Blersch, Jeffrey N. John 1:29.
>   Mitchell, Tom. John 1:29.

Lamb of God, grant us peace. John 1:29. Soper, Scott.

Das Land ist voll erkenntnis des Herrn. Isaiah 11:9.
Peter, Johann Friedrich.

Laudate! Psalm 150:00. Liebergen, Patrick M.

Laudate Dominum (Sing praise to God above).
>   Chant (Gregorian) (ed. J. Ritter Werner). Psalm
>   117:00.
>   Hovland, Egil. Psalm 150:00.
>   Mozart, W. A. (ed. Nancy Telfer). Psalm 117:00.
>   Mulet, Henri. Psalm 117:00.
>   Pitoni, Giuseppi O. (ed. Patrick M. Liebergen).
>   Psalm 117:00.

Lay up your treasures in heaven. Matthew 6:19-34.
Choplin, Pepper.

Lead me, Lord. Psalm 5:8. Wesley, Samuel S.

Lead me, O Lord. Psalm 5:8. Molique, Wilhelm B.

Leaning. Deuteronomy 33:27. Showalter, Anthony J.
(arr. David M. Hines).

Led by the spirit. Joel 2:12-13. Vaughan Williams, Ralph.

Let all the gates be opened wide. Psalm 42:7-10. Brahms, Johannes (arr. Hal H. Hopson).

Let all the people praise thee. Psalm 67:3 (based on). Sleeth, Natalie.

Let all the peoples praise God. Psalm 67:00. Christopherson, Dorothy.

Let all the peoples praise you! Psalm 67:00. Johengen, Carl.

Let all the rivers clap their hands. Psalm 98:00. Schweizer, Mark.

Let all the world. Psalm 67:3-5. Scott, K. Lee.

Let creation raise the strain. Psalm 148:00. Mengel, Dana.

Let everything that has breath praise the Lord. Psalm 150:00. Neaveill, Ryan.

Let light shine. II Corinthians 4:6. Roth, John D.

Let my prayer rise. Psalm 141:2. Walker, Christopher.

Let my prayer rise before you. Psalm 141:00. Inwood, Paul.

Let not troubled be your hearts. John 14:1-4. Murphy, Michael Patrick.

Let the children come. Matthew 19:14. Murphy, Michael Patrick.

Let the heavens praise your wonders. Psalm 89:00. Butler, Eugene.

Let the people praise Thee, O God. Psalm 67:00. Kauffmann, Ronald.

Let the words of my mouth. Psalm 19:14. Baumbach, Adolph.

Let us come and praise the Lord. Psalm 95:00. Aks, Catherine.

Let us go rejoicing.
 Cotter, Jeanne. Psalm 122:00.
 Hurd, Bob. Psalm 122:1-9.
 Roberts, Leon C. Psalm 121:00.

Let us go to the altar. Psalm 42:00. Schutte, Dan.

Let us love one another. I John 4:7-11. Sherman, Arnold B.

Let us rejoice and sing. Psalm 118:24. Schultz, Larry E.

Let us sing to the Lord. Psalm 149:00. Emig, Louis Myers.

Let us, with a gladsome mind. Psalm 136:1, 7, 25. Hopson, Hal H.

Let your light so brightly shine. Matthew 5:16. Shields, Valerie.

Let your restless hearts be still. John 14:00 (taken from). Irish traditional (arr. John Bell).

Life tree. John 15:5. American folk tune (arr. David M. Cherwien).

Lift up your heads.
 Holden-Holloway, Deborah. Psalm 24:7-10 (adapted).
 Larson, Lloyd. Psalm 24:7-10.
 McCray, James. Psalm 24:00.
 Williams, Thomas J. (arr. Stan Pethel). Psalm 24:7-10.

Lift up your heads, O gates. Psalm 24:7-10. Owens, Sam Batt.

Lift up your voice and sing. Psalm 100:00. Handel, G. F. (arr. Hal H. Hopson).

Like a dove. John 1:29-34. Purifoy, John.

Like a river in springtime. Philippians 1:4-7. Williams, Paul and Donna.

Like as a father. Psalm 103:13. Haan, Raymond H.

Like cedars (arr. Randall DeBruyn). Psalm 92:00. Schutte, Dan.

Like eagles, you will fly! Psalm 103:1-5. McDonald, Mary.

Like the deer. Psalm 41:1-2. Sr. Maria of the Cross.

Listen, O heavens. Deuteronomy 32:1-4. Day, James R.

Listen to what the Lord is saying. Psalm 85:8-9, 13. Behnke, John A.

A living hope. I Peter 1:3-5. Guimont, Michael.

Living sacrifice, A. Romans 12:1-2. Johnson, Ralph M.

Locus iste. Isaiah 40:1. Martinson, Joel.

Look at the birds of the air. Matthew 6:25-34. Dengler, Lee.

Look to this day. Matthew 6:26, 28-29, 30. Wetzler, Robert.

The Lord bless you and keep you. Numbers 6:24-26. Lau, Robert.

A Lord-built house. Psalm 127:00. Lentz, Roger.

Lord, for the years. Psalm 134:00. Pote, Allen.

Lord, have mercy.
 Christianson, Donald G. & Carrie L. Kraft. Psalm 40:00.
 Dengler, Lee. Isaiah 53:3, 6.

Lord, hear my prayer. Psalm 4:1. Schütz, Heinrich (arr. David W. Music).

Lord, I cry unto thee. Psalm 141:1, 2, 3, 8. Tschaikovsky, P.

The Lord is exalted. Isaiah 33:5, 8, 10. West, John E. (arr. Ellen Jane Lorenz).

The Lord is in his holy temple. Habakkuk 2:20. Hastings, Thomas.

The Lord is king.
 Behnke, John A. Psalm 99:1-3.
 White, David Ashley. Psalm 99:1-3, 9.

The Lord is mindful of his own.
 Mendelssohn, Felix (arr. Ellen Jane Lorenz). Psalm 115:00.

The Lord is my keeper. Psalm 121:5, 7. Page, Anna Laura.

The Lord is my light.
 Burson, John Wyatt. Psalm 27:00.
 Cox, Michael. Psalm 27:1, 3.
 Drennan, Patti. Psalm 27:00.
 Murphy, Michael Patrick. Psalm 27:00.
 Walker, Christopher. Psalm 27:00.

The Lord is my light and my salvation.
 Kosche, Kenneth T. Psalm 27:1, 7, 11.
 Leavitt, John. Psalm 27:00 (from *Requiem*).

The Lord is my shepherd.
 Bell, John L. Psalm 23:00.
 Grier, Gene and Lowell Everson. Psalm 23:00.
 Leavitt, John. Psalm 23:00 (from *Requiem*).
 Liddle, Samuel. Psalm 23:00.
 Mozart, W. A. (ed. Ellen Jane Lorenz). Psalm 23:00.
 Schubert, Franz (arr. Walter Ehret). Psalm 23:00.
 Sensmeier, Randall. Psalm 23:00.
 Smith, Timothy R. Psalm 23:00.
 Stearns, Peter Pindar. Psalm 23:00.

The Lord is my strength and my song.
Exodus 15:2, 11. Schwoebel, David.

The Lord is righteous. Lamentations 1:18. Schalk, Carl.

Lord, make us turn to you. Psalm 80:2-3, 15-16, 18-19. Roberts, Leon C.

Lord, now let thy servant go in peace. Luke 2:29-32. Brown, Grayson Warren.

The Lord now rules. Psalm 92:1-5, 12. Willcock, Christopher.

Lord, O Lord, your name is wonderful. Psalm 8:00. Hopson, Hal H.

The Lord says, I will make a covenant. (Offertory: Advent III). Ezekiel 37:26-27, Kohrs, Jonathan.

Lord, send out your spirit. Psalm 104:00. Cotter, Jeanne.

Lord, Thou hast been our dwelling place. Psalm 90:1-6, 12, 17. Landes, Rob.

Lord, who may enter your house? Psalm 15:00. Bell, John.

The Lord will soon appear. Isaiah 40:3-4. Bach, J. S. (setting Hal H. Hopson).

Lord, you have been our refuge. Psalm 90:00. Bell, John L.

Lord, you have searched me. Psalm 139:00 (based on). Hobby, Robert A.

Lord, you have the words. John 6:68. Joncas, Michael.

The Lord, your God, will come. Isaiah 35:4c-61. Westra, Evert.

The Lord's my shepherd.
Behnke, John A. Psalm 23:00.
Kosche, Kenneth T. Psalm 23:00.

The Lord's prayer.
Arensky, Anton. Matthew 6:9-13.
Clausen, René. Matthew 6:9-13.
Dengler, Lee. Matthew 6:9-13.
Schütz, Heinrich (ed. George Guest). Matthew 6:9-13.
Walker, Christopher. Matthew 6:9-13.

The lost boy. Luke 2:41-52 (based on). Kemp, Helen.

Love. John 14:15. Bales, Gerald.

Love is kind.
Bach, J. S. (arr. Dale Grotenhuis). I Corinthians 13:00 (based on).
Broughton, Edward. I Corinthians 13:00 (based on).

Love is of God. I John 4:7-11. Harris, Ed.

Love never fails. I Corinthians 13:8-10, 13. Scott, K. Lee.

Love one another.
Causey, C. Harry. John 13:34.
Dufford, Bob. John 13:34.
Hopson, Hal H. John 13:34-35.

Lover of us all. Ephesians 2:7-10. Schutte, Dan.

Loving and forgiving. Psalm 103:00 (based on). Soper, Scott.

M

Magna et mirabilia. Revelation 15:3-4. Neswick, Bruce.

Magnificat.
Rubalcava, Peter. Luke 1:46-55.
Zacharia, Cesare de. Luke 1:46b-55.

Magnificat anima mea.
Near, Gerald. Luke 1:46, 47.
Porter, Steven. Luke 1:46-55.

Magnificat: God who is mighty. Luke 1:46-55. Schiavone, John.

Magnificat in C major. Luke 1:46. Aldgasser, Anton Cajetan (ed. David Stein).

Make a joyful noise.
Friedman, Mark. Psalm 150:00 (based on).
Harlan, Benjamin. Psalm 100:00.
Kalbach, Don. Psalm 100:00.

Make a joyful noise unto the Lord.
Heck, Lyle. Psalm 100:00.
James, Layton. Psalm 100:00.

Make our hearts burn with love. Luke 24:32. Englert, Eugene.

Mandatum. John 13:34-35. Farlee, Robert Buckley.

Maranatha. Isaiah 35:00. Schoenbachler, Tim (arr. Patrick Loomis).

Mary. Luke 1:26-38 (based on). Williams, Amy Tate.

Mary at the tomb. John 20:00. Ellingboe, Bradley.

Mary's canticle. Luke 1:45-55. Roberts, Leon C.

Mary's song. Luke 1:46-55. Brown, M. Susan.

May God be gracious. Psalm 67:1-2. Lantz, David, III.

May God bless and keep you.
Lovelace, Austin. Numbers 6:24-26.
Walker, Christopher. Numbers 6:22-27.

May God bless you now. Psalm 115:14. Bach, J. S. (arr. David W. Music).

May love be ours, O Lord. I Corinthians 13:00 (based on). Gieseke, Richard W.

May the Lord bless you. Numbers 6:24-26 (based on). Brown, Grayson Warren.

May the Lord watch over you and me. Genesis 31:40. Grotenhuis, Dale.

May the peace of the Lord be with you today. John 14:6, 27. McChesney, Kevin.

May we never boast. Galatians 6:14-16 (inspired by). Connolly, Michael.

May you know God's grace. Philemon 0:3-7. Larson, Lloyd.

Mbiri Kuna Mwari (Shona Gloria). Luke 2:14. Kesselman, Lee R.

Meditations on the cross. Philippians 2:8. Malmin, Olaf G.

The mercies of God. Romans 12:1, 9, 10. Butler, Eugene.

Mercy, God have Mercy. Psalm 51:00. Mozart, W. A. (arr. Theron Kirk).

Micah's song. Micah 6:6-8. Brown, Grayson Warren.

Miserere mei. Psalm 51:1. White, David Ashley.

The music of earth. Psalm 147:00. Routley, Erik (arr. Austin C. Lovelace).

My faith is sure. Psalm 116:10-13. Ducis, Benedictus.

My friend, do not forget. Proverbs 6:20-22 (based on). Martin, Joseph M.

My God is an awesome God. Psalm 24:00 (based on). Hampton, Keith.

My heart is full today. Psalm 111:00. Proulx, Richard.

My heart is ready.
Barnard, Mark. Psalm 108:00.
Butler, Eugene. Psalm 108:00.

My heart is ready to sing. Psalm 108:1-5. Leaf, Robert.
My heart is steadfast, O God.
    Powell, Robert J. Psalm 57:7-11.
    Young, Philip M. Psalm 57:7-11.
My life is in your hands. Psalm 31:00. Soper, Scott.
My shepherd is the Lord. Psalm 23:00. Choplin, Pepper.
My shepherd will supply my need.
    American folk melody (setting by Howard
      Helvey). Psalm 23:00.
    American folk tune (arr. Austin Lovelace). Psalm
      23:00.
    Mengel, Dana. Psalm 23:00.
My soul doth magnify the Lord. Luke 1:46, 47.
    Baker, Richard C.
My soul is thirsting. Psalm 63:1-8. Hurd, Bob.
My soul is thirsting for you, O Lord, my God. Psalm
    63:2-6. Callahan, Charles.
My soul longs for you, O God. Psalm 25:00.
    Beethoven, Ludwig van (arr. Hal H. Hopson).
My soul proclaims. Luke 1:46-55. Toolan, Suzanne.

N

Na rekakh Vavilonskikh. Psalm 137:1-5, 7-9. Vedel,
    Artemiy.
Nativity. Luke 2:00. Hastings, Thomas.
The nativity of our Lord. (*Alleluia verses*, Set 2).
    Luke 2:11. Blersch, Jeffrey.
Never the blade shall rise. John 12:00. Powell, Kathy.
New beginnings. John 4:00. Bourgeois, Louis (arr.
    Wayne Wold)
A new commandment. John 13:34. Murphy, Michael
    Patrick.
A new creation. Revelation 21:5. Callahan, Charles.
The new Jerusalem. Revelation 21:1-5. Gawthrop,
    Daniel E.
A new magnificat. I Samuel 2:1-20. Jennings, Carolyn.
A new song. Psalm 96:00 (based on). Pote, Allen.
A new song of praise. Psalm 98:00. McClellan, Michael.
Ni wangu. Romans 8:35, 38. Swahili song from
    Kenya (arr. Hal H. Hopson).
No longer I. Galatians 2:19-20. Hurd, Bob.
No other foundation can anyone lay. I Corinthians
    3:11, 16, 17. Bouman, Paul.
Noah. Genesis 7:00. Harlan, Benjamin.
Not unto us, O Lord.
    Busarow, Donald. Psalm 115:1.
    Mozart, W. A. Psalm 115:1, 2 (arr. William
      Livingston).
Nothing can come between us. Romans 8:35-39.
    Young, Jeremy.
Now bless the God of Israel. Luke 1:67-79. Haugen,
    Marty.
Now Paul, he was a servant. II Corinthians 11:23-27.
    Brazzeal, David.
Nunc dimittis.
    Archangelsky, Alexander. Luke 2:29-32.
    Walker, Christopher. Luke 2:29-32.

O

O be joyful.
    Carr, Benjamin. Psalm 100:00.
    Wanger, Douglas E. Psalm 5:00.
O be joyful, all ye nations. Schütz, Heinrich (ed.
    Leonard Van Camp). Psalm 100:00.
O be joyful in the Lord.
    James, Donald. Psalm 100:00.
    Selby, William. Psalm 100:00.
O be joyful, joyful in the Lord. Psalm 100:00. Schubert,
    Franz (arr. Walter Rodby).
O bless the Lord, O my soul. Psalm 100:00.
    (paraphrased). Pergolesi, Gian Battista (arr. Hal H.
      Hopson).
O clap your hands.
    Lau, Robert C. Psalm 47:00.
    McChesney, Kevin. Psalm 47:1, 2, 6.
O clap your hands, all ye people! Psalm 47:00.
    Staplin, Carl.
O come, let us sing to the Lord. Psalm 95:00. Lantz,
    David, III.
O exult yourself above the heavens. Psalm 57:5, 7-8.
    Handel, George F.
O for a thousand tongues. Psalm 98:00. Glaser, Carl
    (arr. Theron Kirk).
O for a thousand tongues to sing.
    Glaser, Charles (arr. David M. Music). Psalm 98:00.
    Glaser, Charles (arr. Walter Pelz). Psalm 98:00.
    Young, Gordon. Psalm 98:00.
O give thanks. Psalm 136:00. Purcell, Henry.
O give thanks to the Lord.
    Brown, Jody & Jeff McGaha. Psalm 105:00.
    Pelz, Walter. I Chronicles 16:00.
O give thanks unto the Lord. Psalm 118:00. Roth, John.
O God, creator. Psalm 8:00. Marcello, Benedetto
    (ed. and arr. Dale Grotenhuis).
O God, have mercy. Psalm 51:00. Purcell, Henry
    (arr. Hal H. Hopson).
O God, my heart is ready. Psalm 108:00. Lindley,
    Simon.
O God of font and altar. Psalm 29:1-2. Scott, K. Lee.
O God we do exalt your name. Psalm 95:00
    (adapted). Larson, Lloyd.
O God, wherefore art thou absent. Psalm 74:1-3.
    Blow, John (ed. George Guest).
O God, you search me. Psalm 139:00 (based on).
    Farrell, Bernadette.
O holy city, seen of John. Revelation 21:00. Powell,
    Robert J.
O how amiable are thy dwellings. Psalm 84:00.
    Rutter, John.
O Jerusalem. Luke 12:34-35 (paraphrased). Haas, David.
O lamb of God. John 1:29. Starr, David.
O Lord from the depths I cry. Psalm 130:00.
    Hopson, Hal H.
O Lord, hear me. Psalm 143:00 (paraphrased).
    Hopson, Hal H.
O Lord, I am not worthy. Matthew 8:8. Frank, Melchior
    (ed. and arr. Henry V. Gerike).
O Lord our governor. Psalm 8:1, 4-7, 10. Hancock,
    Gerre.

O Lord, our Lord. Psalm 8:1-6, 9. Powell, Robert J.

O Lord, you are my God and king. Psalm 145:1-3, 8-13. Parry, C. Hubert (arr. Donald Busarow).

O Lord, you know my heart. Psalm 139:00. Ford, Sandra T.

O love of God (arr. Craig Kingsbury). I Corinthians 12:4-6, 12-13. Hurd, Bob.

O my people, turn to me. Hosea 14:1, 4-7. Farlee, Robert Buckley.

O praise God in his holiness. Psalm 150:00. Mason, Lowell.

O praise the Lord. Hodges, Edward. Psalm 100:00.

O praise the Lord with one accord. Psalm 135:00. Handel, G. F. (arr. Walter Rodby).

O praise ye the Lord.
    Callahan, Charles. Psalm 148:00.
    Parry, C. Hubert (arr. Mark White). Psalm 150:00.
    Parry, C. Hubert H. (arr. S. Drummond Wolff). Psalm 148:00.

O rest in the Lord (Elijah). Psalm 37:7. Mendelssohn, Felix (arr. Jonathan Willcocks).

O sing to the Lord a new song. Psalm 96:1-4. Martinson, Joel.

O sing unto the Lord. Psalm 96:1. Handel, G. F. (arr. Robert N. Roth).

O sovereign God. Psalm 8:00. Wold, Wayne L.

O taste and see.
    Goss, Sir John. Psalm 34:8-10.
    Kosche, Kenneth T. Psalm 34:1-8.
    Larkin, Michael. Psalm 34:00.
    Neswick, Bruce. Psalm 34:8.

O taste and see how gracious is the Lord. Psalm 34:8. Nikolsky, A.

O vos omnes.
    Croce, Giovanni (ed. Jerald Hamilton). Lamentations 1:12.
    Pinkham, Daniel. Lamentations 1:12.
    Victoria, Tomas Luis de (ed. Raymond Sprague). Lamentations 1:12.

O, ye wise maidens. See: *Virgines prudentes.*

Of the kindness of the Lord. Psalm 33:1, 51, 6, 9 (based on). Proulx, Richard.

Offering—Take my life, that I may be. Romans 12:1. Collins, Dori Erwin.

Oh, clap your hands. Psalm 47:00. Leavitt, John.

Oh, for a thousand tongues. Psalm 98:00. Wetzler, Robert.

Oh, for a thousand tongues to sing. Isaiah 43:1, 3. Wetzler, Robert.

Oh, how beautiful! Psalm 84:00. Horman, John D.

Oh, sing to God a new song. Psalm 96:1-4. Swedish folk tune.

The old and the young. Joel 2:28. Thompson, Randall.

Omnes gentes plaudite manibus. Handl, Jacob. Psalm 47:00.

On eagles' wings. Psalm 91:00. Joncas, Michael (arr. Edwin Earle Ferguson).

On the journey to Emmaus. Luke 24:13-15. Haugen, Marty.

One thing I ask of the Lord. Psalm 27:1, 4, 6. Rudolph, Glenn L.

One thing I seek. Psalm 27:5. Proulx, Richard.

Only this I want. Philippians 3:7-16. Schutte, Dan.

Open to me the gates of righteousness. Psalm 118:19-22, 24. Scott, K. Lee.

Orietur stella. Numbers 24:17-18. McCray, James.

Otche nash (The Lord's prayer). Matthew 6:9-13. Arensky, Anton.

Our blessing cup. I Corinthians 10:16. Joncas, Michael.

Our God has done great things for us. Psalm 125:00. Foley, John.

Our Lord's prayer. Matthew 6:9-13. Larson, Loyd.

Our soul waits for the Lord. Psalm 33:20-22. Schalk, Carl.

Out of the depths.
    Owens, Sam Batt. Psalm 130:1, 4.
    Schalk, Carl. Psalm 130:00.

P

Parable. Ecclesiastes 3:1-9. Ridge, M. E. (arr. Patrick Loomis)

Peace. John 14:27. Schultz, Timothy P.

Peace be with you. John 14:1-14. McDonald, Mary.

Peace, I give to you. John 14:27. Larkin, Michael.

Peace I leave with you.
    Landes, Rob. John 14:27.
    Mendelssohn, Felix (arr. Hal H. Hopson). John 14:27.
    Pelz, Walter L. John 14:27.
    Perti, Giacomo (arr. Hal H. Hopson). John 14: 6, 27.

The peace of Christ. Colossians 3:12-17. Landes, Rob.

The peace of God.
    Scott, K. Lee. Philippians 4:6-7.
    Spong, Jon. Philippians 4:7.

Peace to you all. Ephesians 6:23, 24. Grotenhuis, Dale.

Pentecost. Acts 2:1-2. Hopson, Hal H.

Peoples of earth. Psalm 100:00. Dean, Stephen.

Pilgrim church of God. Ephesians 4:13. Scott, K. Lee.

Praise awaits you. Psalm 65:00. Bober, Melody.

Praise God from whom all blessings flow. Psalm 100:00. Anonymous (ed. William P. Rowan).

Praise God in heaven. Psalm 9:11-12. Schütz, Heinrich.

Praise God with the trumpet. Psalm 150:00. Young, Jeremy.

Praise him, Alleluia! Psalm 107:8. Butler, Eugene.

Praise, my soul, the God of heaven. Psalm 103:00. Jennings, Carol.

Praise, my soul, the king of heaven. Psalm 103:00. Ellis, John.

Praise the almighty, my soul adore him. Psalm 146:00. Pelz, Walter L.

Praise the goodness of God. Psalm 145:00 (based on). Pote, Allen.

Praise the Lord, his glories show. Psalm 150:00. Niedmann, Peter.

Praise the Lord in a song. Psalm 69:30. McDonald, Mary.

Praise the Lord in song. Isaiah 12:2-6. Fortunato, Frank.

Praise the Lord in the highest. Psalm 148:00. Clemens, James E.

Praise the Lord! O heavens adore him. Psalm 148:00. Hopson, Hal H.

Praise the Lord, O Jerusalem. Psalm 147:12-13.
Maunder, J. H. (Wilson).
Praise the Lord who reigns above.
Courtney, Craig. Psalm 150:00.
Foundry collection (arr. Alice Parker). Psalm 150:00.
Praise to the Lord, the Almighty.
Hughes, Robert J. Psalm 103:1-6.
Steffy, Thurlow. Psalm 103:1-6.
Praise ye the Lord. Psalm 150:2, 3.
Tschaikovsky, P. I. (arr. Homer Whitford).
Praise ye the name of the Lord. Psalm 135:1, 3, 21.
Tschaikovsky, P. I.
Prepare ye. Isaiah 40:3. Robinson, Marc A.
Prince of peace. Isaiah 9:2, 6. Causey, C. Harry.
Processional for Christmas. Luke 2:14. Harlan,
Benjamin.
Proclaim with me. Psalm 34:1-9. Busarow, Donald.
Psalm 4. Psalm 4:00. Ure, James.
Psalm 8. Psalm 8:00. Hoekstra, Thomas.
Psalm 8 (O Lord our God). Psalm 8:1, 3-9. Levine,
Elliot Z.
Psalm 17: When your glory appears. Psalm 17:1, 5-
6, 8, 15. Cooney, Rory.
Psalm 14. Psalm 14:00. Ives, Charles (ed. John
Kirkpatrick and Gregg Smith).
Psalm 20. Psalm 20:00. Brown, Grayson Warren.
Psalm 23.
Burkhardt, Michael. Psalm 23:00.
Lawson, Gordon. Psalm 23:00.
Mulholland, James Quitman. Psalm 23:00.
Zimmermann, Heinz Werner. Psalm 23:00.
Psalm 27. Psalm 27:00. Mulholland, James Quitman.
Psalm 27: The Lord is my light. Psalm 27:00.
Honoré, Jeffrey.
Psalm 27 - Trust in God. Psalm 27:00. O'Hearn, Arletta.
Psalm 32. Psalm 32:00. Callahan, Charles.
Psalm 34. Psalm 34:00. Chepponis, James.
Psalm 42: My soul is thirsting. Psalm 42:00.
Brown, Grayson Warren.
Psalm 46.
Burkhardt, Michael. Psalm 46:00.
Kosche, Kenneth T. Psalm 46:00.
Psalm XLVI. Psalm 46:00. Luther, Martin (setting by
John Ness Beck).
Psalm 47. Psalm 47:00. Handl, Jacob.
Psalm 47: God mounts his throne. Psalm 47:00.
Palmer, Nicholas.
Psalm 50, Offer unto God. Psalm 50:14-15.
Christiansen, F. Melius.
Psalm 51: Create in me. Psalm 51:3-4, 12, 14, 17, 19.
Hurd, Bob.
Psalm 51: Create me again. Psalm 51:00. Cooney,
Rory.
Psalm 63. Psalm 63:00. Kosche, Kenneth T.
Psalm 84.
Mackie, Ruth E. Psalm 84:00.
Mulholland, James Quitman. Psalm 84:00.
Psalm 85. Psalm 85:00. Martinson, Joel.
Psalm 85: Show us your kindness. Hurd, Bob (arr.
Craig Kingsbury).

Psalm 91. Psalm 91:1-7, 9-12. Courtney, Craig.
Psalm 91: Be with me. Psalm 91:00. Hurd, Bob
(arr. Craig Kingsbury).
Psalm 95: If today (arr. Craig Kingsbury). Psalm
95:00. Hurd, Bob and Joe Bellamy.
Psalm 97 (from *Sacred Service*). Psalm 97:00.
Zaimont, Judith Lang.
Psalm 98. Psalm 98:00. Martinson, Joel.
Psalm 100.
Diemer, Emma Lou. Psalm 100:00.
McHugh, Charles R. Psalm 100:00.
Psalm 103.
Honoré, Jeffrey. Psalm 103:00.
Kosche, Kenneth T. Psalm 103:00.
Larson, Sonia. Psalm 103:1-4.
Mulholland, James Quitman. Psalm 103:00.
Psalm 103: Our God is rich in love. Psalm 103:00.
Moore, Bob.
Psalm 104: Send out your spirit. Psalm 104:00.
Cooney, Rory.
Psalm 110. Psalm 110.00. Kosche, Kenneth T.
Psalm 117, Praise the Lord, all you nations. Psalm
117:00. Busarow, Donald.
Psalm 118. Psalm 118. Kosche, Kenneth T.
Psalm 121.
Barta, Daniel. Psalm 121:00.
Caesar, Anthony. Psalm 121:00.
Hildebrand, Kevin. Psalm 121:00.
Psalm 123. Psalm 123:00. Bullard, Janice M.
Psalm 126: The Lord has done great things for us.
Psalm 126:00. Honoré, Jeffrey.
Psalm 128: All the days of our lives. Psalm 128:00
(based on). Cooney, Rory.
Psalm 130: Out of the depths.
Ferguson, John. Psalm 130:00 (based on).
Johnson, Stephen P. Psalm 130:00.
Psalm 138. Psalm 138:00. Hoekstra, Thomas.
Psalm 143. Psalm 143:00. Kosche, Kenneth T.
Psalm 146. Psalm 146:2, 6-10. Chepponis, James J.
Psalm 147. Psalm 147:1-11. Courtney, Craig.
Psalm 148. Psalm 148:00. Diemer, Emma Lou.
Psalm 150.
Hayes, Mark. Psalm 150:00 (based on).
Rowan, William P. Psalm 150:00.
Schütz, Heinrich. Psalm 150:00.
Psalm 150 – Hallelujah! Psalm 150:00. Cann, Jesse.
A Psalm of celebration. Psalm 96:00. Pelz, William L.
A Psalm of confession. Psalm 51:1-4, 7-9. Hopson,
Hal H.
Psalm of joy. Psalm 95:00. Choplin, Pepper.
Psalm of joy. Psalm 104:00 (based on). Boyce, William
(alt. and arr. Jane McFadden and Janet Linker).
Psalm of praise. Psalm 135:1, 21. Ivanov, P. (arr.
Ellen Jane Lorenz).
A Psalm of the redeemed.
Cooney, Rory. Psalm 1:00.
McCabe, Michael. Psalm 1:00.
Put on love. Colossians 3:12-17. Powell, Kathy.
Put on therefore as the elect of God. Colossians 3:12-
17. Sowerby, Leo

Q

Quam dilecta.   Psalm 84:1, 2, 4, 12. Bales, Gerald.
Qui biberit aquam.   John 4:13, 14. Busch, Richard.
Qui tollis peccata mundi.   John 1:29. Thayer, Fred.

R

A radiant light.   Isaiah 9:5, 6, 9. Proulx, Richard.
Rain down.   Psalm 33:00 (based on). Cortez, Jaime
    (arr. Craig Kingsbury).
Raise a joyful sound.   Psalm 95:00. Sedio, Mark.
The record of John.   John 1:19-23. Hurd, David.
The reign of God.   Revelation 19:00 (based on).
    Dufford, Bob.
Rejoice!   Philippians 4:4, 6, 7. Courtney, Craig.
Rejoice and sing out his praises.   Psalm 104:33-34.
    Hayes, Mark.
Rejoice, be glad, give praise.   Revelation 19:6-7.
    Wood, Dale.
Rejoice in the Lord always.
    Hopson, Hal H. Philippians 4:4-7.
    Martinson, Joel. Philippians 4:4-7.
Rejoice, rejoice, believers.
    Honoré, Jeffrey. Matthew 25:1-13 (based on).
    Swedish folk tune (arr. Theodore Beck). Matthew
    25:1-13 (based on).
Rejoice, the Lord is king.
    Darwall, John (arr. Jimmy Owens). Philippians
        4:4 (Wesley).
    Darwall, John (arr. Courtney, Craig). Psalm 33:12,
        18-22.
    Handel, G. F. (setting S. Drummond Wolff).
        Philippians 4:4 (Wesley).
    Saint-Saëns, Camille (ed. George Martin).
        Philippians 4:4 (Wesley).
    Willcocks, Jonathan. Philippians 4:4 (Wesley).
Rejoice, ye people.   Psalm 100:00. Sweelinck, Jan P.
Remember me.   I Corinthians 11:23-25. Pethel, Stan.
Remember, O Lord.   Lamentations 5:1, 7, 15, 16.
    Schalk, Carl.
Remember this.   I Peter 4:8-9. Burroughs, Bob.
Remember your Lord God/Prayer of Habakkuk.
    Deuteronomy 8:2. Powell, Robert J.
Responsorial Magnificat, A.   Luke 1:46-55.
    Rotermund, Donald.
Return, Lord.   Isaiah 40:3. Keesecker, Thomas.
Return to the Lord.   Joel 2:13. Gerike, Henry V.
Revelation 19.   Revelation 19:00 (based on).
    LaValley, Jeffrey.
Revelation canticle.   Revelation 15:3-4. Callahan,
    Charles.
Ride on! Ride on in majesty.
    Darst, W. Glen. John 12:12-15.
    Gippenbusch, J. John 12:12-15.
    Norris, Kevin. John 12:12-15.
    Stocker, David. John 12:12-15.
    Titcomb, Everett. John 12:12-15.
    Young, Gordon. John 12:12-15.
Rise up in splendor.   Isaiah 60:1-2. Goemanne, Noël.

Rise up, Jerusalem.   Beruch 5:5. DeBruyn, Randall.
Rise up, my love.   Song of Songs 2:10-12.
    Laubengayer, Paul.
Rise up, my love, my fair one.
    Entsminger, Deen E. Song of Songs 2:10, 11, 12.
    McConnell, David A. Song of Songs 2:10-12.
    McCray, James. Song of Songs 2:10-12.
Risen! Go and tell.   Luke 24:4-7. Nelson, Ronald A.
The risen Christ.   I Corinthians 15:55-56. Martin,
    Gilbert M.
Rorate caeli.   Isaiah 45:8. Proulx, Richard.

S

The sacrifice of God.   Psalm 51:17, 18. Handel, G. F.
    (arr. Richard Langdon).
Salmo 150 (Psalm 150).   Psalm 150:00. Aguiar, Ernani.
Sanctus
    Evans, John E. Isaiah 6:3.
    Fauré, Gabriel (ed. Robert Roth) (*Requiem*).
        Isaiah 6:3.
    Fauré, Gabriel (ed. Nancy Telfer) (*Messe Basse*).
        Isaiah 6:3.
    Haydn, F. J. (ed. Rod Walker). Isaiah 6:3.
    Mozart, W. A. (ed. Anthony Howells). Isaiah 6:3.
    Mozart, W. A. (ed. Henry Kihlken). Isaiah 6:3.
Save me, O God.   Psalm 69:1, 3, 7, 10, 13, 14. Blow,
    John (ed. George Guest).
A scarlet robe.   Matthew 27:27-37, 51, 54. Larson,
    Lloyd.
Search me, O God.   Psalm 139:23-24. Day, J. R.
The second song of Isaiah.   Isaiah 55:66-11.
    Callahan, Charles.
See the place where Jesus lay.   Mark 16:6. Kihlken,
    Henry, arr.
Seek ye first.
    Lafferty, Karen and Johann Pachelbel. Matthew
        6:33.
    Lau, Robert. Matthew 6:3.
    Pachelbel, Johann and Karen Lafferty. Matthew
        6:33 (arr. Douglas E. Wagner).
Seek ye the Lord.   Isaiah 55:6, 7. Roberts, J. Varley.
Send out thy light.   Psalm 43:3, 4. Gounod, Charles.
Send us your strength, O God.   Psalm 104:6-10.
    Callahan, Charles.
Send your bread forth.   Ecclesiastes 11:1, 2, 7, 8.
    McLarry, Beverly.
Set me as a seal.
    Conte, David. Song of Songs 8:6-7.
    Grotenhuis, Dale. Song of Songs 8:6-7.
Set me as a seal upon thine heart.   Song of Songs
    2:10-12. Hoddinott, Alun.
Set me as a seal upon your heart. Song of Songs
    8:6-7. Micheltree, John.
Share this covenant of love.   John 4:7-16 (based on).
    Page, Paul F.
Share your bread with the hungry.   Isaiah 58:7-10
    (inspired by). Haas, David.
Shelter.   Psalm 91:00 (based on). Lisicky, Paul.
Shepherd and teacher.   Matthew 6:30-34. Kreutz,
    Robert E.
The shepherd song.   Psalm 23:1. Haan, Raymond H.

Surely the Lord is in this place. Genesis 28:16, 17.
Lau, Robert.

Surge illuminare (The third song of Isaiah). Isaiah 60:00. Boles, Frank.

Surgens Jesus. John 20:19-20. diLassor, Orlando (ed. Lawrence Doebler).

Suscepit Israel (Magnificat). Luke 1:54. Pergolesi, G. B. (arr. Gregory M. Pysh).

T

Take my heart. Psalm 51:9-13. Wilkinson, Sandy.

Take up the tambourine. Psalm 117:00 (based on). Larson, Lloyd.

Taste and see.
Barnard, Mark. Psalm 34:00 (adapted).
Smith, Timothy R. Psalm 34:1-7, 9.

Taste and see that the Lord is good. Psalm 34:8-10. Gehring, Philip.

Taste and see the Lord is good. Joshua 5:9-12. Thompson, J. Michael.

Teach me now, O Lord. Psalm 119:00. Marcello, Benedetto (ed. and arr. Dale Grotenhuis).

Teach me, O Lord, the way of your statutes. Psalm 119:00. Mitchell, Tom.

Teach me your way, O Lord.
Bisbee, B. Wayne. Psalm 86:11-12, 15-16a.
Sedio, Mark. Psalm 86.

Tell all the nations. Psalm 96:1-3, 7-8, 10 (adapted). Connolly, Michael.

Thanks be to God. I Corinthians 15:57-58. Beebe, Hank.

That I may know him. I Corinthians 1:22-2:9. Dennis, Randall.

There is a balm. Jeremiah 8:22. Fairbanks, Brian.

There is a balm in Gilead.
Owens, Sam Batt. Jeremiah 8:22.
Spiritual (arr. James Furman). Jeremiah 8:22.

There is a river. Psalm 46:4, 5. Traditional Irish melody (arr. Richard Dickinson).

There is a time. Ecclesiastes 3:1-8. Courtney, Craig.

There is no greater love. John 14:00. Canedo, Ken.

There shall a star. Numbers 24:17. Mendelssohn, Felix (ed. Ken Fleet).

These words. Deuteronomy 6:4. Löwenthal, Tom.

They have taken away my Lord. John 20:13-16. Stainer, John (arr. Ellen Jane Lorenz).

They rolled the stone away. Mark 16:00. James, Layton.

They that wait upon the Lord.
Purify, John. Isaiah 40:1-2, 11-31.
Wilson, Russell. Isaiah 40:31.

Think on these things. Philippians 4:8. Murphy, Michael Patrick.

This body. I Corinthians 11:24-25. Willcock, Christopher.

This is my son. Matthew 3:3, 13-17. Ore, Charles W.

This is my word. Isaiah 55:10-12. Choplin, Pepper.

This is the day!
Brown, Grayhson Warren. Psalm 118:1, 4, 24.
Caceres, Abraham. Psalm 118:24.
Callahan, Charles. Psalm 118:24.
Cooke, S. Charles. Psalm 118:24.
Fadek, Alfred V. Psalm 118:1, 17, 24.

Joncas, Michael. Psalm 118:1-2, 16-17, 22-23, 24.
Kirkland, Terry. Psalm 118:24.
Owens, Sam Batt. Psalm 118:24.
Roberts, Leon C. Psalm 118:00.
Shute, Linda Cable. Psalm 118:00.
Wright, Paul Leddington. Psalm 118:24.

This is the day the Lord has made.
Hayes, Mark. Psalm 118:24 (adapted).
Renick, Charles R. Psalm 118:00.
Shoemaker-Lohmeyer, Lisa. Psalm 118:24, 27-29.

This is the day the Lord hath made. Psalm 118:24. Young, Gordon.

This one will be our peace. Micah 5:00. Schram, Ruth Elaine.

Those who observe the day. Romans 14:6-8. Gehring, Philip.

Those who sow in tears. Psalm 125:00. Farrell, Bernadette.

Thou wilt keep him in perfect peace.
Neswick, Bruce. Isaiah 26:3.
Stearns, Peter Pindar. Isaiah 25:3, 4, 8.

Though we are many, in Christ we are one.
I Corinthians 10:17. Proulx, Richard.

Three Psalm settings. Psalm 46:00, Psalm 96:00, Psalm 98:00. Burkhardt, Michael.

Through all the changing scenes of life. Psalm 34:00 (based on). Schulz-Widmar, Russell.

Throughout every age. Psalm 90:00. Breedlove, Jennifer.

Thy holy wings.
Burkhardt, Michael. Psalm 25:00.
Hobby, Robert A. Psalm 25:00.

Thy law is within my heart. Psalm 40:4-8. Powell, Robert J.

Thy light is come. Isaiah 40:00 (adapted). Sartor, David.

Thy perfect love. Ephesians 5:1-2a. Scott, K. Lee.

A time and a purpose. Ecclesiastes 3:1-8. Ore, Charles W.

A time for all things. Ecclesiastes 3:1 (adapted). Wagner, Douglas E.

The time for singing. Song of Songs 2:10-12. Grotenhuis, Dale.

The time of singing. Song of Songs 2:11-12. Snyder, Audrey.

Timeless song. John 3:16 (and other). Choplin, Pepper.

To build your kingdom. Psalm 127:1 (based on). Causey, C. Harry.

To everything there is a season. Ecclesiastes 3:00. Caricciolo, Stephen.

To God be joyful. Psalm 100:00. Mozart, W. A. (ed. Hal H. Hopson).

To love our God. Ecclesiastes 1:00. Hayes, Mark.

To render thanks. Psalm 92:00. Butler, Eugene.

To see your glory. Colossians 2:6-10. Scott, K. Lee.

To thee, O Lord do I lift up my soul.
Kalinnikoff, P. Psalm 25:1-2.
Rachmaninoff, Sergi. Psalm 25:1, 2.

To thy pastures. Psalm 23:00. Lau, Robert C.

To you, O Lord. Psalm 25:00. Haugen, Marty.

To you, O Lord, I lift my soul. Psalm 25:00. Roberts, Leon C.

Toda la tierra (All earth is waiting). Isaiah 40:3-5. Taulè, Alberto (arr. Jerry Gunderson).

Together we are love. Romans 5:1-2. Atkins, Jean and J. W. Snyder.

Train up a child. Proverbs 22:6. Choplin, Pepper.

The transfiguration of our Lord. Psalm 45:2. Blersch, Jeffrey.

Treasure. Matthew 6:19-21. Graham, Michael.

The treasure and the pearl. Matthew 13:44-45. Hopson, Hal H.

Treasure in heaven. Matthew 6:19-21. Frahm, Frederick.

Tres sunt, qui testimonium. I John 5:7-8. Haydn, Johann Michael.

Tribulationes cordis mei. Psalm 25:17-18. Haydn, Johann Michael (ed. David Stein).

Tristis est anima mea. Matthew 26:38. Pinkham, Daniel.

True builder of the house. Psalm 90:1, 2, and other. Martin, Gilbert M.

Truly blest. Psalm 23:00 (based on). Pooler, Marie.

Truly God is good. Psalm 93:00. Barrett, Michael.

The trumpeters and the singers were as one. II Chronicles 5:13. Young, Gordon.

Trust. Psalm 31:14-15. Proulx, Richard.

Trust in the Lord.
  Martin, Joseph M. Proverbs 3:5.
  McDonald, Mary. Proverbs 3:5-6.

Tu es Petrus. Matthew 14:16. Bauer, Marie Rubis.

Turn thy face from my sins. Psalm 51:9-13. Locke, Matthew (ed. George Guest).

U

Unto us a child is born. Isaiah 9:6. Kosche, Kenneth T.

V

Venite, Exultemus Domino. Psalm 95:00. Aks, Catherine.

Vere languores nostros. Isaiah 53:4. Victoria, Tomás Luis de.

Verse for Palm Sunday (Alleluia verses). John 12:23. Blersch, Jeffrey.

Verse for the ascension of our Lord (Alleluia verses). Romans 6:9. Blersch, Jeffrey.

Verse for the holy trinity (Alleluia verses). Isaiah 6:3. Blersch, Jeffrey.

Verse for the resurrection of our Lord (Alleluia verses). Romans 6:9. Blersch, Jeffrey.

Verses for Sundays in Lent. Mark 10:45. Hyslop, Scott M.

Vespers canticle. Revelation 15:00. Hoddinott, Alun.

Vinea mea electa. Isaiah 5:1-7. Pinkham, Daniel.

Virgines prudentes. Matthew 25:4-6. Handl, Jacob (ed. Mary Lycan).

Vo tsarstvii Tovoyem (The Beatitudes). Matthew 5:3-10. Panchenko, Semyon.

Vocem jucunditatis. Isaiah 48:20. Busch, Richard.

A voice cries out. Isaiah 40:1-11. Joncas, Michael.

A voice cries out, 'Prepare the way of the Lord.' Isaiah 40:1, 3-5. Larson, Lloyd.

W

Walk in love. Ephesians 4:25-32. Lantz, David, III.

The walk to Calvary. Matthew 26:36-66. Anderson, Norma Sateren.

We are a light. Acts 13:47, 52. Canedo, Ken (arr. John Purifoy).

We are God's people. I Peter 2:4-10. Helgen, John.

We are singing for the Lord is our light.
  South African freedom song (arr. Hal H. Hopson). Psalm 27:1-4 (based on).
  Zulu traditional song (arr. Hal H. Hopson). Psalm 27:1-4.

We come rejoicing. Psalm 63:00 (based on). Pethel, Stan.

We will need no candle. Revelation 22:5. Martin, Joseph M.

We will serve the Lord. Joshua 24:15. McDonald, Mary.

Well done, faithful servant(s). Matthew 25:23. Martin, Joseph M.

Wenn es meines Gottes Wille (Cantata 161). Luke 7:11-17. Bach, J. S.

What shall I give. Psalm 116:00. Soper, Scott.

What shall I render to the Lord? Psalm 116:12-14, 17-19. Tiefenbach, Peter.

What then. Romans 8:31-39. Ferguson, John.

When fully came the day of Pentecost (Dum complerentur dies Pentecostes). Acts 2:1-2. Palestrina, G. P. (ed. Dwight Weldy).

When He appears. I John 3:2-3. Schramm, Charles W., Jr.

When I look at the heavens. Psalm 8:00 (based on). Lung, Richard Ho.

When I survey the wondrous cross.
  Ferris, William. Galatians 6:14.
  Franck, Melchior (ed. Edward Klammer). Galatians 6:14 (Watts).
  Gustafson, Dwight. Galatians 6:14 (Watts).
  Harris, Ed. Galatians 6:14 (Watts).
  Lau, Robert. Galatians 6:14.
  Miller, Edward (setting by Bruce Saylor). Galatians 6:14 (Watts).
  Murry, Lyn. Galatians 6:14 (Watts).
  Parks, Joe E. Galatians 6:14 (Watts).
  Schoenfeld, William. Galatians 6:14 (Watts).
  Young, Gordon. Galatians 6:14.

When Israel came out of Egypt's land. John 114:00. Bell, John L.

When Jesus was a growing lad. Luke 2:41-52. Horman, John D.

When the morning stars together. Job 38:7. Scott, K. Lee.

When we eat this bread. I Corinthians 11:25. Joncas, Michael.

Whence then comes wisdom. Job 28:20-21, 23-24, 28. Rollins, Joan E.

Whenever you do this. Matthew 25:40. O'Sheil, Judy.

Where, O death, is your victory? I Corinthians 15:55. Connolly, Michael.

Where two or three are gathered. Matthew 18:20. Colgan, Tobias (arr. Craig Kingsbury).

Wherefore I put thee in remembrance (Two Emmanuel motets). II Timothy 1:6-9. Harbison, John.

Who do people say that I am? Matthew 16:13-16.
    Courtney, Craig.

Who knows where the wind blows? John 3:7-8.
    Martin, Joseph M.

Who shall separate us. Romans 8:35-39. Schütz,
    Heinrich (ed. Larry L. Fleming).

Whoever would be great. Matthew 20:26-28. Hughes,
    Robert J.

Whoever would be great among you. Matthew 20:26-
    28 (based on). Nelson, Ronald A.

Whosoever. Romans 10:13-15. Burroughs, Bob.

Wilt not thou turn again, O God? Psalm 85:6, 7.
    Dietterich, Philip R.

Wind, fire and heat, bless the Lord. John 3:8.
    Proulx, Richard.

Wings of the dawn. Psalm 139:00. Spencer, Linda.

With a voice of joy. Psalm 42:4-8 (based on).
    Drennan, Patti.

With a voice of singing. Isaiah 48:20b. Jennings,
    Kenneth.

With grace and carefulness. Psalm 65:10-11, 14.
    Bell, John L.

With my voice I cry out to the Lord. Psalm 142:00.
    Clemens, James E.

With my whole heart. Psalm 9:1, 2, 10. Nelson,
    Ronald A.

With one heart. Romans 15:6. Patterson, Mark.

With what shall I come before the Lord. Micah 6:6-8.
    Bush, Gladys Blakely.

Without love it will all pass away. I Corinthians 13:
    1-13. Larson, Lloyd.

Wondrous cross. Galatians 6:14. Hamil, Paul, arr.

The wondrous cross. Galatians 6:14. English folk
    song (arr. K. Lee Scott).

The word became flesh. John 1:1-5, 14. Roberts, Paul.

Worthy is Christ. Revelation 5:12-13. Leavitt, John.

Worthy of the Lord. Colossians 1:9-14. McDonald, Mary.

XYZ

Ye that stand in the house of the Lord. Psalm 135:2,
    3. Spinney, Walter.

Yes, Jesus is my savior. Philippians 2:1-11 (adapted).
    Swahili song from Kenya (arr. Hal H. Hopson).

You are a chosen race. I Peter 2:9. Hobby, Robert A.

You are my son. Psalm 2:7-8. Schramm, Charles W., Jr.

You are the branches. John 15:1-11. Jothen, Michael.

You are the Christ. Matthew 16:13-20. Angerman,
    David.

You are the light. Matthew 5:13-16. McDonald, Mary.

You are the light of the world. Matthew 5:14-16.
    Hillert, Richard.

You are the salt of the earth. Matthew 5:13.
    Patterson, Joy F.

You are the vine. John 15:00 (based on). Martin,
    Joseph M.

You fill all creation. Ephesians 4:00 (based on).
    Welsh tune (arr. Ronald A. Nelson)

You shall be as the tree. Psalm 1:00 (adapted).
    Killman, Daniel.

You shall go out in joy.
    Martin, Gilbert M. Isaiah 55:12-13 (based on).
    Schalk, Carl. Isaiah 49:6.

You will keep in perfect peace. Isaiah 26:3-4.
    Kosche, Kenneth T.

You will not be left alone. John 14:00. Joy, Dawn.

Your wonderful name. Psalm 8:00. Haas, David.

Your word is a candle. Psalm 119:105. Vantine,
    Bruce.

Your works, O God. Psalm 104:00 (based on).
    Foley, John.

Collection Information

9 x 2. Hopson, Hal H. Sacred Music Press. (1981) CS 75

10 anthems for about 10 singers (compiled by Larry Pugh). Lorenz (2001) 45/1094L

Anthems for limited choirs (SAB, SA or unison) (compiled by Eugene McCluskey). Lorenz (1970) CS 11

Anthems for limited choirs II (SAB, SA, or unison) (compiled by Eugene McCluskey). Lorenz (1972) CS 12

Anthems for the SAB choir (compiled by Hugh S. Livingston, Jr.). Lorenz (1988) CS 871

Augsburg choirbook, Sacred music of the twentieth century (ed. Kenneth Jennings). Augsburg (1998) 0800656784

Christ will be lifted up (compiled by Mary McDonald). Lorenz (2001) 45/1106M

Early American sacred choral library, Vol. I (compiled by Barbara Owen). Boston Music Co. (1991) BM14174

Early American sacred choral library, Vol. II (compiled by Barbara Owen). Boston Music Co. (1992) BM14232

Easy anthems. Hopson, Hal H. Concordia (1990) 97-6040.

Easy hymn tune anthems I (compiled by Roger C. Wilson). Lorenz (1961) CS 36

Easy standard anthems I (compiled and edited by Ellen Jane Lorenz). Lorenz (1949) CS 38

Easy standard anthems II (compiled and edited by Ellen Jane Lorenz). Lorenz (1969) CS 39

Exaltation (*Ten SATB anthems for the church year*) (compiled by Larry F. Pugh). Lorenz (1990) CS 902

Festive Bells 'n' Choir (arr. Gregg Sewell). Lorenz (1985). CS 151

Go out in joy! (compiled by Larry Pugh). Lorenz (2001) 45/1097L

Instant anthems of praise (compiled by Larry Pugh). Lorenz (2001) 45/1091L

Psalms/Anthems, Set 1. Concordia (1990) 97-5902

Psalms/Anthems, Set 2. Concordia (1990) 97-6041

Sacred anthem book (compiled by Dale Wood). Sacred Music Press (1986) CS 166

Simplified standard anthems for mixed voices, I (compiled and edited by Ellen Jane Lorenz and Roger C. Wilson). Lorenz (1956) CS 94

Sing to the Lord a new song I (compiled and edited by Dale Wood). Sacred Music Press (1990) CS 898

Sing to the Lord a new song II (compiled and edited by Dale Wood). Sacred Music Press (1991) CS 904

Songs of joy (compiled by Dale Wood). Sacred Music Press (1980) CS 101

Twenty-five anthems from the Russian liturgy. J. Fischer (1976) FE 09757

The two-part mixed choir. (adaptations by Thomas Chesterton). Lorenz (1986) CS 165

About the Compiler

James H. Laster is Professor Emeritus at Shenandoah Conservatory of Shenandoah University, Winchester, Virginia, where he has taught since 1973. He holds degrees in Music History and Biology from Maryville College, Maryville, Tennessee; the M.A. in Musicology and the Ph.D. in Church Music from George Peabody College in Nashville; as well as a Master of Science in Library Science (music emphasis) from Catholic University, Washington, DC. He also holds a Certificate in Organ from the Mozarteum Summer Academy, Salzburg, Austria. In addition to professional film and stage credits, he has been musical director for over fifty different musical theatre productions. He has choral works published by Augsburg, Concordia, Boosey & Hawkes, Treble Clef Press, and Hinshaw. Other publications include *A Catalogue of Choral Music Arranged in Biblical Order*, *A Discography of Treble Voice Recordings*, *A Catalogue of Vocal Solos and Duets Arranged in Biblical Order*, and *So You're the New Musical Director*, all published by Scarecrow Press. He and Dr. Nancy Menk have compiled an annotated bibliography of materials dealing with women's choral ensemble published as issues #149, #150, #166, and #175 of The Research Memorandum Series.